THE MIDDLE SEA

BOOKS BY L. G. PINE

The Stuarts of Traquair
The House of Wavell
The Middle Sea
The Story of Heraldry
Trace Your Ancestors
The Golden Book of the Coronation
They Came with the Conqueror
The Story of the Peerage
Tales of the British Aristocracy
The House of Constantine
Teach Yourself Heraldry
The Twilight of Monarchy
A Guide to Titles
Princes of Wales
American Origins
Your Family Tree
Ramshackledom
Heirs of the Conqueror
Heraldry, Ancestry and Titles
The Story of Surnames
After Their Blood
Tradition and Custom in Modern Britain
The Genealogist's Encyclopedia
The Story of Titles
International Heraldry
Sons of the Conqueror
Acteon : History of Hunting in Britain
The New Extinct Peerage
The Highland Clans

St Peter's Square in Rome

L. G. PINE

B.A.Lond., F.S.A.Scot.
F.J.I., F.R.A.S., F.R.G.S.
Barrister-at-Law, Inner Temple

THE MIDDLE SEA

A SHORT HISTORY
OF THE MEDITERRANEAN

DAVID & CHARLES
NEWTON ABBOT

To
My Mother and Father

0 7153 5232 6

First published 1950
Revised edition 1973

© L. G. PINE 1973

Set in 10/12 point Pilgrim
and printed in Great Britain
by W J Holman Limited
for David & Charles (Holdings) Limited
South Devon House Newton Abbot Devon

CONTENTS

LIST OF ILLUSTRATIONS

PREFACE

'The grand object of travelling is to see the shores of the Mediterranean. On these shores were the four great empires of the world: the Assyrian, the Persian, the Grecian and the Roman. All our religion, almost all our law, almost all our arts, almost all that sets us above savages, has come to us from the shores of the Mediterranean.'—*Dr Samuel Johnson*

This book originated in 1943 when, as a newly commissioned officer I had been posted to No 500 (County of Kent) Squadron RAF, at a tiny place called Tafaroui, some twenty miles from Oran in Algeria. The squadron's work at this time involved long non-operational periods when training was essential and, as its intelligence officer, I was naturally expected to take my part in the programme. My C.O. told me to give some lectures and, provided that they dealt with the war, there was no restriction as to subject.

I chose as my theme—The Mediterranean, its background and importance in our war strategy. I was deeply interested in Mediterranean history and gave a sketch of it in the course of four lectures. These proved so popular that I was asked to give them again and again to other units. From sketches and notes I gradually built up a narrative of some length, which eventually developed into a manuscript of 70,000 words. After all, my audiences had consisted of a cross-section of the male population in England and, as they had liked the lectures, it seemed that an expanded version might be well received.

So I wrote the book in North Africa and Italy, finishing it in India where I was able to check dates and facts in the large libraries of the Secretariat in New Delhi. There, too, the book was typed, and I brought it home with me. I had had one previous book published in 1940, in New York, a small work on the ancestry of the Earls of Traquair. *The Middle Sea* was my first book published in England, and I shall always remember with very kindly feelings the directors of George Philip and Edward Stanford, not only because they were my first English publishers, but also because dealing with them was a pleasant and friendly experience. My book was to be included in a series of very good travel books which Stanfords were then preparing and as I had written *The Middle Sea* as a straight narrative of historical events, I was asked to introduce passages of a travel nature. Hence the subtitle in the 1950 edition. David & Charles have preferred my original plan for this revised edition, and the book is, in consequence, now purely an historical narrative.

L. G. PINE
Squadron Leader RAF (ret.)

THE MIDDLE SEA

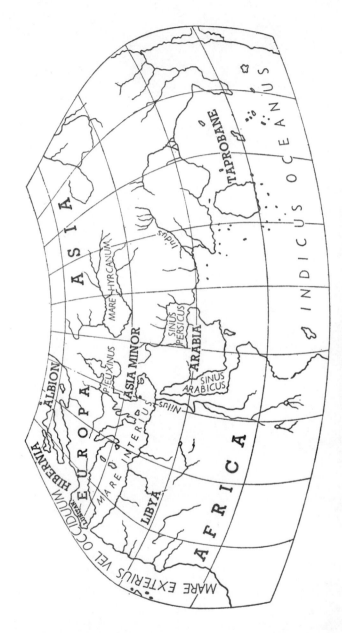

Map 1: The World as conceived by Ptolemy (c AD 150)

CHAPTER ONE

THE IMPORTANCE
OF THE MEDITERRANEAN
IN THE HISTORY OF THE WORLD

THE LITERAL meaning of the word 'Mediterranean' is 'middle of the earth', a Latin description, and to the Romans who first used it, this almost land-locked sea was indeed situated in the middle of what to them constituted the world.

Take a map of the world drawn on any projection you choose. Cover the Americas, north and south, Australia, New Zealand, and most of Africa below the opening wastes of the Sahara. Blot out likewise Europe north of the Baltic Sea, all Russia north of the fringe around the Black Sea, and the whole of Central Asia. What is left? So much of the continents of Europe, Asia and Africa as are within a comparatively short distance of the Mediterranean, or to adopt Gibbon's computation of the boundaries of the Roman Empire, an area having a breadth of some 2,000 miles from the line of the Rhine and Danube to the Sahara Desert, and a width of 3,000 miles from the Atlantic to the Euphrates.

On the map as conceived by the astronomer and geographer Ptolemy, who lived circa AD 150, the *Mare Interius* appears, it is true, to be in the middle of a westward extension of the great Asiatic land mass. We have to remember that, to quote Gibbon again, the Roman Empire 'in the second century of the Christian era ... comprehended the fairest part of the earth, and the most civilised portion of mankind'. To a Roman, the empire was the civilised world. What was there outside its boundaries? To the west beyond the Pillars of Hercules, at the western end of the Mediterranean, there appeared a seemingly endless waste of waters which, in ignorance of its true nature, had from ancient times been described under the Homeric name of Oceanus, the ocean surrounding the world. Stories of islands—the Canaries, possibly the Azores—were known to the Roman world before the time of Christ, and in the last century of the republic when trouble was the order of the times, some Romans in despair of their country had sailed out to reach these islands.

To the south, the empire included the fertile North of Africa and the Valley of the Nile. Roman dominion ended with the beginnings of the Sahara. The northern frontier of the empire was roughly coterminous with the rivers Rhine and Danube. To the Romans, the mass of central and eastern Europe outside their own limits was a wilderness sparsely inhabited by wandering barbaric tribes. Eminently practical in their outlook, the Romans saw no value in acquiring territory for its own sake. Even if a conquest would have served a useful purpose, as with the attempted subjugation of western Germany, they abandoned it when the obstacles proved too great. Nor had they any of the intellectual curiosity which has driven Europeans to explore remote parts of the earth. Mallory's famous reason for his wish to climb Mount Everest, 'because it is there', would have seemed fantastic to a Roman.

Under the governor of Britain, Agricola, whose life written by his son-in-law has come down to us, the Roman navy accomplished a great feat of exploration in circumnavigating Britain and demonstrating it to be an island. This was done as part of Agricola's policy of combined operations by which he hoped to reduce the whole of North Britain. He also thought of invading Ireland, but his recall to Rome put a stop to conquest from the east for more than another thousand years. After this there was no attempt by the Romans to explore the coasts of Ireland, or of the North Sea. Content to refer vaguely to Scandinavia as the Cimbric Chersonese, the Romans knew of the Baltic because amber came from its shores to the marts of Rome, but they were quite prepared to people both Baltic and North Sea with monsters and even supernatural beings when their warships were driven by storms into these waters. Even in the third century AD when incursions by Saxon pirates caused the establishment of the Count of the Saxon Shore (*Comes Saxonici littoris*), Roman war vessels were employed only in a defensive capacity; there was no attempt to raid the pirates' nests across the North Sea.

The eastern limits of the empire were imposed by a 'sandy desert, alike destitute of wood and water', which 'skirts along the doubtful confines of Syria, from the Euphrates to the Red Sea'. Unlike the southern frontier of the empire, in the Sahara, possession of this eastern desert area was often disputed with an oriental power, the empire of Parthia, later replaced by that of the Sassanids and loosely described as Persian. In conflict with these foes, the Romans experienced as many defeats as victories. As late as the second part of the fourth century AD, the Emperor Julian contemplated the conquest of Persia, but his death ended that possibility. In the seventh century the Persians overran the whole of Asia Minor, though subsequently defeated by the Emperor Heraclius in a long struggle which left both powers too weak to meet the new attack coming from Arabia with the rise of Islam.

Granted then that the existence of the Parthian power prevented the extension eastward of Roman rule, what of the enormous areas of Asia beyond the Parthian Empire? In the Far East, in the past of thousands of years ago, there existed of course the great empire of China, and the huge area of India. Communications between the Chinese at one end of the great land mass of Europe-Asia, and the dwellers around the Mediterranean at the other have always existed either by sea or land. Marco Polo in the Middle Ages journeyed to China by land and returned to Europe by sea—nor was his an isolated achievement. Long before his time Imperial Rome had, it is said, received an embassy from the court of China, and possibly sent one thither, but otherwise there was no official knowledge by one empire of the other's existence. In the last century of the Roman Republic, when Roman armies were operating in the Caspian region, a far-flung Chinese army was within a week's march of the Roman force but they never met. Trade did exist between China and Rome, probably by junk across the seas, or by caravans over land during settled periods. It was a somewhat one-sided traffic, for while the Chinese supplied many articles of luxury, such as their porcelain, the Romans paid for this in gold and silver, but did not supply the Chinese with any of their goods, hence a resulting drain on the Roman economy.

Some useful knowledge must have filtered through from the Far

East to the Roman world, as Ptolemy's map shows the peninsula of Arabia and the country as far as the mouth of the Indus with some approach to accuracy, but the southern extent of India is hopelessly foreshortened and its place taken by a great enlargement of Ceylon under the name of Taprobene. It is strange that Ptolemy should have so miscalculated the shape and size of India and Ceylon when his delineation of the Far East was far less inaccurate. Such knowledge as he possessed of the extent of the Far East may have come from the commercial intercourse between the two empires. The Roman ignorance of India is the more strange as they had knowledge of Alexander the Great's expedition into the Punjab. Here then existed two mighty empires of Rome and China with no significant contact. 'The frontiers of each were threatened by barbarians. The Chinese built a wall along the outskirts of the steppes; the Romans built a wall along the Danube and the Rhine. In China, a man dressed in yellow received divine honours; in Rome, a man dressed in purple received divine honours; in each country the religion was the religion of the state, and the emperor was the representative of God.' (Winwood Reade, *The Martyrdom of Man*, p479, 26th edition.)

Is there not then some validity in Oswald Spengler's contention that the writing of world history is impossible; as well write the history of two separate planets as try to combine the stories of Rome and of China. At the beginning of the Christian era, we see— with of course the knowledge denied to both Romans and Chinese —several areas of civilisation, like fires burning brightly in a surrounding penumbra, shading away into a great outer darkness. In Europe, and particularly around the Mediterranean, there is the Roman civilisation which has gathered within itself the Greek and near Eastern civilisations. In the Far East, China, and in what ought really to be called the Middle East, India. Right across the world in Central America there is the intricate Maya culture, and in Peru perhaps the precursor of the Inca system. In some little known places—Zimbabwe and Easter Island—possibly other beginnings of ordered life.

How can the story of all these be combined, or are we merely to have a series of episodes, disjointed, unconnected? Toynbee's thirty or more recorded cultures, each meeting or failing to meet a challenge? Surely the answer is to be found in the close inter-connection of the modern world. Affairs in Israel, in Vietnam, in Korea, in the Congo, in Bolivia now have a significance for all man-kind. How and when has this unity of our planet come about? Several periods can be assigned to it; 1945 and the explosion of the first atomic bombs could be said to have united all mankind in a nightmare of mutual terror. The nineteenth century, according to a saying once current, made the world one neighbourhood. Some modern historians see the eighteenth century with its beginning of the industrial revolution as the time of a binding together of the human race. Yet others would go back to 1492, when the New World was discovered, and they would point with some justifica-tion to the fact that a century after that time the true shape of the land masses of the earth was known, the world had been circum-navigated, and there was hardly a corner of a silent sea into which the triumphant Europeans had not penetrated.

Whatever the date assigned to the world's history as having a common theme, the nature of that theme is clear. It is the civilisa-tion of Europe, a civilisation derived from the Mediterranean lands. In seeking the one Pou Sto of world history, we may say in the trite expression to which Einstein's genius gave rise, 'All is relative'. In superficial theory one can begin in the Yukon or Yucatan; in fact, not. We speak of the Old World (Asia, Africa, Europe); and of the New World. It is Europe which discovered America, not vice versa.

The world known to Europeans before the age of discovery began in the fifteenth century consisted of a mass of land extend-ing from Britain and France to the coasts of China and Japan. The two island groups of the British Isles and the Japanese Islands were situated at the western and eastern extremities of the known world. Each was separated from the mainland not only by a narrow sea passage but by a mental barrier. Though each received much from its neighbours, each was careful to adapt all that it received to the spirit of its own national tradition. Neither group made any great contribution to the world until the boundaries of the old world were enlarged. To the west of Europe and to the east of Asia

B

alike there extended an unknown ocean, while to the north and south of the land mass described there were deserts or other territories difficult of access.

Is it a piece of European conceit, a species of continent-wide chauvinism, to call the Mediterranean the centre of world history while away to the Far East flourished the mighty cultures of China and India? Might not a Chinese historian be able to write the history of the world on the lines that China's growth was the centrepiece, to which the western nations had gradually been drawn? To do so would be to falsify the course of history, for it is not China which has opened up Europe, but Europe which has opened up China and the whole of the East, as of Africa and every area outside Europe.

The effort of man to understand his world begins in Europe and goes on from there, haltingly it may be, but it proceeds. Whatever may be the contribution of the Chinese and Indians to human progress, and our knowledge of both lands is still very imperfect, it cannot be disputed that these countries are not on the main path of human development. The thread of history is unravelled from the empires of Egypt and of Mesopotamia, through Greece and Rome into medieval Europe until, with the discovery of the New World, the civilisation of Europe, which is built partly on that of Greece and Rome, spreads all over the world so that today everywhere life is conducted on a European model. This fact is the cause of a phenomenon which may at first occasion surprise as one reads modern world historians: although they endeavour to treat comprehensively of all parts of the world, the outline of their story is the growth of European civilisation and its spread throughout the world. The contrary view expressed by Spengler, although superficially accurate, does not satisfy. It gives us no explanation or even description of the process by which the world has been united. If, on the other hand, following the plan adopted by most world historians, we group the story of the nations around the development of western civilisation as a central theme, we can, without doing injustice to any other great culture, produce a readable and coherent story. Today the culture originating in Europe has become world-wide for good or for ill, probably for both, and other cultures are most conveniently studied in their relation to it.

The story of the development of European influence will be told in detail in the succeeding chapters, but it is of interest here to summarise the process whereby European discovery began the unification of the world, followed by European domination, and lastly by the adoption of European ways of life by other civilisations. For think of the facts of the spreading of western influence. Henry the Navigator, the famous Portuguese prince, died in 1460. Through his insistent efforts Madeira and the Azores were discovered by the Portuguese. Before this, the realms of Europe were confined to the small area of half that continent, with eastern Europe dominated by the Turks, and Russia still gripped by the Tartars. Even in the Iberian peninsula, the Moorish kingdom of Granada still held out. Half of a continental peninsula, and that a peninsula jutting out of Asia—that was Europe in 1460.

Since then Europeans have taken over and colonised North and South America, and in so doing have obliterated the Mayan, Mexican and Peruvian cultures. The whole of this brave New World has been Europeanised to such an extent that American scholars are much preoccupied in trying to reconstruct from archaeological remains, and the few poor remnants of Indian tribes, the nature of pre-Columbian civilisation.

Fifty years ago a school child learned of five continents—Europe, Asia, Africa, America (North and South) and Australia. Today, it is customary to speak of seven—North and South America being treated as two, and Antarctica making the seventh. On this basis, European control exists in five of the seven continents. Not only has Australia been completely Europeanised but if we use the term Australasia, then Europe's influence has triumphed in New Zealand, Tasmania and the adjacent islands. In the archipelagoes of the Pacific, native ways of life have declined, where they have not altogether disappeared before the western traders, politicians and missionaries. No one will dispute that the Antarctic continent is a European and American preserve.

In regard to Asia, the first efforts of Europe after the great awakening of the European mind following the age of the discoveries were directed towards shaking off the yoke of the Asiatic powers. Notably was this the case with Russia. In the sixteenth century, Russia broke with the Tartars and soon went on to subdue them in her turn. She reached the Pacific coast in the seventeenth century, and in the next 200 years conquered the Siberian tribes, the peoples of the Caucasus and many Moslem races in central Asia. Whatever the Tzars held over this enormous tract, the Soviet Union retains but with a much more vigorous control, the dominant power being in Moscow.

During the nineteenth century the Balkan countries freed themselves from Turkish rule. Against the destruction of their power in Europe must however be set the complete defeat of the Greeks in Asia Minor in 1922, and the expulsion of the remaining age-old Greek communities from that area. Also, the Turks retained control of Constantinople. The Turks have been subjected none the less to a Europeanisation on a most thoroughgoing scale, and that by one of their own leaders.

In Africa, after the overthrow of the pirate regimes in the north, the whole continent, with the exception of two countries, came under European control during the 'scramble for Africa' in the nineteenth century. Only Ethiopia and Liberia remained independent, and Liberia was an American creation. Ethiopia managed to resist Italian pressure towards the end of the century, only to fall under its rule later.

In Asia, the home of the most ancient civilisations, the case was to some extent different. Every land came under European influence, but not every country was directly ruled by Europeans or colonised by them. India was the most obvious example of direct European rule, where a company of mere traders succeeded in the course of three and a half centuries in acquiring complete political control of the vast peninsula. The Dutch ruled the huge archipelago of the East Indies; France acquired Indo-China; Russia pressed forward steadily towards India and the Chinese borders; small settlements of Portuguese, Germans, and others existed in Asia, and the United States of America took over the Philippines from Spain. The enormous country of China with its huge population was brought under European influence and plans existed for its partition in certain eventualities.

Only one Asiatic country succeeded in keeping itself free from European rule, either direct or indirect. This was Japan, and the means by which the Japanese managed to retain their freedom aptly illustrate the extent to which western influence and outlook had pervaded the world. By 1900 the world was controlled by European or European-derived powers, except for Japan. Now, when European influence has receded in the sense of political rule and tutelage from Asia and Africa, it is instructive to observe that Japan, in order to remain free to develop independently, had to adopt the ways of the west. Between 1866 and 1905 the Japanese transformed their country from a picturesque feudal-style state, ready, so it seemed, to become a white man's colony, into a modern power able to meet a great western nation on equal terms and win. In the Russo-Japanese war of 1905, the Japanese inflicted a very heavy defeat on Russia, and brought the colossus of the steppes to her knees. In the 1914-18 war Japan sided with the western allies as an equal, and as equal sat down at the peace conference; but her very success was a decisive proof of the way in which western influences had taken over in every land. *Fas est doceri ab hoste*—was the message sent around the world following the Japanese victory.

The case of China was much more complex. It is the country which has the longest history of any state in the world: 4,000 years of record as a centralised, civilised country. To assess so vast a subject would be impossible but for the labours of many learned Sinologists who have made available the results of their deep research. From these studies we know that there has been a regular pattern, until our own time, in Chinese history. It follows the rule of the establishment of a dynasty over a wide empire, the gradual enfeeblement of that dynasty and its eventual fall, to be replaced after a period of misrule by another royal house. Each succeeding family has assumed connection with its predecessor and thus the succession of the Son of Heaven is assured. As late as 1916 the pattern could have been repeated, when a Chinese general Yuan Shih-Kai was preparing to ascend the Dragon Throne, vacated by the last of the Manchu dynasty in 1912. (The last Manchu emperor died recently as a communist gardener in Pekin.) Then, for the first time in 4,000 years, there was a change in China's history and a republic set up on democratic lines was proclaimed. Needless to relate, the idea of such a regime had come from study of western ideas. New leaders had been educated in western ways, and China, wrapped for ages in her own self-satisfied wisdom, was compelled to accept new conceptions of life from the formerly despised western 'hairy barbarians'.

Even stranger transformations of the Chinese scene were to follow. For many troubled years China was in a state of disorder. The republican regime could not bring effective democratic procedures to so enormous a population as that of China. Various war lords and self-appointed leaders controlled parts of the country. At last, after attempts by the Japanese to conquer China, there arose a powerful communist movement under the leadership of Mao-Tse Tung, which in the period following the 1939-45 war succeeded in unifying the country. The remnants of the former so-called democratic government of China, under Marshal Chiang-kai-Tshek, escaped to Formosa but the whole of mainland China came under the rule of Mao in Pekin.

How was it that the ancient culture of China should adopt so drastic a change as to become a communist state? Briefly and simply, through European influence.

The sequence of events which brought this about was of a very curious nature. The growth of industrialisation in the west caused much suffering and hardship to the majority of working people. Previously, work had been mainly agricultural, or in crafts which did not entail working in crowded factories and living in huge urban conglomerations of mean streets and cramped dwellings. With the herding together of millions of human beings, without prospect of earning anything beyond their weekly or daily pittance, ideas of socialism and communism were not unnatural. The financial system of capitalism came under severe criticism. The greatest critic of this system was a German Jew, Karl Marx, who found it expedient to seek refuge in England, where he became a diligent reader at the British Museum library. He set out his theories in many writings, the largest of which is his famous but little-read *Das Kapital*. During his lifetime he was poor and without influence. He believed that the capitalists would grow even richer, and the mass of workers even poorer, a theory completely disproved by the present state of the workers in such countries as the USA, Britain and Germany. He believed that a revolution would occur, and that the workers would take over power in a highly industrialised land such as Germany or Britain. Today his writings have a curiously old-fashioned flavour, and it is admitted by all that he did not foresee the growth of the managerial class, or the diffusion of benefits with a higher standard of living among the workers in industrial countries. He certainly would have been astonished to have been told that his desired revolution would come in Russia, which at the time of his death was a most backward country where the vast majority of workers were peasants.

Yet this is precisely what happened. The war between Russia and Japan mentioned above brought about a liberal revolution in Russia which resulted in an attempt at a democratic regime. This liberal experiment was never likely to succeed, and the autocracy of the Tzars went on despite the existence of an elected Duma or Parliament. However, the tyranny of the Tzarist system was not efficient, and it blundered badly into the war of 1914, in which the Russians suffered terribly. At last, in 1917, the Tzar was compelled to abdicate, and a democratic regime was set up. It did not last, but in the meantime the Russian government made efforts to continue the war.

There was further chaos and immense suffering. The chief exponent of Marxist ideas, Lenin, a Russian exile, was allowed by the Germans, for their own ends, to travel into Russia in a sealed train. He soon succeeded in driving out the liberal leader, Kerensky, and set up his own Soviet, communist organisation. Peace was made with Germany, the separate peace of Brest-Litovsk in 1918. Freed from war on two fronts, the Germans made a supreme bid to beat the western allies and failed when within sight of victory. Meanwhile in Russia a violent revolution took place. Large numbers of people were killed, including the Tzar and his whole family. Immense disorganisation occurred, but the Russian communists, Bolsheviks as they were called, succeeded in gaining control over the whole vast area of Russia in Europe and Asia.

Within a few years the rest of the world accepted the existence of the communist system, and the Russian government set out to turn the country from a backward agricultural state into a modern industrial community.

Right up until the end of the war of 1939-45 communism was the system with one state only, Russia, but the result of the second world war was to widen the boundaries of the system until it embraced fourteen countries. Russia was on the winning side in that war, and indeed her stand against Hitler of Germany and his horrible system had been so magnificent that immense goodwill existed for Russia after the war. The Russians had also been strategically placed to take over eastern Europe and this they did, gaining control of Poland, Czecho-Slovakia, Hungary, Rumania, Bulgaria, and several other states. Even when a country slipped outside the Russian network, it tended to remain communist, as with Yugo-Slavia and Albania.

The greatest gain for the communist system was, however, the mastery of China. The Chinese population is the largest of any country in the world—reputed by the Chinese themselves to be 700 million. That this huge total should be added to the hundreds of millions of Russia and her satellites is indeed a triumph for communism.

It is also proof outright of the spread of western modes of thought. It is a western system of philosophy which has been taken up by the Chinese. In place of their own ancient ways of thought, they have now adopted the works of the western master Karl Marx. They even go so far—in a way reminiscent of the quarrels of Catholics and Protestants—as to proclaim that they in China are the true followers of the Master, and that the Russians are deviationists. In this way in a most grotesque form there is a revival of the bitter controversies which have disgraced the Christian Church, first between the Latin and Greek Churches, and then after the Reformation between the Roman Church and the Protestant bodies. That is by the way, but the most important feature of the Russo-Chinese dispute is that China has taken to its heart a system derived entirely from the West.

In other Asiatic countries, too, western political ideas have been adopted: the system of voting in use in a democracy, parliamentary government, and even more important, the industrial system which began in Europe and America in the latter part in the eighteenth century. Every country in Asia and Africa which has attained its independence from the white man—and nearly all countries have now done so—has economic ambitions to get wealth in the way that the west gets it, by industry. In many other ways—the adoption of western inventions, the use of western styles of dress, in speech and in general behaviour—the influence of the west, derived from the Mediterranean, has prevailed.

Only in one most important respect has western practice and influence failed. This is in the sphere of religion. Even the most determined atheist must know that in the millennium from the fall of western Rome (476) to the capture of Constantinople (1453) it was the Catholic Church which taught and guided the peoples of Europe. Under her aegis they grew to nationhood. One of the tragedies of the human condition is that when at last in the fifteenth and sixteenth centuries the westerners broke the bonds imposed on them by Islam, they almost at the same time became sundered by religion. Half of western Christendom revolted from the Catholic Church and became Protestant. Yet even so, the Christian faith was still professed by Europeans and was transplanted to every land open to European influence. Far and wide Catholic missionaries travelled, reaching China, India and Japan. In Japan they achieved a great initial success, which was only checked and finally overcome by savage persecutions in which many of the converts died. In China and in India the Catholics set up churches which have endured to this day. The Philippines were converted, so that the majority of the modern inhabitants are Catholics. After the Catholic effort came the more belated but still powerful Protestant missionary crusade, which has brought into existence various non-Catholic churches all over Africa, Asia and the Pacific.

It could have been that among the exports of the west would have been included its spiritual philosophy, but unfortunately in the middle of the nineteenth century a questioning of religious beliefs arose from the discoveries and the theories of scientific men.

The geological discoveries of Sir Charles Lyell, the biological theories of Charles Darwin, accompanied by destructive criticism of the Bible coming from Germany, led to an undermining of Christian belief in most countries. As a result, it must have appeared to many thinking men and women in oriental lands that if the western leaders of the world did not themselves believe in their own religion, there was little incentive for men of other cultures to embrace Christianity. In fact, when the Japanese were making their extraordinary effort to catch up with modern life and were adopting wholesale western techniques and inventions, their leaders did seriously consider whether such adoption should include the assumption of the westerners' religion. In all likelihood it was owing to the signs of decline in western religious belief that the Japanese decided against the acceptance of Christianity.

However, the work of Christian missionaries has had an unexpected effect on the non-Christian world, and that is in the quickening of other world faiths. Buddhism, Islam and Hinduism have all felt this stimulation and, far from being moribund, they have put forth signs of renewed strength. In addition, the adherents of all faiths have been brought a degree nearer to one another owing to the fact that communism is officially opposed to all religions. Religion is regarded in the communist philosophy as the opiate of the masses, and the official teaching is of a militant atheism, a form of philosophy which has, incidentally, all the characteristics of a religion, albeit in an inverted form.

It thus comes about that with the exception of religion, the features of the western civilisation have been carried over to the rest of the world, and consequently the bases of modern culture throughout the entire planet are derived from the civilisation which originally was centred around the Mediterranean.

NOTES : As to the position of Europe vis-a-vis Asia, and the use of Europe as the centre of world history, few passages in modern writing can be more illuminating than the following: 'Till the period of European dominance over Asia, there was no Asian history as such. Asia consisted of three cultural areas, the Islamic, the Hindu Buddhist and the Sinic, each continental in its proportions. Separated by deserts and impassible mountains, the relations between these areas were limited and intermittent. The dominance which the western nations exercised over them in the nineteenth century and in the first half of the twentieth gave to Asian political developments a unity which entitles it to be considered a definitive period of history.'

This is from the foreword written by an Asian, K. M. Panikkar, to Professor Jan Romein's work, *The Asian Century*, 1962. The author, a distinguished Dutch historian, is pro-Asian in his outlook, but he adds (p 25) a most convincing account of the failure of the East, after its great initial successes in building a civilisation, to continue the good work. 'Thus lived the Asian masses, generation after generation, century after century, living in AD 1500 just as they had lived in 1500 BC, uncoveting, undesiring, and so renouncing the effort to gain an existence worthy of a human being.' Previously he had pointed out that there was no advance beyond the level of skill reached by the earliest pioneers of civilisation. 'Men did not strive to better themselves as did the peasants and workers in later Europe who made their own betterment their main objective.'

As to Africa, the most scathing comment comes again from a writer who cannot be accused of ecclesiastical bias. Hugh Trevor-Roper, in *The Rise of Christian Europe* (1965), writes (p 9): 'Perhaps in the future, there will be some African history to teach. But at present there is none, or very little; there is only the history of the Europeans in Africa. The rest is largely darkness, like the history of pre-Columbian America. And darkness is not a subject for history.'

As a corrective of Trevor-Roper's statement, the reader can examine some of the attempts (made, by the way, by Europeans) to set out what is known of African history. *A Short History of Africa* by Roland Oliver and J. D. Fage (1962); *Kingdoms of the Savanna*, by Jan Vansina;* and *Africa*, by Richard Hall. The last work contains a useful bibliography of books on African history, and also deals with the Chinese discovery of and commerce with East Africa before Europeans knew of it. The idea, however, that central Africa had a history comparable to that of Europe is not in anyway realistic. Finally, there may be added a quotation from Arnold Toynbee's *The World and the West* (1953) in which he explains his choice of title: 'It has not been the West that has been hit by the world; it is the world that has been hit—and hit hard—by the West.' (pp 1 & 2.)

---

* Sub-title: 'A history of Central African states until European occupation.'

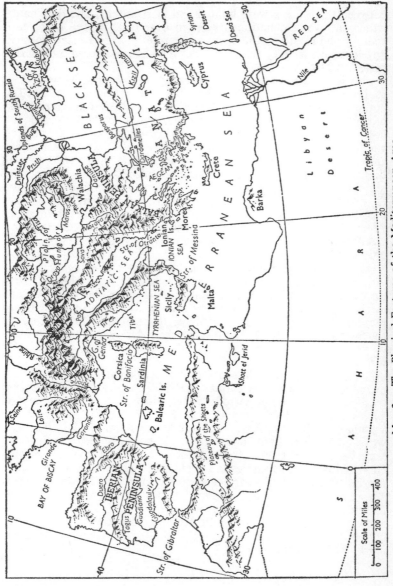

Map 2: The Physical Features of the Mediterranean Area

CHAPTER TWO

PHYSICAL FEATURES
OF THE MEDITERRANEAN

THE MEDITERRANEAN is almost entirely enclosed by land. The exit through the Suez Canal has existed only for a short space of time and is an artificial channel.* The only natural exit, through the Strait of Gibraltar, is very narrow, smaller than the Strait of Dover, and the connection with the wide ocean thus set up does not affect the movement of tides in the Mediterranean to any appreciable extent.

The Strait of Gibraltar was known in ancient times as the Pillars of Hercules, which were supposed to mark the limit of the journeys of Hercules on his labours. The actual pillars were the Rock of Gibraltar on the European side and the Apes' Hill near Ceuta on the African shore.† In fact, the African pillar is twice the height of the Rock, but receives nothing like the same publicity. The best way to see the two pillars at once is to approach from the Atlantic, especially on a fine sunny evening when the African peak is shining rosy red in the setting sun and has, perhaps, a loose girdle of fleecy clouds about its middle. One can feel something of the relief with which the poor voyager who had been blown outside the strait and who had managed by a change of wind to get back

---

* A canal was constructed by the Pharaoh Seti I and this work is depicted in the temple of Karnak; but the canal appears soon to have fallen into disuse. For full details of the history see Chapter 16. It was not until Ferdinand de Lesseps took up the project that the canal became a workable and permanent achievement.

† These mountains were known more euphoniously in classical times as Calpe and Abyla.

would have greeted the sight of the pillars. It is a fascinating though macabre thought how many unfortunate wretches were carried away over the broad Atlantic to starvation by adverse winds when they were too near the oceanic end of the strait.

As the sea is almost tideless (there is a very slight rise and fall in eg, the North Adriatic), it may for practical convenience be referred to as an inland sea, the largest as well as the most important in the world. It is some 2,400 miles in length and about 600-700 miles at its greatest width. Owing to the numerous indentations made by natural action in the coastline around it, the Mediterranean has several arms or branches opening from it which are considerable seas in themselves. Apart from minor areas, such as the Ligurian, Tyrrhenian and Ionian Seas, there are large stretches of water opening from the central sea : the Adriatic, Aegean, and Black Seas. The last named is the only one which can be considered an independent sea, for although it is connected with the Mediterranean, the channel is through the narrow straits of the Bosporus and Dardanelles and the little Sea of Marmora. The ancients had an excellent nomenclature for these waters which open from the Aegean branch of the Mediterranean. The Sea of Marmora was the Pro-Pontic (the Fore-Sea), or antechamber of the Pontic or Euxine Sea, as the ancients styled our Black Sea. The Sea of Azov, which opens out of the Black Sea behind the Crimean peninsula, was evidently regarded by them as a lake, a hated and dreary spot— the *Maeotis Palus*, or Maeotic Swamp, into which flowed the gloomy Tanais, the modern Don. The name Euxine is probably a Greek euphemism (εὔξενος 'kind to strangers', similar to the name given to the Fates, Εὐμενίδες 'the kindly ones').* The word Pontus (πόντος), meant 'open sea' and the awe inspired in ancient times by the Black Sea is shown by the description of the Euxine as though it were exposed to the full fury of the ocean winds.

---

* The Euxine was anciently called also ἄξενος 'the inhospitable' from the savage tribes who dwelt around it, as also from the climate. The poet Ovid, who was exiled to the region by Augustus, bewailed his fate in such surroundings. *Dictus ab antiquis Axenus ille fuit.* Trist. 4. 456.

The Mediterranean does not compare in depth with the oceans proper. The deepest sounding is 2,538 fathoms (15,228ft), which is less than half that of the famous Mindanao deep in the Pacific. The average depth, taking Mediterranean and Black Sea together, is 780 fathoms. The volume of water is over 1,000,000 cubic miles, which is only 0.3 per cent of the Atlantic. There is constant evaporation in the Mediterranean as part of the climatic conditions, but this is made good by the inflow of water from the Atlantic through the Strait, and from the Black Sea where evaporation is offset by rainfall and run-off from the rivers. Otherwise the Mediterranean might by now have become a sea comparable in salinity to the Dead Sea.

Three peninsulas break the even outline of the sea, the Iberian (the Spaniards, anciently known as the Iberians, appear to have achieved geographically that dominion over the Portuguese which they sought in vain politically), the Italian and the Greek. The Iberian peninsula forms the western boundary of the sea and should perhaps be more accurately compared with the huge headlands of Asia Minor on the east. The Italian peninsula, however, very definitely divides the sea into two basins, the western and eastern. Italy and its continuation, Sicily, approach so nearly to the southern shore of the sea that at the closest, the Sicilian Narrows, the distance is little more than eighty miles. The third peninsula, that of Greece, is very near Italy in geographical measurements, but in much of its history, its harbours and important towns have lain on its eastern side, while the corresponding Italian towns and harbours were on the western coast of Italy. Thus, by the fact that in earlier days intercourse between Greece and Italy was comparatively rare, a situation of great historical importance was created. The Greek peninsula also has, owing to its numerous mountains and ensuing difficult communications, served as a buffer to absorb attacks from Asia which might otherwise have overrun Italy and western Europe.

The sea is rich in islands. The Balearics, which now belong to Spain but whose possession has been so much disputed in the past; Corsica, birthplace of the most publicised soldier in the world's history; Sardinia, renowned as the abode of Roman criminals or

exiled Christian confessors of earlier days; Sicily, rich in history
and legends; Crete, home of a very early civilisation; Cyprus, famed
alike in myth and in Christian and profane history—these are
only the larger islands. There are many others which, though small,
have become famous: Elba, Malta, Pantellaria, Lampedusa, Vis,
Cos, Rhodes, and the rest of the Dodecanese; there is the vast collection of the Greek archipelago, which makes the Aegean Sea
resemble a flood which has overrun the lowlands between the hill-
tops. In addition, there are many islands and islets the names of
which mean little even to people who have travelled the Mediterranean. They are small, often uninhabited, and lie off the normal
shipping routes. In fact, it is quite within the bounds of possibility
for a person to be shipwrecked on an island in the Mediterranean
and to stay there for years. In the 1939-45 war, when every channel
was important, there were constant patrols of the most out-of-the-
way routes as well as the more normal, and it was astonishing to
find islands which were hardly ever entered on maps, save on
Admiralty charts or special plans. Some of these did not lie very
far off the beaten tracks; places like Albaron island, for example,
which belongs to Spain and lies between its southern coast and
that of Africa.

Some of these smaller islands are very grim and forbidding when
seen in the Mediterranean winter. The Liparian group, often covered with lowering clouds so that visibility is very poor, include
the harsh sombreness of Stromboli, where smoke rises always in a
great plume to meet the clouds. In some ways, it is more impressive
on a gloomy day than at night, for at night the flames from the
volcano give it beauty, but in the day it is simply harsh and horrible, stark and cruel. Below the volcano lies the dingy little town
where a few poor inhabitants eke out a scanty living. The rest of
the islands in this group are mostly a few acres of bare, desolate
rock. They are only a comparatively short distance from Italy or
Sicily, but they give the impression of being at the world's end,
near an *Avernus* more dreadful than any poet could conceive. It
was to this place that Mussolini sent his political opponents to
drag out an existence for thirty years, and to return—if they
returned—old and broken men.

By contrast, when the sun smiles nothing can exceed the loveliness of the island-strewn sea. Over the Aegean, for instance, it is
easy to understand how the culture of the Ionian land made its
way across the sea from legend-haunted island to island, for on
these isles of the Aegean are centred many of the stories of the
Greek mythology, such as the birth of Apollo. Many are only rocks,
but others are fairly large, quite a few miles in extent, having little
villages and towns. The houses are beautifully white, glinting in
the sun like newly-washed dolls-houses, and each village has its
little church round which it clusters. Such islands are like stepping-
stones across the Aegean.

Many rivers of great historic importance, but few of any great
size, flow into the sea. In the former class may be reckoned the
Tiber, the Strymon, and the Metaurus; in the latter, the Ebro, the
Rhone and the Po. There is only one river outstanding both in size
and importance which has its outlet into the sea, and that is the
Nile. Only the Nile (and the Rhone to a much smaller degree)
has the many-mouthed opening known as a delta. To approach the
Nile by air from across the western desert is to come suddenly
upon a great V-shaped stretch of green after passing over hundreds
of miles of sand. At once one can see why Egypt has been described
as the gift of the Nile, for there is the stream winding through the
sand like a vast ditch, surrounded in all directions by the sand,
except in the immediate vicinity of the bank where a thread of
green shows the influence of the precious water. The V-shaped
patch is the famous Delta of the Nile, and lovely is the view after
the stretches of barren desert, though bright with colour as this
can be when seen from above.

The land around the sea is generally mountainous. Starting from
the Strait of Gibraltar and proceeding in a northerly direction there
are mountains which form the plateaus of Spain, broken here and
there by river valleys but containing very little ground suitable for
military movements, despite the numerous wars which have been
fought in Spain. Between Spain and France is the Pyrenean range.
In France, the southern coast, except around the mouth of the
Rhone, is a land of mountains, while the great chain of the Alps
forms the boundary between France and Italy. The Apennines take

C

up the mountainous character of the country almost from the point where the Alps joins the sea, and run the length of the Italian peninsula. Except for the valley of the Po, the plains of Italy are small in extent and few in number. Italy is a country of mountains, as allied troops found to their cost in the campaigns of 1943-45. North of the Adriatic, the Alps continue into the Velebit mountains and the Dinaric Alps of Yugo-Slavia, while these latter ranges join the Pindus mountains of Greece. The whole Balkan peninsula is mountainous. Similar country is found in Asia Minor, and on the coastline of Syria the Lebanon range runs parallel with the sea until it merges into the hill country of Palestine. From the southern borders of Palestine across Egypt and Libya lies the only portion of the Mediterranean coastline which is not high ground. This area is mostly desert, save for the coastal strip, and even the desert is broken into plateaus. The typical Mediterranean country appears again in Tunisia and thereafter North Africa is filled with mountain ranges, the Atlas and its offshoots, which eventually disappear only on the shores of the Atlantic.

In Algeria, the mountains are much lower than in the rest of North Africa, but even there they constitute formidable obstacles to travel. The islands of the sea are also mountainous and in some cases, such as Sicily with its 10,000ft Etna, they contain high ranges. But even islands like Sardinia, which do not attain a great height, are still above the level of merely hilly country and are exceedingly rocky and difficult for communications.

In so mountainous an area it is not strange that traces of volcanic activity should be found. Everyone knows the fame of Vesuvius, Stromboli and Etna. Few remember the fact that within historic times there were active volcanoes in southern France (the rogation days of the English Book of Common Prayer take their names from the prayers instituted to obtain relief from this visitation), that Blida and Djijelli in Algeria were overthrown within the last century by earthquakes. Lisbon was destroyed by an earthquake in the eighteenth century. Asia Minor has been scourged in like manner, and continues to be, as witness the seismic disturbances in modern Turkey. There is a reference in one of the Minor Prophets to an earthquake in Palestine.

Perhaps the presence of so many mountains on either side of the sea and in its islands, together with the continuing volcanic activity, may give some help to solving the problem of the origin of the Mediterranean. Possibly when the ice melted at the end of the last Ice Age, masses of water poured down from the Alpine chains of Europe through the valleys and overwhelmed the lowlands of the area now covered by sea waters. This would explain the rocky and lofty nature of the islands, if they are the unburied relics of land covered by a flood. Such phenomena have occurred in various parts of the world; the Marianas Group in the Pacific, which is both rocky and volcanic, is simply the summit of land buried by ancient shiftings in the level of the sea bed. On the other hand, in some remote period the ocean undobutedly broke in through the Strait of Gibraltar. Perhaps the flooding of the Mediterranean is remembered in the story of Noah's Flood. Whatever its origin, the sea has exerted a great influence on the fate of humanity for it has facilitated the passage of races and therefore of ideas from East to West.

Of the climate of this area, it can reasonably be said that it is temperate and approaching the sub-tropical. The summers are hot and dry, the winters wet but fairly mild, though snow and ice make for lower temperatures in various parts. The Mediterranean climate does not equal the heat of the tropics; it does not provide the cold of far northern regions, and the seasons are constant, so that from May to August dry weather can be predicted, while wet and cold occur from September to April, though between January and April there is often some pleasant weather. On the whole, the Mediterranean area does not provide those horrible features which are scourges of nature in other parts. The sirocco when it blows in Algeria is very unpleasant, lashing the skin and burning it, making the atmosphere very heavy and penetrating into every house, but it is a small trouble to endure compared with a sandstorm in the Sahara.

In fact, the Mediterranean has a climate peculiar to the region, just as its geographical features are peculiar. Essentially the lands of the Mediterranean, while forming part of Europe, Asia, and Africa, have a homogeneous character of their own. North Africa, though united physically with the rest of the African continent, has little in common with the land south of the Sahara, but bears a much stronger resemblance in geography, climate, productions and people to southern Europe. The south of Europe, again, though united to the north and centre of that continent, has in its mountain ranges an isolating factor which cuts it off from the northern lands and joins it to the rest of the Mediterranean lands.

Ethnologists have spoken of a Mediterranean race as distinct from the Nordic and Alpine races. This is a matter in which it would be easy to dogmatise and to create controversy, but it is true that the people of the Mediterranean area have features in common, just as climate and geographical phenomena are common to these lands. In going from North Africa to Malta, Sicily or southern Italy, one notices differences between the inhabitants of those different lands rather in their clothes and other incidentals than in their physical appearance. There is not much to choose between the so-called Arabs of Algiers and the Sicilian peasants as regards the colour of their skin, their stature, facial characteristics and type of hair.

CHAPTER THREE

HISTORY TO THE
ESTABLISHMENT
OF THE PERSIAN EMPIRE

ONLY ONE state has ever succeeded in dominating the Mediterranean from end to end, and in controlling its entire coastline and hinterland. That state was the empire of Rome. The Moslem powers from the seventh to the seventeenth century conquered the whole southern and eastern shores and penetrated inland in Spain and the Balkans, but they failed to complete their conquests and were eventually driven out from both the Spanish and Balkan peninsulas.

We use the Roman name for the sea, and it was under Roman rule that it became the highway between Europe and Asia. Under the empire, the Mediterranean became an Italian lake and the Romans called it *Mare Nostrum*. Rome had gathered within the boundaries of her empire not only Greece, but also Carthage, Egypt and the Near East. What of the empires which preceded Rome?

Dr Samuel Johnson in the quotation prefixed to this book, referred to the four great empires of the world—the Assyrian, the Persian, the Grecian and the Roman. This was reasonable enough, though he knew of the Egyptian Empire also. Up to the nineteenth century, our knowledge of ancient pre-classical civilisation was confined to the writings of the Greek and Roman historians and to the Bible. The monuments of ancient Egypt were obviously known, but since the hieroglyphics were not deciphered very little exact information was available. Herodotus begins the second book of his History with an account of the Egyptians. He derived such information as he set down from conversations with the Egyptian priests by means of interpreters. By the time of Herodotus the Egyptians had greatly declined in power, and from the middle of the eighth century BC were ruled by dynasties which, though Egyptian in habits and outlook, were foreign in origin. In the fifth century the country was conquered by the Persians, and although it regained its independence its old institutions began to decline. Quite apart then from the linguistic difficulties which Greek travellers encountered in Egypt, it is highly probable that even among the Egyptian priests knowledge of their country's history was already beginning to fade. In the fourth century BC an Egyptian priest, Manetho, wrote a history of his country in Greek, but as only fragments remain we cannot judge how much information he was able to transmit.

As early as the fifth century BC the attractions of Egypt as a tourist country had been realised, and many famous Greeks made the journey there. Some sought esoteric knowledge, one of the perennial quests of the human mind. Just as modern Europeans and Americans imagine they will discover an all-revealing wisdom in what is vaguely known as 'the East', so the ancient Greeks, and later the Romans, expected to find the clue to life's riddle in Egypt. 'You Greeks are always children', as an Egyptian priest said to Solon of Athens, and no doubt from the standpoint of the 3,000-years-old civilisation of Egypt, the Greeks must have appeared parvenus indeed.

If in the sixth or fifth centuries BC there was discussion as to whether the Egyptians were the most ancient of mankind, as Herodotus relates, then the question was worth discussing. The researches of savants following upon Napoleon's expedition to Egypt in 1798 led to the deciphering of the hieroglyphics and we now have a considerable amount of historical information about Egypt. The history of Egypt begins towards the end of the fourth millennium BC. The rulers of Egypt are divided by historians into dynasties following Manetho's scheme of arrangement. The first king of Egypt was Menes, king of Upper Egypt, who conquered Lower Egypt, so that the Pharaohs were said to hold the sceptres of the two lands. The dating of Menes and the first dynasty is thus put at about 3000 BC. The thirtieth and last dynasty reigned until 341 BC. After the death of Alexander the Great, one of his generals, Ptolemy, became ruler of Egypt, founding the dynasty of the

Ptolemies, which lasted 300 years and culminated in the famous Cleopatra. It was under the fourth dynasty that the Great Pyramid at Giza was built by the Pharaoh Cheops (Khufu). The second pyramid at Giza was built by the Pharaoh Chephren (Khafra), and the third edifice of the same kind and at the same place was constructed by Mycerinus (Menkaura). The famous Sphinx is impossible to date but modern scholars think that it may have been built by order of Chephren, circa 2900 BC. It has clearly contributed to the world's storehouse of allusion, by its name and the mystery which its presence evokes—the idea of a sphinx-like insoluble enigma. (Picture, p 65)

The three pyramids, and particularly the Great Pyramid at Giza, form with the Sphinx the greatest works of the ancient world which have survived, apart from the Wall of China. Just as the latter is regarded as a useless construction—since its ostensible purpose, to keep out the barbarians, was never fulfilled—so, too, the pyramids have been described as monuments of vast but futile labour. They were, as far as we can conjecture, the burial-place of kings, and we can but marvel at the awe in which the early Pharaohs must have been held, in that they should have been able to bring their people to erect so mighty a monument to the dead. These monuments having been built before the ruler's death, a material power alone would not have sufficed for such a work; only a belief in the divine nature of the Pharaoh could have compelled the labour of thousands over so many years.

Nor are the pyramids the product of brute labour alone. High architectural and mathematical skill went into their construction. The Great Pyramid covers an area of thirteen acres and is 150ft higher than St Paul's Cathedral in London, and yet the four sides of the base have a mean error of only 6/10th of an inch in length and 12 in angle from a perfect square. There are many passages and chambers in the Great Pyramid which show yet again the marvellous skill and workmanship of those who built it. Two chambers, commonly called those of the king and queen, once contained a sarcophagus in each, but no trace of bodies, jewels or other ornaments has been found in the pyramid. In eerie darkness broken only by an acetylene flare in the hand of a guide, one may stand in the heart of this mass of stone, beside a tomb-like object on the chamber floor and ponder the thought that here, 5,000 or 5,500 years ago, probably rested the body of the most powerful monarch in the world. Long before the Christian era the tomb had been plundered; indeed it is one of the rarest of archaeological finds to discover a Pharaoh's tomb which robbers have not already opened and ransacked. It was the fact that although robbers had gained access to Tutankhamun's tomb they had not been able to remove its wonderful treasures that made the discovery of this comparatively unimportant Pharaoh so memorable, but how even the most skilful and well-equipped robbers could have made undetected entry into a pyramid, especially the Great Pyramid, remains a mystery, since bodies of guards were posted to prevent such outrages.

The intricate nature of the interior of the Great Pyramid, where some of the passages are dangerous to use and all are extremely hard of access, together with the extreme accuracy of the measurements and the unexplained origin of the Sphinx have all given rise to many stories in ancient and later times. It is therefore not surprising that a modern sect has arisen which seeks to find in the measurements of the Great Pyramid a key to the past and future history of the world.

The history of Egypt is divided into three sections; the Ancient Kingdom; the Middle Kingdom (beginning with the eleventh dynasty but of indeterminate date) which was terminated by the period of the Hyksos or Shepherd Kings who ruled from about 1720 to 1570 BC. These were invaders from Asia who by means of horse-drawn chariots—weapons then new to the Egyptians—were able to conquer the land. They appear to have been driven out by a Pharaoh of the seventeenth dynasty. Egypt then entered upon the period of the New Kingdom under which Egyptian greatness rose to its full height. The Pharaohs in reign after reign led their armies into Western Asia and conquered as far as the Caspian Sea. It is commonly assumed that it was during the rule of the Shepherd Kings that the Israelites entered Egypt, and that the 'Pharaoh who knew not Joseph' was one of their successors. The Egyptians regarded the Hyksos period as one of national degradation and national suffering. The passage in Genesis xlvi, 34, 'for every shepherd is an abomination unto the Egyptians', is evidently a reference to this Egyptian hatred of the Hyksos.

The last Pharaoh to achieve great conquests and assert Egypt's power was Rameses III, who reigned from 1198 to 1166 BC. After this the country declined. One authority sums up the rest of Egyptian history as 'a melancholy story of disintegration and defeat relieved but occasionally by a short spell of recovery'. (Chamber's Encyclopedia.)

How old was the Egyptian civilisation? All that we can say is that there must have been settled communities in the Valley of the Nile for many centuries before the first dynasty of Menes. Some three to four thousand years before the Christian era, settled populations meriting to be called civilised arose in the great river valleys in Egypt, in Mesopotamia (Iraq), in India and China. It is usual to assume that agriculture dates back some 10,000 years. Without it, the form of life in fixed communities which we call civilised, as having evolved cities, could not have existed. The argument as to the oldest state, or succession of states in the world, is unlikely ever to be settled, but some conclusions can be taken for certain. That the civilisations of the New World were much later than those of the Old World, and that the history of China and India, despite talk of immemorial antiquity, cannot be traced as far as that of Egypt or of the Middle East, are not debateable propositions but statements which can easily be verified by consulting any modern encyclopedia or some of the numerous and attractively written works on archaeology.

Which was the older civilisation, the Egyptian or that which it encountered in the land between the rivers Tigris and Euphrates? It may well be that the Egyptian has prime place as to organisation in a large community, or as the precursor of the numerous imperial systems. Other communities, smaller though they were or may have been, were much older. According to excavators who work on the basis of radio carbon analysis, Jericho was settled about 7500 BC, and by 6800 BC had grown to the size of a town of nearly ten acres with an estimated population of 2,000. These facts postulate a much older antiquity for city life than anywhere else in the world, and antedate Egyptian history by more than 3,000 years. It can be said that Jericho was only a small community as against a much larger prehistoric population in the Nile valley. In South Babylonia there are remains of human culture in the Eridu period, which is dateable to about 4500 BC or a little later. These remains are found in prehistoric graves in Mesopotamia, where the possessions of the deceased buried with them—pots, implements, ornaments—seem to imply belief in an after life.

About 3500 BC the Eridu settlement was made by the Sumerians, the people to whom the origin of Mesopotamian civilisation is generally attributed. In a slightly Irish form of statement, one of the greatest modern authorities has said that wherever the Sumerians came from, it was not Sumer. The best view is that they came from somewhere east of Babylonia. 'And it came to pass, as they journeyed from the east, that they found a plain in the land of Shinar, and they dwelt there.' Thus Genesis, XI, 2, which goes on to recount the attempt to build the Tower of Babel and the subsequent confusion and scattering of humanity throughout the whole earth. In the preceding chapter there is a reference to the kingdom of Nimrod, the mighty hunter before the Lord. 'And the beginning of his kingdom was Babel, and Erech, and Accad, and Calneh, in the land of Shinar' (Chap X, 10). Here we have the mention of Accad or Akkad, one of the city states which contested supremacy with Sumer, but beyond the preservation of names such as Erech and Accad nothing was known in classical antiquity about these beginnings of Mesopotamian civilisation.

In Egypt, the nature of the climate and the extremely massive monuments ensured that the Egyptian civilisation was not forgotten. Men could hardly overlook the Great Pyramid. In Babylonia, the monuments were not quite so large and the various empires fought each other with a fury which resulted in great destruction. Nineveh, the mighty capital of Assyria, which survived the preaching of Jonah, fell in 612 BC before a coalition of Nabopolassar of Babylon, the Ummanmanda (some Scythians) and Cyaxares of Medea, and was obliterated or buried beneath the sands. Much the same fate befell the later empires in this area. The city of Babylon still existed in the time of Alexander the Great, but 300 years later,

by the first century AD, it had declined to a place of small importance. Alexander's troops had marched past mounds beneath which
were the remains of the old civilisations of Babylonia, and it was
not until the nineteenth century that re-discovery of these ancient
cities began. Two Englishmen, Henry Rawlinson and Austen Layard,
played a great and honourable part in recovering the true history
of the ancient civilisations. It was a European enterprise throughout.

The Greek civilisation borrowed much from the achievements of
states in Egypt, the Near and the Middle East. Writing alone would
have been a priceless gift, and writing developed from lowly and
obscure beginnings in the eastern cultures. In addition, the whole
apparatus of civilised living developed in the east—in agriculture,
irrigation, building, suitable clothing, ships and roads.

Of writing, a leading modern authority on Babylon has this to
say, 'The origin of writing was lowly. It arose not as the servant of
religion (except indirectly), not as a vehicle for transmission of
history or literature or noble thoughts, but simply in connection
with the prosaic task of keeping the temple accounts.' (*The
Greatness that was Babylon*, H. W. F. Saggs, 1962. p 22.) To hold
in one's hand a small cylindrical tablet of baked clay, knowing
that it is one of the earliest pieces of writing, is to experience the
sense of wonder. Here is the beginning of the vast storehouse of
human thought and knowledge; the commencement of the process
which has given to mankind the possession of great literature. Yet
what is written on these earliest memorials of man's attempt to
hand on something to speak for him when he is gone? Only a bare
reckoning of the amount of oil or fuel required in a temple; almost,
one might say, a ledger account.

In the period of some 6,000 years during which writing has
existed, many systems have been developed. First there was the
mnemonic system, where some object is used to aid the memory.
The system of the quipu among the ancient Peruvians, or of beads
among the Maoris, was of this type, though whether such a method
would always have gone on to another stage cannot be known.
Secondly there is the system of pictographs, used among the Indian
tribes of North America and, in a much more intricate form,
providing the basis of the ancient Egyptian hieroglyphics. From

this developed the ideographic method in which the original picture becomes a symbol, so that a sceptre represents kingship. Several great nations in antiquity reached this stage, among them the Sumerians and the peoples who succeeded them. They used what has been called the cuneiform or wedge-shaped style of writing, and there are still several scripts of this type—Hittite, Cretan etc— not yet fully deciphered. This style of writing is cumbersome and requires an ever increasing number of symbols. Chinese, with its derivative the Japanese syllabary, is the only one to survive, and it is the most involved of all these ideographic systems. In course of time up to 1500-1000 BC, rudimentary alphabets developed from the earlier methods using fewer symbols to denote sounds. The credit for this must go to the Phoenicians who developed the alphabet of twenty-two letters to speed up their business transactions.

The older systems of writing were not only cumbersome but were also so involved that they could never become media for popular use. It is reported that the communist rulers of China are trying to simplify their script and it was with this same object in view that the Phoenicians worked out their alphabet. From this original, from around 1000 BC, has come the alphabet now in use in the modern world, derived from Phoenicia and the Hebrew system and on to the Greek and Latin languages. The Phoenicians were the schoolmasters of Europe, but for purely utilitarian reasons. Once their pupils had learned their lesson, they applied it to the production of the many forms of literature in poetry and prose, and for the purpose of abstract thought.

The old eastern civilisations contributed the groundwork of European culture, but they could not give something which they did not possess. The utilitarian, yes, that the barbarous peoples of Europe could acquire from Egypt and Asia, but the finer flower of civilisation at its best is Europe's own. There was art in Egypt and Assyria but it was not art for art's sake or for beauty, but solely in the service of monarchy or of the temples. There was applied science, too, in the erection of mighty buildings or in the study of the stars, but not the pursuit of truth and knowledge as its own reward.

A necessarily brief sketch of the Babylonian civilisation before the establishment of Persian rule begins with the Al'Ubaid or Prediluvian period (?4000-3500 BC). The Sumerians had a tradition of a great flood. So did most nations of the ancient world, but the evidences of a flood in the deep layer of silt discovered by Sir Leonard Woolley is now thought by many archaeologists to refer to a local flood, and not to the deluge described in Genesis and encountered elsewhere as Deucalion's Flood etc. The early dynasties of Ur of the Chaldees are derived from king lists which mention the Flood and give particulars of sovereigns who reigned before and after that event.

The first dynasty of Ur is dated at approximately 3000 BC. The king of Umma, one Lugalzagesi, overthrew the state of Lagash shortly after 2400 BC. Babylonia consisted then of various small city states which were in frequent conflict with each other. A dynasty was founded by Sharrum-kin (better known as Sargon of Agade) which lasted from 2371-2230 BC. His third successor and grandson was Naram Sin (2291-2255 BC). The fall of this dynasty was caused by a barbarous race, the Gutians, coming from the east of Babylonia, Elam, whence invaders often troubled the civilised states. The third dynasty of Ur showed Sumerian civilisation in its most developed form (2113-2006 BC). There are about 15,000 tablets in existence of this period—legal, administrative and economic documents. The end of this dynasty came with the destruction of Ur, and an Elamite garrison was left on the ruins of the devastated capital.

The Ur of the Chaldees from which Abraham set out in obedience to divine summons to found the people of Israel, was already ancient at that time (circa 2000 BC). Egypt, too, was ancient with more than 1,000 years of recorded history. The appearance of the Israelites on the scene of the ancient world does not acquire much significance until around the year 1000 BC, in the brief splendour of the monarchy of David and Solomon.

Babylon was an ancient city which, about 1790 BC, was under the rule of a king, Hammurabi, whose name has been discovered after being unknown and neglected for ages. He now has a considerable place in history as the author of a code of laws.

In the course of some hundreds of years there began to arise the great power of the ancient world before the age of the Persian dominion. At the time of Hammurabi there was an Assyrian king named Shamshi Adad I ,who conquered far and wide, even claiming an empire which reached from the Mediterranean to east of Babylon. He assumed the title 'King of the World' but for several centuries after his time, Assyria was depressed and even had to endure a Babylonian garrison in its capital, Nineveh. There were comings and goings of peoples in Babylonia and Asia Minor during the second millennium BC, with waxing and waning of several powers. Just before 1200 BC, the Hittite power collapsed before an invasion by land and sea of a group of peoples out of eastern Europe, of whom the Philistines were a part. Rameses III of Egypt inflicted a naval defeat on them but they secured control of Syria and Palestine. They proved great oppressors of the Israelites, as the Old Testament so frequently records.

A great king arose in Assyria, Tiglath Pileser I (1115-1077 BC) who was constantly engaged in warfare, reaching the Mediterranean shores in his conquests. His hard-fought wars were apparently looting campaigns for there was no attempt to annex territory and weld it into an empire. Consequently, the tributary peoples were ready to rebel at a favourable opportunity. The Assyrian answer to rebellion or its possibility lay in a policy of frightfulness, and there are many pictorial records showing captives impaled by the conquerors. In the Old Testament they do not receive a good word; their downfall is prophesied and fervently hoped for.

The fortunes of Assyria shifted over the centuries from experience of excessive power brutally employed to an enforced subservience to some stronger power. Tiglath Pileser II (966-935 BC) and Ashur-nasir-pal III (883-859 BC) have left records of their many savageries to the conquered. The latter established a new capital at Kalhu (Biblical Calvah, modern Minrud) in 879 BC, and his son and successor, Shamshi-Adad V (823-811), was compelled to admit the king of Babylon as his suzerain. About this time the Medes, later partners of the Persians, emerged as an important people. In 871 Shamshi-Adad V defeated Babylon and offered sacrifices in the city. This king's line was wiped out by murder in 764, and there came to the throne Tiglath-Pileser III (Pul in the Old Testament), among whose allies was Ahaz of Judah. He took vast numbers of prisoners, 73,000 in one campaign. The Chaldeans began to gain control of south Babylonia, and Merodach-baladan (Marduk-apil-iddina), who is mentioned in second Kings XX, 12, was king of Babylon.

In 722 BC Shalmaneser V succeeded Tiglath-Pileser IV and brought to an end the state of Israel, the larger of the two kingdoms into which Solomon's realm had been divided at his death. Shalmaneser captured Samaria, the capital of Israel, and deported some 27,000 of her people, a method often employed by the Assyrian kings in dealing with the conquered. In this case it seems probable that many more were deported or driven away, as from this time the ten tribes of Israel are lost to history, except for a brief reference in the second book of Esdras, ch 13. The Israelite deportees were removed to the province of Guzanu (Gozan) and to the region south east of Lake Urmea. A king named Sargon, who may have been in command of the army which captured Samaria, succeeded Shalmaneser. His son, Sennacherib, rebuilt Nineveh and made it again the Assyrian capital. In 689 he captured Babylon and assumed the title of King of Sumer and Akkad (that is, of south and north Babylonia). In 681 he was murdered by two of his sons and succeeded by another, Esarhaddon, who twice invaded Egypt and captured Memphis. He died in 669, while on the march for the third time against Egypt.

It was now no longer possible for the Egyptians to keep their own frontiers secure and once again, under Ashurbanipal, the Assyrians invaded Egypt and sacked Thebes (mentioned by the prophet Nahum as No-amon, ch iii, 8-10). Gyges, king of Lydia, formed an alliance with Ashurbanipal, who appointed Psammetichus as king of Egypt under him. It seemed that Assyria was at the height of its power and glory, yet forty years later, in 612 BC, Nineveh was captured and destroyed (see above). As so often happens with coalitions, the allies were soon to fall out, but before that happened there was to be a short Babylonian empire.

It began with Nabopolassar, whose son and successor was the famous Nebuchadnezzar. He met and completely defeated the Egyptian army under Necho II at Carchemish (the Egyptian king had defeated King Josiah of Judah at Megiddo). This was in 604. By 597 Nebuchadnezzar had begun the siege of Jerusalem. The king of Judah, Jehoiakim, died during the siege and his son Jehoiachin was led captive to Babylon, along with Judean nobles, craftsmen and soldiers. The country rebelled again against the Babylonians and in 586 Jerusalem was finally starved out. The king Zedekiah was blinded and taken to Babylon, as were a large section of the remaining population.

Nebuchadnezzar was succeeded by his son Amel-Marduk (Evil Merodach) who was killed in a revolution in 560. There is proof of his kindness to Jehioachin (II Kings, xxv, 27-30) under the Assyrian form of Ya'u-kinu of Yahuda. Nerg-shar-usur (mentioned in Jeremiah XXXIX, 3 as Nergalsharezer) was Nebuchadnezzar's son-in-law and succeeded to the throne. He died in 556 BC. Nabuna'id (Nabonidus) was then placed on the throne. He was not of the royal family but the son of a nobleman and of the high priestess of the god Sin at Harran, who may have been of the Assyrian royal house. Nabonidus invested his son Bel-sharusur (the Belshazzar of Daniel) as regent in Babylonia.

In 540 Babylon fell to the Medes and Persians who were closely akin. Cyrus the Persian, king of Anshan in 553, overthrew Astyages, king of Medea, and set up a kingdom which stretched from the south of the Caspian to the river Halys in Asia Minor. Mesopotamia was exhausted and easily fell when Cyrus and his Persians swept down from their uplands upon states which were unable to oppose them. Under Cyrus and his two immediate successors, Cambyses and Darius, the empire of the Persians spread from the borders of India right across to the Aegean Sea, south-westwards to include Egypt and northwards to the Caspian and the Crimea. It was the largest empire yet seen in the world. Its ruler, the king of Persia, was referred to as the King of Kings and the Great King. He so much impressed the Greeks that in their literature he is called simply 'The King'. To show his universal dominion, it was his wont to have a cup presented to him in which water from the Nile, Danube and Indus was mixed. He lived in a style of great magnificence and the wealth accumulated in the royal palaces was immense.

The founders of his empire were simply hardy mountaineers. When they had overthrown the Medean and Babylonian kingdoms they reached the river Halys, which formed the eastern boundaries of the kingdom of Lydia. Lydia embraced the whole of western Asia Minor and the Greek cities along the coast paid tribute to the Lydian king. The reigning monarch of Lydia in the time of Cyrus was one Croesus, whose name has become synonymous with wealth. Indeed, the Lydians are credited with the invention of coined money. Cyrus does not appear to have intended at first to invade Lydia, but Croesus started the trouble. Croesus was anxious to know what would happen if he attacked Cyrus, so he sent an embassy to consult the oracle of the god Apollo at Delphi, in Greece. He asked a question but the oracle replied as ambiguously as a modern astrologer, saying that if Croesus went to war he would destroy a great empire. Hitler used the same words in speaking of the British declaration of war in 1939. The prophecy was fulfilled, Croesus was beaten in the field and his capital, Sardis, was captured. Cyrus ordered him to be burned. When placed on the funeral pyre, Croesus was heard to cry out for one called Solon. On this being translated for Cyrus, he stopped the proceedings to inquire who Solon might be. Croesus then explained that some years before he had entertained at his capital a wise man from Athens. He had showed this Solon all his wealth and treasures and when the visitor obstinately refrained from any comment, Croesus had asked him if he did not think him, Croesus, the happiest of men. To this Solon had replied first by naming two completely obscure Greeks as the happiest of men, and then added that no man could be called happy until dead, and that when one might come with iron sufficient he would be master of Croesus's gold. Cyrus felt the force of this anecdote. He pardoned Croesus, who later became one of his counsellors. The Lydians were reduced to dependence on Persia.

Following the conquest of Lydia, the Persians imbibed the idea that Persian rule must extend until it was co-extensive with the earth. Cyrus himself seems to have fallen in battle against some savage tribes to the north of his newly-won empire, and his head, it is said, was used as a drinking cup by the savages' Amazonian queen.

D

His successor, Cambyses, appears to have been both madman and good soldier. His principal exploit was the conquest of Egypt, which for the next two centuries was part of the Persian empire. He then proceeded to indulge in all sorts of excesses against the Egyptians, particularly against their religion. The Egyptians were then perhaps more firmly attached to their old beliefs than in the days of their greatness, and Cambyses deliberately outraged their feelings by slaying their sacred animals.

Cambyses died and his reign was followed by a period of anarchy. Darius, a kinsman of the two previous kings, then succeeded to the throne and within a short time was supreme throughout the empire. Either from the wish to employ his unruly subjects in foreign wars, or because he was filled with the Persian desire for empire, he undertook fresh conquests. He was the first would-be conqueror of Russia, and the first great warrior to invade her from the west. He had as much good fortune in this venture as those who were later to follow his example—Charles XII, Napoleon and Hitler. Crossing into Europe, he marched as far as the Danube where his Greek mercenaries had prepared a bridge of boats for the crossing of his army. He then passed over the river with a great army to seek the Scythians, who at that period were the nomadic possessors of southern Russia. They followed a strong 'scorched earth' policy and refrained from open battle with Darius, contenting themselves with guerilla and partisan warfare along his lines of communication. For some sixty days Darius marched into the wastes of southern Russia around the Black Sea.

In the meantime, his communications across the Danube were being menaced by some of his paid Greeks, who saw that Darius would eventually turn upon the little Greek states around the Aegean. The more mercenary-minded Greeks prevailed, however, and when Darius returned from his long trek he found to his great relief that he could cross the Danube into more settled territory. Had his bridge not been intact he would have been cut off, for he had no fleet on the Black Sea to transport his troops and behind him were the Scythians. They had sent him a contemptuous message which consisted of specimen animals: a mouse to suggest that he should burrow out of the country, and a bird to show him that wings would be equally useful as a means of escape. The Great King took the hint and was no doubt thankful to retire to his Asiatic dominions, having left a large proportion of his soldiers to occupy southern Russia for ever.

The court chroniclers must have had a difficult task explaining away the defeat of Darius, but no more efforts were made to conquer the wild regions he had invaded. Darius himself retired to his capital, but left his general with 80,000 troops in the north of Greece to reduce that country. Darius had presumably heard of the attempted treachery of his Greek allies, and in any case he was in need of a triumph which would offset his failure against the Scythians.

In the event, he was bitterly disappointed in his belief that the Greek states would fall easily. Each of them individually was weak and he knew from the many 'Quislings' in his pay that unity did not come easily to them. But sometimes in face of great danger the Greeks could unite and against Persia they now did so, led by Athens and Sparta. In 490 BC, at the battle of Marathon, a small Greek army beat the Persian host. No more attempts to conquer Greece were made while Darius lived, but ten years later his successor, Xerxes, renewed the effort with a much greater force. The Greeks had had time to prepare, particularly the Athenians, who had built a fleet. At Thermopylae, a small body of Spartans was overwhelmed after slaying masses of Persians, but Salamis was a great naval, and Plataea an equally great land victory, of Greeks over Persians. Never again were the Persians a menace to the Greeks. The victories won against them by the Greeks produced little if any resentment in their minds. They appear to have learnt the lesson of their defeats and to have abandoned the dream of an ever expanding empire. With the Greeks the case was very different. They had been the victims of an unprovoked aggression. Their cities, temples and homes had been burnt and many of their people slain. The fact that Greece had been saved from the Persians was not enough. Persia must be punished in full and that could only be done by invading her and conquering her as she had intended to conquer others. The chronic lack of unity among the Greeks, however, proved stronger even than their resentment against the

Persians and, although schemes for overthrowing Persia were always present in Greek minds, no serious attempt to realise them was made until 336 BC, when Alexander invaded the Persian Empire. The empire founded by Cyrus lasted about two centuries. It was the largest empire yet seen in the world and probably the most efficient.

It took Darius three years to restore order in his empire and he then set about establishing a proper organisation of the whole Persian realm. 'The empire was divided into twenty satrapies and over each were set three Persian officers, the satrap, the general and the secretary of state. These were independent of each other and in direct communication with Susa (O.T.: Shushan). Each satrapy was perfectly autonomous in its internal affairs, except for the tribute which was fixed and regularised; but the control of the central government was maintained by a system of travelling commissioners, and by the development of an imperial postal service carried on by official couriers. Within the satrapies, some districts were allowed to have their own native rulers.' (*Israel in World History*, by A. W. F. Blunt. 1927, p 93.) This is in remarkable contrast to the rule by terror exercised by the Assyrian and Babylonian kings.

Persian rule was, of course, a despotism, but that was nothing new. In religious matters the Persians approximated to monotheism, for they were fire worshippers. This may have been their reason for destroying the Greek temples and it may also have helped them into the good graces of the Jews. In the pages of the Old Testament the Persians, unlike the other foreign rulers of Israel, were spoken of with respect. Cyrus received terms of praise in the later chapters of Isaiah which many a king of Israel would have liked instead of the melancholy and monotonous 'He did evil in the sight of the Lord'.

The Persians appreciated the goodwill of their Jewish subjects, whom they allowed to return to their own land and to whom they granted various privileges. This was perhaps the most peaceful period in the history of the Chosen People. Other parts of the Persian Empire were distracted by vain attempts to regain liberty, but Palestine was at peace. The Jewish feeling regarding the Persians can be gauged by the favourable views taken in the book of Esther of the marriage of Esther with King Ahasuerus. One can imagine the terms in which a marriage between a Jewish maiden and Nebuchadnezzar would have been described.

The Persian king after the time of Darius surrounded himself with great pomp. He lived in magnificent style and made progresses between various parts of his dominions when he changed his summer and winter residences. He governed by means of satraps or provincial governors, and largely because of the need for constant supervision of the provincial governors, there existed an excellent system of roads running for thousands of miles throughout the empire. The royal couriers came and went along these highways which were also useful for the passage of troops.

Nevertheless, the Persian Empire did not endure longer than it took for a powerful enough enemy to arise. After the repulse of Xerxes from Greece, the Greeks carried the war into the enemies' sphere, and Persia lost control of Thrace, and of the Ionian cities in Asia Minor. Disunity and internal warfare among the Greeks delayed the full Greek revanche. In the meantime, the Persians had no other form of redress against the Greeks than to take Greek mercenaries into their pay and to seize every opportunity of intriguing in Greek affairs, thus setting Greeks against Greeks. One of the Persian royal family, Cyrus the Younger, revolted against his brother, the Great King, in 404 BC, and but for his death in battle might have reached the throne. Cyrus was using a force of Greek mercenaries and, when they found themselves cut off in the heart of the empire after Cyrus's death, they made their way under the leadership of Xenophon to the Black Sea coast and to safety. Xenophon's famous work, the *Anabasis*, or *Retreat of the Ten Thousand*, was a standing exposure of the weakness of Persia.

The Persian character deteriorated under the influence of unlimited wealth and luxury. That the noble Persians employed slaves to help them out of bed may be only an exaggeration, but for such a story even to have been credited shows how greatly the character of the once-hardy soldier race had been corrupted. To speak the truth, to ride, and to draw the bow were the main elements in the old Persian education. Plutarch's *Life of Themistocles* and the Old Testament Book of Esther show us, by contrast, a court in which prostration was required of those who approached the Great King, and where life could be forfeited by those to whom he did not extend his golden sceptre.

The Persian Empire included in its extent the old empires of Egypt, Babylon, and Assyria, also the lands such as Palestine over which they had fought. It summed up the many excellent features of those civilisations. To the old civilisation of the Near East modern civilisation is indebted for many things without which civilised life could not exist. In the river valleys in Egypt and Mesopotamia agriculture was highly developed, irrigation was a necessity; astronomy was studied in order to assist in the management of agriculture. Tools were developed and building advanced to a high degree. Many skilled trades flourished and the useful arts were discovered. As far as can be ascertained, nothing was done in the direction of original research. Learning in the old civilisations was in the hands of priesthoods and would tend to be conservative. All the great advances made were in obedience to purely utilitarian purposes; there does not appear to have been any conception of research for its own sake. These two features of the old civilisations of the Near East may have accounted for their failure to progress beyond a certain level of achievement.

Whatever their failures, these Mesopotamian cultures did produce a civilised mode of life which was probably quite pleasant for a multitude of the citizens and no doubt infinitely better ordered and cleaner than that of its successors. Centuries of misrule and mismanagement have ruined the lands watered by the Tigris and Euphrates. To fly across the great Syrian desert is to view a land where the prevailing feature is sand until one comes to what look like two great ditches cutting through the desert. These are the Two Rivers.

A new factor in the development of mankind was now about to appear, that of the Greek mind. So important has Greek influence been in history that it is necessary to study the Greeks and their way of life in some detail.

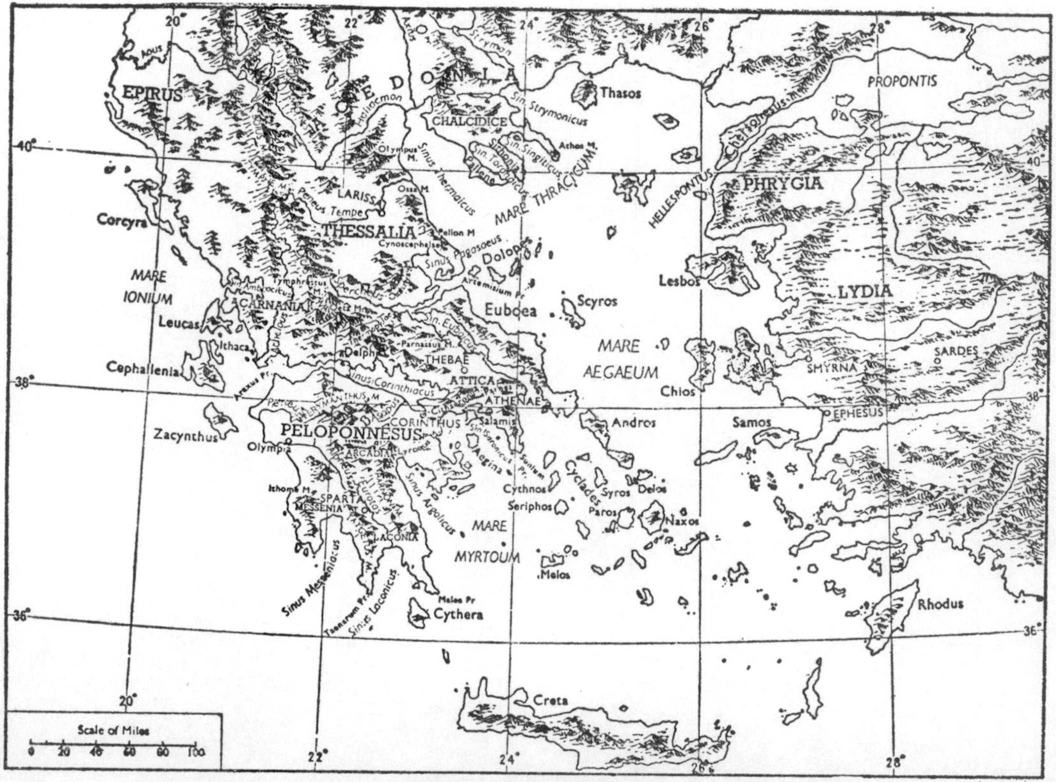

Map 3: Ancient Greece

CHAPTER FOUR

THE GREEKS
AND THEIR CIVILISATION

WE DESCRIBE the ancient people of Greece by a word which the Romans, in mistaking a tribe for the entire nation, erroneously bestowed upon them. They called themselves Hellenes and their land Hellas. As far as can be judged from researches in the Homeric poems and in archaeology, about 1000 years BC the Greeks (it is impossible to avoid the use of this name) came down through the Balkans into Greece and subjugated the more civilised peoples who lived there. We know that in various parts of Greece there are monuments of pre-Greek cities which are certainly not the result of barbarian efforts. Crete was a centre of civilisation long before its capital was sacked and overthrown by the pirates from the mainland. The Tale of Troy recounts the expedition of some of the Greek princes against a city on the shores of the Dardanelles, and archaeology has revealed that there was a succession of cities on the hill at Troy. The Greek expedition against the city was the effort of a less against a more highly civilised people. A thousand years later Virgil used the various legends which had gathered about the fall of Troy to prove that the Romans were really avenging their remote ancestors when they conquered Greece and turned it into the Roman province of Achaea. The remnant of the Trojans left Troy, according to Virgil's *Aeneid*, and after various wanderings (during which the seeds of discord between Rome and Carthage were sown) found a home in Latium where their descendants afterwards peopled Rome. Thus the feeling of inferiority which the Romans had towards the Greeks was to be put aside in the remembrance that their remote ancestors had been culturally superior to the early Hellenes.

The Greek invaders were tall and fair, but after their conquests of the new homeland they gradually mingled with the dark-haired and dark-skinned natives who are represented by the Greeks of today. In some parts of Greece the distinction between conquerors and conquered lasted almost until the Roman conquest. At Sparta, for example, the Spartans were in a decided minority in the midst of a huge class of aborigines, the Helots, who possessed hardly any rights save that of working for their masters. These Helots were forced to do all the manual work in the country and in consequence of this and their lack of political or economic rights they were full of discontent. During most of their spare time they were either forming plots, or were believed by their rulers to be doing so, which had, of course, the same result, since the Spartans used a most Gestapo-like inquisition against the Helots. Secret police (actually known by that name), informers, spies, concentration camps, political murders, were the instruments of the Spartan 'Herrenvolk'.

Such a state of affairs was unique among the Greek communities, numbered by the score if not by the hundred. Greece was peopled by one race (subject to the distinction, gradually being reduced, between the conquerors and the conquered) who spoke one language and had the same religion. But politically Greece was divided and never did of itself attain unity. The usual pattern of a Greek state was the city with an area around it sufficient for its support, including a number of villages and possibly some smaller towns. Thus, Athens was the capital of Attica, the peninsula which helped to form the bay of Salamis. North of Athens was Thebes, an inland city, which was a separate sovereign state. Across the Bay of Salamis were Megara, Argos and Corinth on the gulf and isthmus of the same name, all separate and independent states. The Isthmus of Corinth prevented the Peloponessus from being a correct name—it means the island of Pelops—for the southernmost peninsula of Greece. In the Peloponessus, Sparta was the chief state, and different architecturally as well as politically from the other states. Sparta did not possess a city, but consisted of a number of unwalled villages on the banks of the Eurotas river in the south of Peloponessus. In the north of this peninsula was the territory of seafaring people, such as that of Corinth, but the bulk of the peninsula was under the control of the Spartans who used their Helot serfs to cultivate the ground.

Not only were the Greeks divided into numerous states, but they were in all the stages of political development. The early form of government had been kingship, but this in its original Homeric form now existed only in outlying Greek or semi-Greek states like Macedonia; though Sparta, with characteristic conservatism, preserved a dual kingship.

Many of the Greek states were oligarchies in which affairs were managed by a few of the more influential citizens. Others, of which Athens was the most prominent example, were democracies. Another political form was the tyranny. The tyrant was a citizen either in an oligarchy or a democracy who made himself a dictator by force and ruled the state despotically. Sparta had a government which united monarchy, oligarchy and democracy. There were two kings who had a considerable amount of power in wartime, there was a popular assembly, and there were eight ephors, or magistrates, who had perhaps the biggest share in determining policy. Sparta was a communist state, the citizens in theory having everything in common, although there were many successful evasions of the laws. The whole system of the state, including the subordination of the individual, was designed to produce efficient soldiers as in Nazi Germany, or among Chaka's Zulus, and the Spartan women had a correspondingly low place in the social scale. The other Greeks professed to admire Sparta, and some thinkers, such as Plato in the *Republic*, suggested that the Spartans should be imitated. But very little imitation took place, and the Spartans in later times tended rather to possess private property and to indulge in intellectual pursuits like their neighbours.

These Greek states were obviously small in extent and population. They could not agree to unite because, in their opinion, union would have meant loss of local independence. They were constantly at war with one another and ultimately the country was so weakened by internal strife that it became an easy prey to Rome.

The Greeks were fond of discussions and sometimes had congresses at which most of the states were represented and where projects such as the invasion of the Persian Empire or the clearing of the seas from piracy were mooted. Nothing came of these discussions because all were afraid that if they joined together to invade Asia, for example, one of them—such as Sparta, the land power, or Athens, the naval power—would predominate. They had a common language and a common religion, in the worship of many gods—Zeus, Hera, Apollo and the rest of the classical pantheon. They held great games and athletic contests at the festivals of the gods and there were occasions when the whole of Greece was represented. They had a general contempt for the barbarians, that is anyone who did not speak Greek as his mother tongue. There were very rare occasions when they could be brought to act together against the common foe. One occasion was the Trojan expedition in the (to them) by no means dim past. Another was against Persia (fortunately for the future of Europe).

The political history of Greece is an account of three or four cities each in turn gaining a supremacy over its rivals. Athens, Sparta, Thebes, each held the leadership for a time. Each became the head of a confederation of smaller states which hoped to gain something for themselves out of the contests, or went in simply for the love of bickering.

We can form a good idea of the condition of ancient Greece if we imagine modern England divided into a number of states— Bristol, Manchester, London, Salisbury, Carlisle, and so on; and if we think of the town council of each as a sovereign independent government. The inhabitants of these states all speak the same language, they have the same contempt for the foreigner, they meet at the great football festivals, but although confronted by a foe as powerful in its day as Nazi Germany, the little states of England can only be brought to a short-lived unity when Kent is invaded. Moreover, the man from Sheffield is a foreigner in Gloucester. He has to be represented by a consul ('proxenos' the Greeks called him, and they still use the word in their consular notices) who is of the nationality of the state in which he lives, not of that which he represents, but who is pro-foreign in his sympathies.

The political differences of the Greeks were exaggerated though not caused by the physical nature of their country. The scenery of

Greece is magnificently beautiful and rarely fails to make an impression on the eyes of foreigners. The sky is a brilliant blue in summer, the sea is sparklingly blue under the sunlight; then there are the mountains, often crowned in summer with snow, the deep gorges, the narrow vales, the deep inlets of the sea, the wooded sides of some hills, the grim bareness of others. One overlooks the absence of rivers and the dry-looking brown soil as one flies above the Gulf of Corinth, a narrow stretch of water with mountainous banks on either side and dotted with the white sails of small vessels contrasted against the blue beneath; or as one flies towards the north of Greece and passes Pelion and Ossa and Olympus, those three mountains famed in poetry and legend.

Yet such beauty has a sinister side. How could a strong central power arise in a land divided in this way, a land in which until even recently there were few railways and where it was difficult to make journeys by land? The beauty of Greece was bought at a price, the price of the political greatness of her people. So it was that in ancient days Greece never achieved political unity. In modern times she only did so when striving to escape from the yoke of the Turks, and even now her unity is sadly disturbed by threats of secession on the part of the north, or Macedonia.

The political bickerings of the old Greeks would be of very little interest but for the fact that these same people were responsible for a greater cultural advance than had yet been made by any other. Not only did the various arts and sciences receive development at the hands of the Greeks, but the ideas of philosophy, drama, metaphysics, political science, physical science and economics all came from Greece.

The Greek language was the most useful medium of thought which had yet appeared. Also, it was not confined to one little country. From very early times the Greeks had found the motherland too small for them and in each generation settlers had left to seek homes elsewhere. In addition to economic distress, which may have been the motive with the majority, many Greeks were forced to leave their original homes by political disagreements with their governments. In this way, Cyrene, which gave its name to Cyrenaica, was founded. The earliest Greek colonies may have been in

Ionia, the strip of coastland with a small amount of hinterland running down the western side of Asia Minor. This land of Ionia contained some of the richest of the Greek cities, such as Ephesus and Miletus and Smyrna, and here it was that Greek civilisation flourished and Greek thought began. Because of the wealth and usefulness of the inhabitants of these cities, the Asiatic kingdoms strove to bring them under their sway. The Greek cities had paid tribute to Lydia, and after the conquest of Lydia by Persia, the Great King became their overlord. After the defeat of the Persians in the Greek war, these cities enjoyed fitful intervals of independence.

There were few areas around the Mediterranean which the Greeks did not try to colonise. In eastern Sicily they founded many cities and towns, the most important being Syracuse, and even now there are reminders of the Greeks in this area. Ruins of Greek temples and theatres are found in many places, and in small towns one comes across little streets named after some Greek hero— Via Timoleoni in Taormina, for example. On consulting the local guide-books, it appears that the individual in question had some interest in the district in which the present inhabitants are living. Through the Straits of Messina and up the west coast of Italy Greek settlers penetrated, keeping near to the sea. Naples (Neapolis, or new city) owes its name and origin to them and there were many other Greek foundations on the Campanian coast.

In the south of France, Marseilles (Masillia) was founded by Greek colonists who had realised the commercial value of this settlement at the mouth of the Rhone valley. Greek ships carrying the products of the east passed through the Mediterranean and called at Marseilles, where they could exchange their cargoes for raw materials coming from the interior of Europe.

For a long time the Greeks strove to wrest the supremacy from the Carthaginians in the western Mediterranean, but although Carthage had relinquished the eastern basin of the sea to the Greeks she would not yield the area which could be more easily patrolled from her home bases. The Greeks were a vigorous people but their shocking lack of political unity prevented them from competing successfully with Carthage, so that with the exception of the places mentioned in Sicily, Italy and southern France, Carthaginian influence prevailed in the western basin.

In the eastern part of the sea conditions were very different. Here, Greek influence became paramount and their ascendancy over the Carthaginians in this area is eloquently reflected by Matthew Arnold in his verses in 'The Scholar Gipsy' (see Note, p 74). Apart from the homeland, the islands of the Aegean Sea were all Greek, as was Crete, and there was the rich land of Ionia. Greeks had established prosperous colonies and trading concerns in the Crimea. The Cyrenaican hump of Libya was filled with their cities—Cyrene, Barca and Sybaris (origin of the term 'Sybarite') being the most important. Apart from these actual settlements, many Greeks had penetrated into the Near East and Egypt as traders and mercenaries. The monarchs of Asia Minor, Syria and Egypt were always glad of additional troops and many of the surplus Greeks sold their services as soldiers.

As may be expected from people who were so prolific in producing sciences, the Greeks were full of curiosity and were great travellers. Even before the time of the Persian wars many of them had travelled widely, including Herodotus, the founder of historical writing, and Solon, the wise man of Athens who had visited Croesus. After the defeat of Persia, the east was even more generally open to the Greeks, who were in great demand as orators, diplomats, doctors, mercenary troops, courtesans and business folk. Thus, before the time of Alexander the Great, the Greeks had entered the oriental world and their tongue was well-known there. It was on the way to becoming a universal language.

Now the time had come for these people to make their great contribution to world progress. They had spread around the world colonising many places, just as we may imagine the development of the great dominions of the British Empire might have taken place without any central government to control and protect.* By a supreme effort the little communities of the old Greece had won their freedom from the Persian domination; and in so doing they

---

* Not that one should exaggerate the part played in Britain's imperial story by Westminster and Whitehall. Usually the British government came in as a reluctant acceptor of territory won for it by a Warren Hastings or a Stamford Raffles. Even so, it was still a strong central power in the development of the Empire, the like of which did not exist in the Greek world.

had saved their colonists to whom they were wont to refer as inhabiting 'Great Greece'. There was never any more political cohesion between the colonists and the mother country than there was between the various states in Greece itself. The position of the Greek world was as if one could imagine Vancouver, Brisbane and Sydney having no bonds with London and Liverpool save those of language and race. It would be difficult to imagine these separate English-speaking states being able to preserve their independence in the world, and so it eventually proved with the Greeks, but the victory over Persia was followed by a period of some two hundred years during which no other world power had arisen to take over Persia's burden of empire. The Greeks had leisure to think, to experiment and to make researches.

Their economic position was based on a slave population. There were, of course, many free workers, but a great deal of the manual, menial work was done by slaves. In Athens, at the height of its prosperity, half of the population were slaves. A leisured class had been created and from these people came most of the intellectuals. The founder of European thought was Thales of Miletus, and his life well illustrates the habits of the Greeks. He lived in Ionia, and had been a successful speculator in the oil business, in which he had secured a corner and become rich. Unlike many modern financiers, when he settled down to enjoy his wealth he turned his attention to pure speculation. It would be difficult, from what we know of his life, to discover that this work had any utilitarian basis, but we do know that his researches, undertaken merely for the sake of finding out the truth, produced practical results. He studied astronomy and was able to predict an eclipse which took place during a battle in Asia Minor and which put a stop to the fighting owing to the superstitious feelings of the combatants. Such a result increased the respect for abstract thought and led to further study of astronomy, with benefit to agriculture. Thales also speculated on an even more useless subject, the origin of the material world. He concluded that there was one original principle, water. Modern science considers that there is more than a little truth in his speculations, especially as it is now thought that life originated in the sea.

Page 65　The Great Pyramid and the Sphinx at Giza

Page 66   (*above*) The Erectheum on the Acropolis at Athens;
(*below*) Virgil's tomb at Posilipo

Other men continued the work of Thales: Anaximander, Anaximenes, Pythagoras, Heraclitus, Parmenides, Anaxagoras and others. Philosophy, which in those days included most of the sciences, was still struggling to divide knowledge into its necessary compartments. A philosopher then meant a man who loved wisdom or knowledge and who sought to know in the widest sense the causes of things, and not as now, a thinker on certain metaphysical problems. These Greek thinkers started with the assumption on which all modern scientific work proceeds—the uniformity of nature. Many of the Greek philosophers also concluded that there was an intelligent cause of the universe, one God. They were thus working in the same direction as the Jews. The Greek effort was in the form of mental speculation, the Jewish was in the direction of religious revelation, but the two streams at last amalgamated in the synthesis of medieval European thought.

The Greeks' adventures in monotheism often led to a charge of atheism, as it did with the early Christians. Having reached the conclusion that there was but one God, the philosophers could not accept the many idols of their contemporaries as real beings, hence they were accused of impiety.

Just such an accusation led to the death of the famous Socrates. Athens had become, after the Persian wars, the most brilliant city in the Greek world, and the philosophers and teachers from Ionia tended to establish themselves there. Soon, Athens had her own philosopher, a singular enough specimen. By profession a sculptor, Socrates showed no signs of any peculiarity in his early life and, like all Athenians, was called upon for military service. On one such expedition he was taken with a trance whilst in the camp, and when he recovered he was a changed man. Although he did not talk much about his vision or trance, it soon appeared that he felt himself commissioned by a higher power to lead men to wisdom. The peculiar method he adopted was to go about asking people questions, his object being to make men think and lead the good life. Insofar as he made some brilliant disciples who helped on the progress of science and thought, he was successful, but in achieving this good he also aroused great hostility and dislike among the bulk of people who did not want to think and hated to be

E

disturbed. As he had abandoned his former occupation for this much less lucrative trade, his financial affairs became, not unnaturally, depressed, and the poverty to which he was reduced probably had a good deal to do with the bad temper of his wife, Xantippe. This unfortunate woman has been handed down as a typical shrew, but we have to sympathise with her when we realise that the speeches of Socrates which so delight us would not have paid for food and clothing for her and her family.

Socrates found it expedient to spend a good deal of his time out of his home. He had a tremendous capacity for food and drink and, fortunately for him, most of his admirers were wealthy enough to invite him to dinner. We have in a contemporary writing a sketch of Socrates at a banquet which lasts until the early hours. When nearly everyone else has been overcome and fallen under the table, Socrates is still calmly drinking and continuing a philosophical discussion with two other survivors.

Socrates wrote nothing, but two of his followers, Xenophon and Plato, wrote about him. Probably the truer picture is preserved in Xenophon, because in Plato's account a very great artist has taken a hand in portraying his master. Master to Plato Socrates certainly was, and his death only served to increase Plato's devotion to him and his doctrines. For Socrates died a martyr. The people of Athens had been amused at first, but later grew so tired of his persistent questionings that it was easy for a minority who hated him to have him put on trial for his life on a charge of impiety towards the state religion. He made an eloquent and humorous defence, but was condemned to death. Capital punishment for an Athenian citizen took the form of drinking a cup of hemlock, or poison. In some splendid dialogues Plato has given us the picture of his master in prison, talking calmly with his friends and preparing to die. When the time comes to drink the cup he does so quite easily and lies down in order not to make an exhibition of himself as some people do who try to stay on their feet after drinking the poison. He tells his friends that he can feel the cold gradually mounting towards his heart. 'Offer a cock to Aesculapius for me', he says, and the friends wait in vain for another word.

Plato took up his work. As well as being a great thinker, Plato was also a very fine literary man, so that his works have lived on and will continue to do so. The *Republic* is the best known of his writings, which are all cast in the form of dialogues. Plato was a great idealistic philosopher and platonic thought has been very powerful in the world's history. He also advanced the progress of the sciences by the necessary task of subdivision. He showed that we must divide the physical sciences from the moral, such as ethics and politics, and that in the realm of science we should divide the formal from the empiric, mathematics and logic from physics, biology and astronomy.

His work in this latter direction was carried much further by his disciple Aristotle, a lad from Stagira in the north of Greece. Plato and Aristotle together have been styled by Coleridge 'supreme lords of the human mind', and certainly they have exercised a very great influence over thought. It is possible that, taking everything into account, Aristotle's influence has been the greater of the two. All through the middle ages in Europe, Aristotle was referred to as 'The Philosopher', and in Dante's poem he is actually represented as receiving homage not only from all the other philosophers, but from Plato as well.

The subordination of Plato to Aristotle may have been due to ignorance in western Europe of Plato's works, and once Greek learning was made more accessible Plato again obtained a great following. None the less, it is to Aristotle that we owe most of the divisions of our knowledge in the present day. Once when studying logic I opened a little treatise which began with these words: 'In logic as in most other things we begin with Aristotle'. There is a school of thought which now repudiates his logic, but even if all his work were to be repudiated, the repudiators would still have the humiliating thought that they had had to begin with him. In any event his work is not likely to be overthrown. He left writings on physics, ethics, logic, metaphysics, economics, politics, poetry and other subjects, and in the main the world has followed his rulings. His works cannot be read as can Plato's. His style is poor, but a more important reason is that the matter has worked itself into our general education and outlook, and to read of the obvious is not interesting. Not only was Aristotle regarded with great respect in the middle ages, but because St Thomas Aquinas, the official philosopher of the Roman Catholic Church, based his theology on Aristotle's metaphysics, Aristotle received a species of canonisation and became as nearly respectable as a heathen can be. But even this accolade could not save his orthodoxy from being called in question by the Athenians of his own day. Saying that he would not allow Athens to sin against philosophy a second time, he went into voluntary exile, accepting an offer from Philip, king of Macedonia, to come and act as tutor to his son, young Alexander.

Greek philosophy had a long course of development from the times of Plato and Aristotle. Most people are familiar with the names of Stoicism and Epicureanism, two schools of thought founded respectively by Zeno, born in Cyprus in 336/5 BC, who died in Athens about 264/3; and by Epicurus of Samos, born in 342/1 BC. A general idea of these two philosophies has been current in the minds of most educated Europeans. Epicurus had the good fortune to gain as a disciple a great Latin poet, T. Lucretius Carus (91-51 BC), who set forth the Epicurean philosophy in his famous poem *De Rerum Natura*, the chief aim of which was 'the liberation of men from the fear of the gods and of death, and the leading of them to peace of the soul.' (*History of Philosophy* vol 1, *Greece and Rome* by F. Copleston, 1951, p402). The later Stoic school found an exponent in Epictetus of Hierapolis (c AD 50-138), and also in the Roman Emperor Marcus Aurelius (reigned from 161 to 180), whose *Meditations*, written in Greek, are famous.

Later in the Christian era came the Neo-Platonic school associated with the names of Plotinus and Porphyry, which has a place in the history of mysticism as well as of philosophy. 'Neo-Platonism was the last breath, the last flower, of ancient pagan philosophy; but in the thought of St Augustine it became the first stage of Christian philosophy'. (Copleston, *op cit*, p506). The schools of philosophy at Athens were closed in 529 by order of the Emperor Justinian, and the leaders of the Neo-Platonists 'went to Persia where they were received by King Chosroes. In 533, they returned to Athens, apparently disappointed with the cultural state of Persia'. (Copleston, p482).

In the 1,100 years from Thales to the closure of 529, Greek

thought had passed through many phases, some of which have greatly enriched the human mind. It had begun as the science of thought, but the various departments of science had branched off and become sections of knowledge within their own right. This is brought out in any history of physical science. In any of such works we find the remote beginnings of the sciences in Egypt and Babylonia; these rudiments are adopted by the Greeks whose brilliant intellects then produce the early developments which lie at the base of modern science. A flaw existed in the Greek approach. The greatest Greek intellects were taken up with mental efforts to deduce the nature of the universe from general principles rather than from observation, the accumulation of facts, and from experiment. In consequence, the greatest of their philosophers refused to condescend to what they termed the mechanic arts. In his essay on Francis Bacon, Lord Macaulay described the attitude of the philosophers to any practical application which might add to the conveniences and comfort of life. Even Plato could not escape this comment. Macaulay quotes Plutarch for the following example. Archytas, a friend of Plato, 'had framed machines of extraordinary power on mathematical principles. Plato remonstrated with his friend and declared that this was to degrade a noble intellectual exercise into a low craft, fit only for carpenters and wheelwrights'.

This being the attitude of the most respected intellects in the ancient world, one can understand the small progress made in investigating the secrets of nature or inventing some of the mechanical devices now taken as commonplace in life. Many discoveries were indeed made, as by Archimedes whose machines of war defended Syracuse in 212 BC against the Romans. 'Archimedes was a mathematician by choice, and a mechanic and inventor only by necessity, whereas in Hero (of Alexandria, lived about a century later than Archimedes. L.G.P.) the parts seem to have been reversed. He invented a great number of conjuring tricks and mechanical toys, one of the more noteworthy being a steam engine.... Here is the first known instance of steam pressure being used to translate chemical energy of burning fuel into energy of motion, the principle underlying the steam engine of today. Hero is also said to have devised the first penny-in-the-slot machine recorded in history.' *The Growth of Physical Science*, by Sir James Jeans, 1947, p81).

Nothing continuous came of inventions such as Hero's because the intellectual climate was unfavourable. It might be thought that war, the most prolific source of inventions, would have given scope to mechanical ability, yet only a few inventions mark the long history of Graeco-Roman warfare. Centuries of strife with the highly mobile cavalry of the Orient did not fit the imperial armies for any better performance against the Arabs of the seventh century AD than they had given against the Parthians at Carrhae in 53 BC. A speedier system of transport or a more powerful offensive weapon would have enabled the legions to defeat the western barbarians, but such things were simply not forthcoming. It was necessary for the human mind to break the fetters it had imposed upon itself in elevating the teachings of Aristotle to a place scarcely inferior to that of Holy Writ. Until this happened there could be no continuous scientific progress.

In the realm of art, the Greek achievement has always been regarded as splendid. In literature, the roll of names runs over the different literary forms. Homer (the epic), Plato (philosophical writings), Herodotus and Thucydides (history), the tragic poets, Aeschylus, Sophocles, and Euripides (drama), Aristophanes (comic drama), Pindar (odes) are only a few names from Greek literature. Greek music has not survived, not surprisingly, yet so gifted a people could hardly have been unmusical. Painting in the form of portraits or scenes on canvas or other non-durable material could not have been expected to traverse the convulsions of a dying empire. Painting on vases has survived in large measure, and the museums of Europe and the United States contain many specimens of Greek art in this form. In statuary we are provided with numerous examples of copying from Greek originals by Roman imitators. The marble Hermes made by Praxiteles in the fourth century BC is the only original of any great Greek master which has survived; many others are thought to have lasted into the middle ages when they were destroyed for the lowest of utilitarian needs, bronze for the sake of that then rare metal, marble to be burnt for lime. But enough is left to us even in often imperfect copies to show how great was Greek sculptural achievement; the perfection of the human form at its best, and the representation of the godhead in human form, as with the Zeus at Olympia wrought in five years of labour by Phidias. 'Let a man sick and weary in his soul, who has passed through many distresses and sorrows, whose pillow is unvisited by kindly sleep, stand in front of this image; he will, I deem, forget all the terrors and troubles of human life'. (Quoted by J. B. Bury, *History of Greece*, 1906, p375). And, it may be added, he will be pardoned for making God in the image of man, when that image is itself so divine.

The ruins of Greek temples and other buildings around the Mediterranean, and the relics which have been salvaged from the ancient world, enable us to recognise the true greatness of Greek art. Perhaps it is tempting to give more admiration to the half-ruined beauty than to the original finished work. The great statue in gold and ivory of the virgin goddess Athena on the Acropolis must indeed have been an awesome sight, and one might even sigh over the triumph of the Christian faith that it should lead to the dismemberment of such majestic loveliness. The remains of the Parthenon frieze, the Elgin marbles, have been saved from further destruction. Their home, the Parthenon, from being the temple of a virgin goddess, became the church of God's Virgin Mother, and as such much of its beauty in frieze and even in statuary was preserved. Then came the unspeakable barbarism of Turkish conquerors, with the final degradation of the church's conversion to a powder magazine. Even so, the glorious place had lived 2,000 years until at last, in the seventeenth century, a chance shot falling in the magazine, wrecked it. Would we restore it if we could? Could anything surpass its enchanting loveliness as it stands half-ruined, yet white and glistening in the sunshine, against the sheer blue of the sky? Will it not always be a symbol to European men that man's thoughts and hopes can rise above the material, soaring into the highest realms of human aspiration?

The Parthenon and other great buildings of Athens were the work of architects, sculptors and artists labouring in the regime of Pericles. For nearly thirty years he ruled Athens, not as a king or tyrant but as the democratically-elected ruler of free men. After the Persian wars, the temples of Attica were in ruins and it became a religious duty to restore them. Restored they were, and with a nobility and beauty that no temples had ever had before. This was due to the genius of Pericles, who was determined to make Athens the queen, or at least the instructress of Hellas. So there arose on the strong place of the city the Acropolis buildings which have stood ever since as the symbol of nobility of thought, of the best of civilisation as it lifts man from his uneasy status among the brutes. Ictinus and Callicrates for architects, with Phidias as sculptor, produced this masterpiece in honour of the city's patron goddess. (Picture, p 66.) Little wonder that the fifth and fourth centuries BC were the golden age of Athens and Greece.

The Periclean era was followed by a time of lesser statesmen, or rather of politicians, who could not lead the sovereign people. Instead of persuading the democracy as Pericles had been able to do, these politicians were forced to seek and discover the desires of the people and to conform to them. The disastrous Peloponnesian war ended in the ruin of Athens. Her political power was gone, though many of her greatest men in other spheres, like Socrates and Plato, were yet to come.

Jealousy of Athens had led her enemies into coalition against her but none of them could take her place. While they quarrelled over the supremacy, a northern power, more than half barbaric and only nominally Greek, was preparing to take over the direction of affairs in the little city states. It was to tutor the son of this country's king that Aristotle had departed from Athens.

NOTE: Following is the extract from 'The Scholar Gipsy' by Matthew Arnold, referred to on p 63.

> As some grave Tyrian trader, from the sea
> Described at sunrise an emerging prow
> Lifting the cool-hair'd creepers stealthily,
> The fringes of a southward-facing brow
> Among the Aegean isles:
> And saw the merry Grecian coaster come,
> Freighted with amber grapes, and Chian wine,
> Green bursting figs, and tunnies steep'd in brine;
> And knew the intruders on his ancient home.

The young, light-hearted Masters of the waves;
And snatch'd his rudder, and shook out more sail,
And day and night held on indignantly
O'er the blue Midland waters with the gale,
Betwixt the Syrtes and soft Sicily,
To where the Atlantic raves,
Outside the Western Straits, and unbent sails
There, where down cloudy cliffs, through sheets of foam,
Shy traffickers, the dark Iberians come;
And on the beach undid his corded bales.

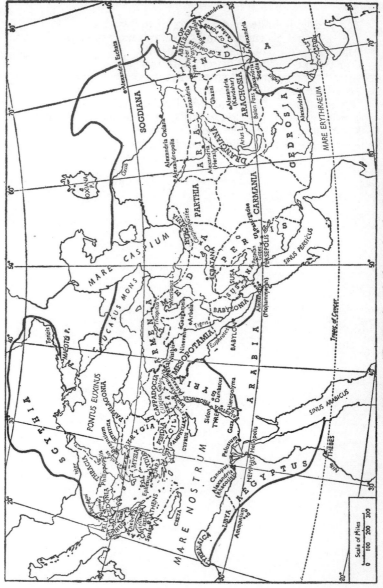

Map 4: The Empire of Alexander the Great

CHAPTER FIVE

THE CAREER OF ALEXANDER THE GREAT

BEHIND ALEXANDER stands his father, Philip, King of Macedonia, a man who, but for an accident, might have robbed Alexander of the glory of conquering the Persian Empire. As it is, Alexander's fame has completely overshadowed that of Philip, but without Philip's preparations there would have been no Alexander.

Macedonia was a wild, mountainous country to the north of Greece. It included the valley of the Strymon, which will serve to identify it in the minds of those who remembered the German campaign in Greece in 1941, and the country around the Gulf of Salonika. In this savage land, over two thousand years ago, lived the tribes of Macedonians, a fierce, unruly nation speaking a variety of Greek. How much akin they were to the rest of the Greeks is difficult to say, but it is certain that they were far behind them in culture. The Macedonians were primarily warriors, delighting in war and doing all they could to encourage it. One of their customs was for a man to wear a rope round his waist until he had killed an enemy in combat. They were ruled by a king who was rather on the Homeric model, save that he possessed much more power, being in fact a despot.

Macedonia had never been much regarded by the great powers of Greece, except when her allegiance had been useful to harry the outlying possessions of a rival. Yet, curiously enough, this half-Greek, half-barbarian land was destined to secure for a time the hegemony over Greece for which Athens, Sparta and Thebes had striven without real success.

After the Persian wars Athens was the leading Greek state. As long as her great statesman Pericles lived, or as long as his advice was followed, she remained such. Her power was in her navy, but ill-advised counsellors induced Athens to undertake great land expeditions with the ultimate result that she declined before Sparta. Athens lost her political pre-eminence, but some of her greatest ornaments, such as Socrates and Plato, appeared in the period of her political decline. Sparta, which was mainly distinguished as a land power, assumed the leadership of Greece. There was never in the real sense of the word an Athenian or Spartan empire, but during the supremacy of each of these states, the other states of Greece found it expedient to base their policy on that of the chief city. Sparta's supremacy was unpopular and it was eventually overthrown by Thebes, a city now only a township, but then the powerful and flourishing capital of Boeotia, which adjoined Athenian territory on the north. The Spartans were vanquished on the field of battle on several occasions by the Thebans, and probably no people in Greece were more surprised by this than the Thebans themselves. They owed everything to their great general, Epaminondas, a brilliant soldier who so manoeuvred his troops that instead of the usual Greek order of battle with lines of warriors in equal depth opposing each other, his line was as much as fifty files deep in one part. The result was that the wing of the Spartan army chosen to meet the heavy Theban thrust was subjected to an overwhelming weight of spears. When it gave way, the rest of the Spartan army which had been kept in play by the thin line of the Thebans was attacked in flank and rear by the heavy Theban wing, which was already victorious in another part of the field.

The Spartans were heavily orthodox in military matters and unable to alter their tactics to meet the situation. But Thebes had neither the finances nor the energy to maintain her position for long as leading power. In his victory over the Spartans at Leuctra, Epaminondas received a mortal wound and with him expired the greatness of his country. He had not been able to secure the leadership of Greece for Thebes, but he had destroyed the supremacy of Sparta and humbled it in the dust. The Spartans had lived for cen-

turies in unwalled villages in their river valley; they preferred to
fight on other nations' territory. Epaminondas taught them the
meaning of war in their own land. Their slaves, the Helots,
revolted against the Spartan 'Herrenvolk'. Sparta never recovered.

Epaminondas had done more. He found it necessary to make
an expedition against Macedonia and one of his terms of peace was
that the boy Philip, the heir to the throne, should come as a hostage
to Thebes. Philip, who thus received a far better education than he
could have had in Macedonia, was an intelligent boy who benefited
by his training. He saw Greek life and politics at close quarters,
and there was much that he admired. The amenities of life in
Greece pleased him, and he studied the military tactics of Epaminondas. He also studied with appreciation, though not with
admiration, the corrupt nature of Greek politics.

When he went back to Macedonia he at once set to work to
apply the lessons he had learned. He trained his subjects to be
disciplined as well as brave, and he improved on the methods of
Epaminondas. He converted the close and heavy section of the
line into the phalanx which was to remain the favourite military
formation until the appearance of the Roman legion. In the
phalanx the men were arranged in rows, with spears of varying
length and so standing that their spears projected far beyond each
others' shoulders. A wall of spears was thus formed which was
impenetrable by cavalry and which by its sheer weight swept
opposition before it. Philip also used cavalry and more lightly-
armed troops to surround the enemy on the flanks.

In all his work Philip was aided by the discovery of goldmines
in his country. The money thus obtained was used partly to equip
his troops in the most modern style and no less usefully to bribe
the leading Greek politicians. In this way Philip planted a 'fifth-
column' and 'Quisling' party in the government of most of his
potential enemies, so that it became extremely difficult for democratic statesmen like Demosthenes to rouse their countrymen to
the danger which was looming up from Macedonia. Arguments of
a type all too frequently used in the democratic governments
before 1939 made their appearance. The Macedonians, said these
paid apologists, were really good friends of Greece. True, they were

building up a large army, but that was because they were facing a very savage enemy in the tribes of the north, and if they were strong enough to resist these tribes they would also keep the barbaric menace away from the rest of Greece. By such treacherous means the states of Greece were lulled into submission until Philip had completed his preparations and the democratic Greek powers had been overthrown at the battle of Chaeronea. Macedon became the supreme head of the Greek states.

Philip prepared to fulfil the old dream of a war of revenge against the Persians. A confederation of the Greeks was summoned. Each state was to contribute money, ships and men in an expedition against Persia under Philip's command. Then Philip was murdered. He had married a Macedonian princess, Olympias, who did not take a tolerant view of her husband's frequent infidelities. After many years of matrimonial difficulties he decided to divorce her in favour of the fair daughter of one of his generals. At the marriage feast there was a scene between Philip and Alexander, his son by Olympias. Soon after, Philip was murdered; perhaps at the instigation of Olympias.

The pan-Greek attack against Persia was again postponed, the various Greek states withdrew their levies and several of them revolted against Alexander. He was a young man of twenty, inexperienced and untried, but he had been carefully trained by his father and by his tutor, Aristotle. Philip had contributed first-hand practical experience of managing Greeks in peace and in war, and in one year's fighting Alexander showed that he had learned these lessons. The wild tribes around Macedon were subdued by his generalship and skill in using heavy chariots, the armoured forces of the time, in hilly country. Thebes, where his father had been brought up, was then attacked and destroyed, only the house of the poet Pindar being left intact among the general ruin. Thebes had been the centre of resistance for the Greek cities and, by smashing it, Alexander left the remaining states in sullen aquiescence of his overlordship.

With Greece quiet behind him, Alexander could resume the Persian expedition. With an army of some forty thousand men, drawn mostly from Macedonia, he crossed the sea of Marmora into

Asia Minor, thus invading the Persian Empire. From now on the contribution to his education made by Aristotle began to have equal weight with that of Philip. Aristotle's method of educating Alexander had been to draw out his intelligence with questions on subjects in which he was interested and then to encourage him to pursue them under his own expert direction. In this way Alexander became a lover of the Homeric poems, an edition of which, specially prepared by Aristotle, he carried with him on all his campaigns.

Thus educated, and gifted with his own original genius, Alexander began to conquer the Persian Empire. We have borrowed from the Greeks the word 'myriads', which they most frequently used when trying to describe the Persian hosts, and against such vast numbers Alexander went forth cheerfully and with success. He stabilised his position in Asia Minor by the victory of the Granicus. He then advanced to the passes which were the gateway to Syria, and there overcame a second and larger Persian army at Issus. He besieged and captured Tyre, a place of great strength. He was aided by his fleet, which gave him command of the eastern Mediterranean. His next exploit was to advance on Egypt where he soon overthrew the Persian power and was welcomed as the son of the Egyptian god, Ammon. Meanwhile, the Persian king, Darius, had gathered a vast army and was advancing against Alexander who, in his turn after the conquest of Egypt, set out to complete the conquest of Persia. The decisive battle was fought near Arbela, in Mesopotamia. The Persians were routed and Darius was never able to gather another army.

These several Persian defeats by much smaller forces may give the impression that the Greek victories were easy; but in fact, all Alexander's actions were hard-fought and achieved by superior military skill and courage. There were in the Persian armies many men drawn from the warlike races of the Middle East and who were often well armed. But they were badly led and their very numbers prevented them from manoeuvring against the much less unwieldy Greek phalanx. There was another and more deep-rooted cause for their failure. The Persian dominion was not popular with the majority of its subjects, whose lives it affected in three main directions: taxation, forced labour and military conscription. The standing army of the Persian monarchy consisted mainly of the corps of guards, and to supplement these it had either to hire mercenaries or to conscript vast numbers of its own subjects. Greek mercenaries had been used very largely and some of them were in the army opposed to Alexander at Arbela. Occasionally, in the quarrels of Persian magnates, Greeks would find themselves opposed to Greeks, as mercenaries on either side; and the fact of their common origin did not prevent them from cutting each others' throats to keep their mercenary bargain. The Greek author Xenophon, as mentioned above, was himself a leader of a force of ten thousand such mercenaries, who found themselves cut off in the heart of the Persian Empire and retreated successfully through Armenia into Asia Minor and so back into Greece.

But the Greeks alone could not supply the necessary numbers for mass slaughter and, in consequence, native levies were called on from all parts of the Persian Empire. Originally, the Persians had supplied their monarch with an army of hardy troops, but with their possession of an empire they ceased to be strong and gradually became more and more degenerate and pleasure-loving. An army composed of such elements, mercenaries, decadent Persians, and conscripts with a sense of grievance, badly generalled and unwieldy by virtue of its numbers, was no effective match for the troops of Alexander, united solidly and zealously behind a leader whom they loved and who had already proved himself supremely capable.

After the defeat of the last large Persian army, Alexander, with a select body of troops, went in pursuit of Darius. He had no intention of ill-treating his rival. He had already taken under his protection the mother and the wife of Darius, and his object was to capture Darius himself. In this he was not successful. When he did reach the Great King, the latter was dying from a wound inflicted by a Persian traitor. His last request was one that Alexander had already fulfilled—to protect his family.

With the death of their king all resistance on the part of the Persians ceased, but Alexander was not content until order had been restored in the whole empire. Susa and Persepolis were the special treasure cities of the Persian kings, and the wealth found there excited the amazement of the Macedonians. One object of great interest was a piece of statuary representing two Athenian heroes, which had been taken from Athens in the invasion of Xerxes one hundred and fifty years before and placed in the Persian treasure house. It was now sent back to Athens.

Whether the story is true or not that Alexander wept because he had no more worlds to conquer, it is certainly the case that he did not rest content with conquering the Persian Empire. Not only did he subdue it more thoroughly than any of his predecessors had done, but he enlarged its boundaries. Towards the east and north the boundaries of the old empire had never been clearly defined. The Great King of Persia could be said in the words of Esther to reign from Ethiopia to India, but in many parts, notably in the wild lands to the east of the Caspian, Persian rule was nominal. This did not suit Alexander, who undertook campaigns against the northern barbarians and forced them to sue for peace. Then he passed with his army into India, into the Punjab. The most powerful of the rajahs, Porus, was defeated in battle and confirmed in his kingship as Alexander's vassal. Alexander then heard of the rich cities of the Ganges valley, and probably stories of the great empire of China had reached him. He was the first conqueror from the west to penetrate into India.

Only just over thirty years of age with apparently many years of life ahead of him, Alexander had enlarged the empire he had conquered, and (perhaps the result of Aristotle's tuition can be seen most clearly here) was full of zest for the discovery of places hitherto unknown, and for further conquests. Had he gone marching on eastwards he might, as the saying goes, have changed the course of history, or he might merely have disappeared, his army either being eventually overthrown in some battle, or simply dwindling away as the result of continual fighting. This remains a great 'if'. Although an absolute monarch, Alexander was not allowed to proceed. No general, however good, can go forward if his staff, his officers, NCOs and rank and file are all resolutely opposed to his going. The Macedonian army had been overseas for a period considerably longer than the five years which caused such

F

hardship in the British army during the last war. True, they had compensations denied to the British soldier. They were allowed to accumulate loot, the only restriction being the difficulty of carrying it with them. But they were weary of travelling on and on into unknown territories; they wanted to return to a civilised land where they might enjoy what they had won. The Macedonian army refused to march further eastwards.

Alexander did everything he could to make them change their minds, but it was useless. They loved their leader, but this one thing they would not do. Alexander had to give the order to march westwards. Many of the troops perished in the deserts of Baluchistan, with the dangers of which they had been unacquainted. Alexander and his troops had made their way into India through Afghanistan and had no idea of the hardships which awaited them as they passed through Sind and Baluchistan. It is all very well to look at these countries from an aircraft as one passes swiftly down the Persian Gulf, but even then one thinks of the horror of making one's way on foot and without adequate guides through such country. In the background are grim-looking mountains, in the foreground great wastes of sand unrelieved by vegetation and broken only by sluggish streams making a gradual way to the sea. In retrospect, such scenery has a rugged grandeur and beauty of its own, but this could not have been any consolation to soldiers dying of thirst.

When Alexander returned to Babylon (which he had made his capital) he rested for a time, but his mind was speedily busy with projects for further conquest. Fresh armies and fleets were gathered, new and great plans made. Arabia was to be reduced by a land expedition from the north, combined with a seaborne landing from the Persian Gulf. The Arabs were to live on unmolested for another thousand years, and to produce their Prophet at the end of this millenium; for Alexander died before the scheme of conquest could be brought into operation. He had always said that there were two things, women and sleep, which put him in mind of his mortality. He might have added death as the third remembrancer. After a short illness he died, leaving as heir to his empire an unborn son, who, when born, was not allowed to live very long in the welter of adventurers, all scrambling for the biggest share of his father's kingdom.

Alexander's was the largest empire yet seen in the world. He had conquered the Persian Empire and many of the lands beyond it. His vision was world-wide. No man and no one nation was destined to inherit his dominions, which were broken up into a number of states, some of them destined to carry on part of his work. After his death, Alexander's generals at once started quarrelling among themselves and it was only after many years that the outline of the new kingdoms could be clearly discerned. One general secured Egypt and founded the dynasty of the Ptolemies, which ruled that country for three hundred years and expired only with Cleopatra. Another founded the kingdom of the Seleucids, which included Syria, Palestine and part of Asia Minor. Macedonia itself was the dubious prize of another adventurer, dubious because the great age of Greece finishes with the death of Alexander. Macedonia remained probably the strongest of the Greek powers, but they could only bicker among themselves, and the period between Alexander's death and the establishment of the Roman province of Achaea—the name which covered the glory that was Greece—is brightened only by the patriotism of Philopoemen, hero of the Achaean League. Other smaller Greek states arose, notably in Bactria, where the influence of their culture remained for a long time. The outlying portions of Alexander's empire, for example the Punjab, resumed their independence.

There have been many conquerors in the world's history and the story of their exploits is apt to become monotonous, for having read one, one has read most. Attila, whose empire stretched from the Volga to the Atlantic, was as powerful as Alexander. Ghengis Khan could be said at one time to have controlled the vast area stretching across the plains of Europe and Asia, from the Pacific to the outskirts of Germany. Had Alexander resembled such conquerors his story would only be as important as theirs in the record of mankind, but he was more than a conqueror. He had very ambitious plans for the future of the world he had won. His adoption of the style of dress worn by the Persian monarch was the product of policy, not vanity. The Greeks had the equivalent of the colour-bar in their conception of barbarians who were not within the proper Hellenic pale. It was probably easier for the semi-Greek Macedonian to overcome this prejudice than it would have been for an Athenian or a Spartan.

Alexander saw himself as the ruler of a state in which his non-Greek vastly exceeded his Greek subjects; he therefore strove to govern them in the way they would understand. The adoption of oriental dress was a concession, and in the really important things he tried to make the Greek influence prevail. The Near East had seen many Greek visitors before his time, as mercenaries, traders, physicians, scholars. After his advent it swarmed with them. Greek became the language of culture and diplomacy, sometimes also of business in the area between Egypt and Mesopotamia. It may be said that this was due merely to the establishment of Greek political influence in these regions, but it is an incontestable fact that Alexander definitely aimed at this very result, the spread of Greek culture. He was the founder of many new cities, among them— to mention only two which have endured to this day and are very far apart—Alexandria and Kandahar. He aimed at overcoming Greek prejudice and oriental backwardness by producing an Eurasian strain which should unite the best qualities of European and Asiatic. To this end he arranged a large number of marriages between the two classes of his subjects. Whatever the result of this particular experiment, Alexander was successful in one respect. The old Greek conception of themselves as a race apart from the rest—the non-Greeks, the barbarians—was undermined. In the Greek kingdoms of the Near East, and gradually in the Mediterranean world in general, the emphasis came to be laid, not on the possession of Greek blood, but on the mental outlook, the possession of an Hellenic mind.

Thus by Alexander's career Greek influence was spread through the East, and Greek became a world language. The way was prepared for the preaching of the Gospel and the writing of the New Testament. Alexander was also the first person to endow scientific research. He continued his relations with his old master, Aristotle, and after his triumph in Asia he placed at the latter's disposal both financial means for research and a body of one thousand men who should carry out Aristotle's orders for procuring specimens and curiosities.

Alexander's achievements and personality not only made a great impression on his contemporaries and on history, but even now in out-of-the-way matters one comes across tributes to his greatness. For instance, in India, where there is a large native cinema industry, many of the films which are concerned with Indian history have a background of reference to the great Macedonian. A film dealing with Chandragupta, the founder of the Mauryan dynasty, the first great native monarchy after the invasion of Alexander, usually contains an oblique reference to him, eg, to Megasthenes who was an ambassador from Seleucus, one of Alexander's successors. It is curious to note the Indian interest in Alexander, especially when one understands that the Mauryan dynasty had arisen largely as a vigorous reaction against the attempt of Alexander and his successors to conquer the Punjab.

Naturally, Alexander's greatest immediate effect was upon his chief followers. Each of the soldier monarchs who succeeded him tried to emulate him in that portion of his empire which they had secured. They tried not only in the military and political spheres, but also in those of science and culture. The Seleucids and Ptolemies liked to be thought cultured, and the early Ptolemies also continued the patronage of science. At Alexandria arose a famous university and in many branches of knowledge advances were made which were not to be surpassed until the fifteenth century AD.

Euclid produced his geometry. The Old Testament was translated into Greek to become the Septuagint, which, as it was the version used by most of the great Christian fathers, has had a considerable influence on the world's thought. The famous lighthouse at Alexandria was built. There were, as we have seen, even such modern developments as the steam-engine made by Hero. The Greek genius was, however, speculative rather than experimental. The practical men of science, as we may call them, or rather the men who turn the inventions of the scientists to profit, were not there, probably because the scientists were much more interested in speculating on how something ought to be rather than in experimenting to see how it actually happened.

After a few generations, then, the science of the Greek world became mostly philosophical and abstract speculation. The results of the first ventures in the physical sciences were recorded in books, and became a tradition to be followed and observed, instead of a stimulus to future effort. Still, they were there on record. The advances had been made, and eventually the effort to master the forces of nature would be resumed. Meanwhile, Greek had been established as the culture-bearing language of the world. It had ceased to be the possession of a small nation and had become the tongue by birth, or by adoption, of a great multitude who had no Greek blood, or but little.

Politically, the results of Alexander's conquests were the destruction of the great empire which had dominated the peoples from Egypt to India, and (as his own empire failed to endure) the replacing of the one Persian state by a number of political units, none of which would be able to stand against a really strong power. The way was thus prepared for Rome, but also as a result of his conquests, Rome would come under the influence of a world culture. This culture, though much debased by the time of its adoption by Rome, would, nevertheless, in company with Roman law and the Christian religion, form the foundation of European civilisation.

CHAPTER SIX

ROME AND CARTHAGE

ALEXANDER THE GREAT died in 323 BC. By 280 BC, the Hellenic world, which he had so largely helped to create, had heard of the existence of a new great power in the western Mediterranean. In a war lasting until 275 BC, the Romans defeated Pyrrhus, king of Epirus (part of modern Albania), a distant relative of Alexander, who had sought to rival in the west Alexander's conquests in the east. The decisive battle was fought at Beneventum on the Volturnus, a place which now bears the name of Benevento.

Until the time of this war between Pyrrus and the Romans, the civilised world had known little of the western Mediterranean peoples. Of the north of Europe, or even of the central portions beyond the Alps, hardly any reliable information was possessed in the third century BC, even by the learned. It was not surprising, for these lands were not destined to play a decisive part in history for many more centuries. Ignorance of the state of affairs existing in the Italian peninsula was much less excusable on the part of the well-informed, yet even the staff officers of Pyrrhus (who had a good modern army) were not prepared for the shock of meeting disciplined troops in place of the barbarians they had supposed the Romans to be.

Italy at this period did not include the valley of the Po, which was inhabited by people akin to those dwelling in France, or Gaul as it was then called. Hence the plain of Lombardy was known as Gaul on this side of the Alps. Ancient Italy was the country dominated by the Apennine range. In the south-west there were some Greek settlements, evidence of which can be seen in the

names of places such as Naples (the new city, to commemorate a
Greek refounding of an older settlement). There were races in
various parts of Italy, not very numerous, alien to the main Italian
stock. Such were the Etruscans, who lived to the north of Rome,
and who were, according to many modern scholars, responsible for
imposing a monarchy upon Rome, the memory of which lived on
in the tales of the seven kings of Rome. The Etruscans were supposed to have come from Asia Minor and used a script which has
not yet been properly deciphered. There were also the Samnites
in the highlands of southern Italy, who were a race of fierce
mountaineers.

The bulk of the peoples of this ancient Italy were, however, akin
to the inhabitants of Rome. They used the same language, Latin.
They worshipped the same gods, Jupiter, Mars, Venus, etc. They
had the same type of economy, and the land was divided among
many city states, each with its own agricultural territory around
the mother city. Rome was only one of these, but it was situated
in the natural position of the capital of Italy and, as events were
to prove, was well placed to be the centre of the Mediterranean
world.

It had been founded in the eighth century BC, and for some
centuries it had been engaged in strife at fairly frequent intervals
with its neighbours. So far there is little in the story to denote any
difference between the history of Italy and that of Greece; but in
the case of Rome a new element came in. After a successful war
the Romans, instead of attempting to hold the vanquished in submission, were willing to accept them as members of the Latin
League. The foreign policy of the member states was determined
by Rome, but internally each was left a considerable measure of
freedom. Thus Rome, instead of being merely the conqueror,
became the natural representative and leader of the Italian states
against foreign aggression.

Parallel with this extension of Roman influence abroad, had gone
internal struggle. Rome had begun as a monarchy, but after a time
the king had been replaced by two magistrates, elected anually.
These consuls were the leaders of the army in time of war. The
patricians of Rome, or at least their leaders, sat in the senate, while

the plebeians met in a popular assembly. Gradually, the plebeians won rights. They had their own magistrates, the tribunes, and in course of time men of plebeian origin rose from the tribuneship to other magistracies and so to the highest of all (the consulate) which carried with it the right of entry to the senate. Although there was much hostility between patricians and plebeians, this progress was accomplished in two centuries without violence and in a constitutional manner.

By the time of the Pyrrhic war, the bulk of the Roman citizens were small, independent farmers. Roman citizenship had been granted to those who sought for the privilege in the Italian states, and in this way Italy was unified. The unification of the Roman Empire was the extension of this system to the whole area around the Middle Sea, first by conquest and then more gradually by the grant of Roman citizenship. Unfortunately, in the process of creating this empire the Romans themselves became more and more corrupt. At the time of their emergence as a great power they were a virile, healthy people with a high moral standard; not possessed of much wealth or culture, but strong and determined. Had they not become involved in wars outside Italy, it is possible that they might have developed a good democratic system, especially as they had not the same reliance as the Greeks on slave labour. It happened that they were almost certain to have gone to war with Carthage, the other great western power which was situated on the African shore of the Mediterranean.

Carthage had hardly anything in common with Rome. She sprung from old Phoenicia and retained the characteristics of the mother country. The western Mediterranean was dominated commercially by Carthage and her seamen had penetrated the sea outside the Strait of Gibraltar, both to the north and to the south. The exploitation of the wealth of the countries around the western basin of the sea was in Carthaginian hands. To protect her commerce, Carthage had a powerful fleet, but it had not been challenged for some two hundred years and was not, therefore, in a very efficient condition. On land, Carthage controlled the north African territories from the Moroccan Atlantic coast to the borders of Libya. The empire did not go far inland but, like the Roman dominion which succeeded it, extended as far as the southern spurs of the Atlas range. Corsica and Sardinia were Carthaginian possessions and Carthage had a strong grip on three-quarters of Sicily. Carthage, the capital city, was situated in what is now Tunisia, and though there were many smaller towns, the capital was the centre of life for the bulk of the Carthaginians. The territories of Carthage were tributary and were held down by force, the tribute being rendered not only in money and goods, but in bodies of men. Carthage employed foreign labour among her slaves, as well as foreigners to fight her battles. Her armies were composed of mercenary troops, men gathered from any and every race within her empire and outside it. Such soldiers were not prepared to fight when their pay ceased to flow, and could then become dangerous and turn against their employers. The generals and staffs of these armies were always Carthaginians and in this way the government of Carthage retained control of its foreign soldiers.

The citizens of Carthage were not afraid to fight. In a tight corner they could fight with Semitic stubbornness, but they thought it foolish to shed their blood when their money could produce other men to war and die on their behalf. The dominating motive in the minds of the Carthaginians was the making of money. All problems were judged in the light of the outlook, 'Will it pay?' If it were likely to pay them, the people of Carthage went to war. If it were likely to pay them, they made peace.

The government was conducted by a group of rich men who stood in the place of the patricians of Rome, and who prided themselves not on their ancient descent but on their wealth. Nominally, the bulk of the people possessed the supreme power, but except in periods of crises (when the popular will aserted itself) the corrupt, self-seeking oligarchy managed the affairs of state to its own satisfaction and advantage.

Only in one department of life did the Carthaginians adopt a non-monetary standard of values, and even in this they were unfortunately led into evil extremes. Their religion, like that of the majority of the oriental peoples in ancient times, was the worship of many gods, and involved human sacrifice. In times of crisis the priests of the gods would claim from the chief citizens of Carthage the sacrifice of their dearest possessions, their children. Flaubert, in his novel *Salammbô*, has drawn pictures of these sacrifices, which render any further description superfluous to those who have read that story. During the unsuccessful turns of a war the dread summons would go forth. The trembling parents waited in an agony for the call which they knew would come, and which they dared not refuse. There was the knocking on their door. When it was opened, a deputation of priests and officials would be found who would grimly and briefly demand delivery of the son of the house. The child would then be brought out, probably quite pleased with the brilliant clothes in which he was dressed for this great occasion, and handed over to the priests. Then he was taken to their temple of Moloch where, after suitable rites, he was dropped into a huge fire which burned between the legs of the gigantic statue. The parents might witness the immolation of their son; they might imagine that in the embers of the fire they could distinguish his bones. Semitic fanaticism would at times overpower natural feelings.

Although the Romans were capable of great cruelty, human sacrifice, as such, was abhorrent to them. In course of time they were to become debased and to pile up a huge account in the bank of human cruelties, but at the time when their struggle with Carthage opened they were still able to feel horror at the cruel obscenities of a Semitic religion. In addition, they professed great indignation at the breaches of plighted word and treaty which they summed up under the heading of 'Punic faith'.

At an early period in the annals of the republic, Rome had made a treaty with Carthage and this was faithfully observed on both sides for a long time. Rome was principally an agricultural state which did not come into conflict with the seaborne commerce of Carthage, and it was not until Pyrrhus's expedition to Italy had been defeated that a sphere of conflict could arise between Rome and Carthage. Then (in 275 BC) all Italy from the south of the Lombard plain to the Straits of Messina was united under the leadership of the Roman Republic. The Italians were bound to the Romans by the Latin League, and by the underlying ties of common race, religion, and political system; the foreign elements in this ancient Italy had either been reduced by a series of wars, as in the case of the Etruscans and Samnites, or had found it expedient to league themselves with Rome, as with the Greek cities on the coast.

The island of Sicily is as much connected with Italy by geography as Ireland is linked with Great Britain. Sicily in 275 BC was divided between territories owned by Carthage, which she had acquired primarily for commercial reasons and had subsequently fortified, and the semi-independent Greek kingdom of Syracuse. This latter would inevitably seek the assistance of Rome against Carthage, because of the Greek preference for Europeans over Asiatics or Africans. Two spheres of influence were thus created, and as Rome increased in strength and importance these spheres were certain to come into conflict. It scarcely needed a pretext such as was supplied by the entry of Roman deserters into Carthaginian territory and the refusal of Carthage to give them up, for the two great powers to go to war in 264 BC. This war was the first overseas expedition of the Romans and it was to be the cause of many changes in their system of government and way of life. Overseas service required more than a stipulated number of days, men were away for months and years, and the foundations of a regular army were laid in this, the first of the three Punic Wars.

The struggle lasted over twenty years and was divided into four fairly clear stages. At first, the Romans thought that all they had to do was to beat the Carthaginian armies in Sicily. This did not present them with a very difficult task and soon most of Sicily was in their hands, with the exception of several powerful fortresses which held out for Carthage. What they had not realised was that Carthage possessed the command of the sea and that she could therefore keep her Sicilian fortresses provisioned and thus stage a successful return to the island. The Romans were never to be lovers of salt water. They were emphatically a land power, but they quickly realised that although the sea was not an element to love, it was certainly one to use. They set to work on the construction of a fleet in order to dispute the control of the sea. Their first encounters with the experienced Carthaginian sailors were, not unnaturally, disastrous, but soon one of the consuls, Duilius, devised a means whereby the superior military power of the

Romans could be made as effective on sea as on land. Powerful gangways, equipped with grappling irons, were attached to the masts of the Roman vessels. When these latter had been brought within reach of the enemy ships, the gangways were let fall and the hooks fastened on the bulwarks of the Carthaginian vessel. Along the gangways the Roman soldiers rushed to make the fighting on the enemy ship resemble a land fight.

By means of this ingenious device the Carthaginians were, for a season, driven from the sea in the central Mediterranean. The Romans not only pressed on their blockade of the strongholds in Sicily, but boldly sent an expedition to invade North Africa. The Roman army landed in what is now Algeria, or Tunisia, and established itself in strength. The Carthaginians were beaten in some battles and as the question of finance now came to the top, the government of Carthage decided to ask for peace terms. The Roman general, the consul Regulus, acting no doubt on orders from his home government, propounded terms which were too harsh. The other great element in the Punic character then asserted itself. A wave of religious fanaticism with the usual immolation of children—'the fruit of my body for the sin of my soul'—raised the spirit of Carthage. A new general was found—this time a Greek mercenary soldier—who was given a free hand in reorganising the army. He realised that the Romans were not skilled in African warfare and had no experience of dealing with an elephant charge. There were many elephants at Carthage, well trained for war. Battle was joined on a plain, the Roman infantry were overwhelmed by an onslaught of living tanks, and only a small body of Roman troops escaped to the port of embarkation. Regulus was captured.

It was now the turn of the Carthaginians to underestimate the Roman character. The Carthaginians re-equipped their fleets, and the Romans had all they could do to hold their own. Naval disasters followed on defeats in North Africa, but with grim tenacity the Romans fought on. A great general appeared on the Carthaginian side, Hamilcar of the house of Barca, and gained notable successes against the Romans in Sicily.

The war had dragged on for over twenty years and both sides now made preparations for a final trial of strength. Everything depended on supremacy at sea. Each side raised a fleet and the rival forces met off the Aegadean Islands, a rocky cluster near the western end of Sicily which lie right across the present-day shipping and air routes from Tunis to Sicily and Italy. Known to the Italians as Isole Egadi, they look barren and are sparsely inhabited, and probably the only important event with which they have ever been connected was the battle between the Romans and Carthaginians which can be called the Trafalgar of ancient times. If the Carthaginians won they could end the siege of their fortresses in Sicily. If Rome won, Sicily would be conquered.

The battle was long and fierce. At the end of it, Carthage, her fleet a wreck, could fight no longer and sued for peace. Rome, though near exhaustion, had won and accepted the chance to end the war to her advantage. Sicily was to be evacuated by Carthaginian troops, an indemnity was to be paid by Carthage, and Roman prisoners restored. Thus the Roman people acquired their first overseas province, Sicily.

The financial resources of Carthage had been depleted by the protracted struggle and at the end of the war she was unable to pay the large number of mercenaries she had enlisted. Rising in revolt, they overran Tunisia and nothing Carthaginian outside the walls of Carthage was safe. Hamilcar, who had never been defeated in battle, was called to aid his country. Gradually, he succeeded in overcoming the mercenaries, the last of whom were given over to refinements of cruelty which only the Carthaginians could enjoy witnessing.

This internal struggle lasted some considerable time, and in the course of it Carthage was unable to maintain effective government in Corsica and Sardinia. The Romans thereupon took these territories under their protection—in violation of the peace terms which had been agreed. Hamilcar was so enraged by this breach of Roman faith that he swore to have revenge on Rome and made his son Hannibal, then a boy of twelve, take an oath never to make friends with Rome. To this act of Roman perfidy may the second Punic War be traced.

Regulus, who has been mentioned earlier in this chapter, has been the subject of a famous story, put into fine poetry by Horace.

During a lull in the first Punic War, when Carthage was temporarily triumphant, Regulus, who had been captured, was sent to Rome as bearer of peace terms. Before releasing him, his captors made him swear that if the Romans did not accept the terms, he would return to Carthage. Regulus, on arrival at Rome refused, as a defeated general, to enter the city and was received by the senate outside the walls. He presented the Carthaginian peace terms, analysed them, and strongly advised against their acceptance. The terms were rejected and Regulus turned away from Rome. His wife and children, his kinsfolk and friends begged him to stay. The senate offered to release him from his oath, but he refused and returned to Carthage to die by torture. Such is the story, and even if its application to Regulus or any particular man is incorrect, it illustrates the harsh nobility of the Roman character in the classical days of the Republic.

NOTE: Mention of Carthage as a colony derived from Tyre, one of the cities of Phoenicia, leads to a consideration of that strip of land along the coast of Syria, running parallel to the Lebanon range. Knowledge of Phoenicia, like that of Carthage, is derived mostly from the records of other nations. Whereas, however, with Carthage, the significance of her three wars against Rome has caused a great deal of information about her to be preserved, the Phoenician mother cities were not so fortunate. Yet it is to the Phoenicians that the world owes the alphabet which, adopted and adapted by the Greeks, was the ancestor of the Latin alphabet and all those of Europe. In navigation and seamanship, the Phoenician sailors were the most skilful of antiquity. Like the Venetians in medieval times, they lent the use of their ships to various masters and, to take one instance only, they supplied Alexander the Great with a fleet.

In the period soon after 3000 BC Phoenicia is found in an alliance with Egypt, with the latter as the senior partner. Supply of goods by Phoenician cities, and particularly timber from the famous cedars of Lebanon, was an important feature in the relationship.

The chief Phoenician cities were Byblos, Berytus, Tripoli, Tyre and Sidon, the last two being the most famous, and frequently mentioned in the Old and the New Testaments. They appear to have formed a confederation with now one, now another city predominant. Hiram, king of Tyre, was a friend of David, and a partner with Solomon, aiding the latter by supplying raw materials, finished goods, and skilled craftsmen, to assist in the building of the Temple at Jerusalem. Later, when Israel was a separate kingdom from Judah, Tyre supplied a queen to King Ahab, and she has passed into history as the famous, or infamous, painted Jezebel. In the book of the prophet Ezekiel there can be read an eloquent catalogue in splendid language of the achievements, the wealth and the alliances of Tyre, accompanied by denunciation on an apocalyptic scale.

Phoenicia was, after a period of independence from about 1100 BC, brought into conflict with the power of Assyria, and her successor in empire, Babylon. The rulers of these states reduced Tyre more than once, although there were frequent rebellions against foreign rule. During the years 585 to 573 BC, while he was engaged in capturing Jerusalem and conquering Judah, Nebuchadnezzar of Babylon was also occupied with a thirteen-year siege of Tyre. He eventually forced it to submit to his rule. Much later Alexander the Great, by a very skilful use of engineering resources, reduced Tyre in less than a year.

Thereafter Phoenicia knew no independence. It was famous in Roman times for the manufacture of Tyrian purple. Tyre met with no catastrophic fall, such as that of Carthage, but underwent a continuous decline to its status as a small town in the Christian and the modern era.

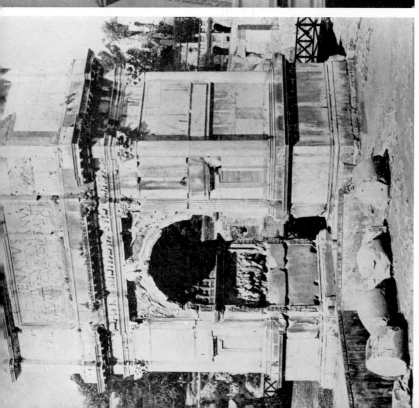

Page 99 (*left*) The Arch of Titus in Rome; (*right*) the Statue of St Paul outside the Walls, Rome

Page 100 (*above*) The Forum at Rome; (*below*) the Amphitheatre at Pompeii

CHAPTER SEVEN

THE SECOND PUNIC WAR

CARTHAGE WAS compelled to acquiesce in the terms of peace as they had been interpreted by Rome, and when she emerged from the struggle with her own mercenaries she found that she had lost her overseas colonies, Sicily, Sardinia and Corsica, while Rome had begun her great experiment in the government of subject peoples. The Carthaginians quickly resumed their sway over the North African territories, and the Libyan and Berber peoples were to wait some years for the overthrow of their tyrants. Carthaginian trade soon recovered and the indemnity due to Rome was paid off.

Hamilcar had become the most distinguished figure in the Carthaginian state, but he could not alter the outlook of the corrupt capitalists who ruled his country. He was a lover of Carthage, but he felt that if she were to be regenerated and become once more a great power, fresh sources of strength must be found and developed away from Carthage itself. As commander of the army which had overthrown the rebel troops, he suddenly ordered it aboard what was left of the Carthaginian fleet and sailed away to Spain. At first, the home government denounced him as one who intended to build a kingdom for himself, but the money-makers of Carthage were soon reconciled to his absence when he not only made no call on public funds for the support of his troops but sent financial presents to the leaders of Carthage. His expedition was showing a profit. Manifestly, then, in the eyes of the rulers of Carthage, it was a good expedition!

By a strange anticipation, Spain, which seventeen centuries later was to exploit the riches of the New World, was itself the exploited

G

El Dorado of the Old. There were silver mines in Spain, and this probably explains the determination with which Romans and Carthaginians fought for the country and the persistent efforts of the Romans to subdue the natives once the Carthaginians had gone. Unhappy Spain was destined then, as in our own century, to be the practice ground in battle for nations mightier than herself. Just as communists and fascists fought at the Alcazar and over Guernica in Franco's war, so the Romans decided several of their wars with Carthage and with each other in Spain.

To exploit the Spanish silver mines the Romans had established a sphere of influence south of the Ebro, in the city of Saguntum, which was an ally of Rome—that is to say it existed in the condition of a foreign state not hostile to Rome, but which she did not as yet find convenient to swallow.

But there was one great drawback to the exploitation of the Spanish wealth, and that was the toughness of the Spanish natives. The whole peninsula was inhabited by tribes who loved battle and seemed never to tire of attacking the invader. The Romans were destined to fight many campaigns in Spain before the country was completely Romanised.

The hostility of the natives was not perhaps as serious for Hamilcar as for the Romans. Certainly, he wanted the wealth of Spain and dealt drastically with any who opposed him, but he also wished to use Spain as a recruiting ground. By offering the hardy natives the chance to serve in his army for good pay, he gradually built up a sphere of influence for himself. Armies were equipped, fleets launched, cities founded. Among those cities was Nova Carthago, so-called as the capital city of Carthaginian Spain, just as the old Carthage was the capital in Africa. Nova Carthago was in later days to be taken by Scipio, but it was not destroyed and has lived on to our days as Cartagena, one of the most important ports of eastern Spain—another example of the resilience of the old names and places.

The Romans could not feel happy over the resurgence of Carthaginian power, but no representations of theirs at Carthage could prevent the empire-building which was going on in Spain. Hamilcar had one objective, the destruction of Rome. He knew that he might not live to carry out his plans, and he therefore trained successors, his son-in-law and his three sons, chief of whom was the future great warrior Hannibal.

For their part, the Romans were not idle in the uneasy twenty years between the first and second Punic Wars. They had been attacked by another of the periodic Gallic invasions from the north, and after its defeat they decided to carry the war into the enemy's country. Under their general, Flaminius, they pushed down through the forests of the northernmost part of the Apennine range and fought a great campaign on the plain of Lombardy. Despite a stiff resistance, the Gauls of this area were reduced, Roman colonies were planted at strategic points, and for the first time the plains between the Alps and the Apennines were brought within the area of Italy.

It was clear that war was bound to come, but it was not until Hamilcar and his son-in-law had died, and Hannibal at the age of twenty-seven had been acclaimed as general of the Carthaginian army, that hostilities began. Even then there was no formal declaration of war by the government at Carthage, and the Romans had some reason on this occasion for complaints regarding Punic faith. Hannibal's army numbered over one hundred thousand men. He was well-equipped with elephants and artillery, and his men were enthusiastic for war which, to them, meant booty. Moreover, the Romans, intent on the development of their new territory, showed no great desire for the fight. Hannibal decided that the time had come to strike.

Hannibal is one of the most fascinating figures of the past. His story has come down to us through the writings of his bitterest enemies, the Romans. No Carthaginian account of him has reached us and the Romans, unlike the English, did not idealise their enemies once they had fallen. Despite this adverse witness, Hannibal remains a great figure, not only as a general and statesman but also as a hero who inspires our affection and sympathy. To us there is an epic quality in his life, a grim and hopeless struggle against fate. As a man of genius alone Hannibal is of the first class, and his greatness as a soldier has been acknowledged by military leaders of all ages and countries. His stature so far surpasses that of the money-makers of Carthage that we marvel at the emergence of such a patriot among them. He was a subtle diplomat, a man of wide-reaching views who waged war by every means and not only on the battlefield with physical weapons.

Our admiration for Hannibal must not, however, blind us to the disaster which would have followed his victories. Rome was the better instrument in the hand of Providence. Her corruption was of a different type from that of Carthage, and by the time it had become deep-seated and deadly, another kingdom had become firmly established in the world, a kingdom which could survive the fall of Rome and carry on the best of her traditions. Had Hannibal made Carthage the supreme power in the Mediterranean he could not have regenerated her, and all that would have happened would have been the exploitation of the whole Mediterranean area without any attempt to protect or develop culture. In the place of the great fabric of Roman law there would have been the law of profit; in place of the development of Greek culture, the book of the merchants; for Christian Rome, the Carthage of human sacrifices.

Hannibal attacked Saguntum merely because the city was an ally of Rome, which barred his progress northward. He knew also that the Romans were not ready for war and that if he could destroy an ally of theirs while they debated the matter, he could strike their prestige a great blow and bring himself before the world in a favourable light. He therefore pressed the siege of Saguntum. The Saguntines begged for aid from the Romans, who sent an embassy to Carthage where the government declined responsibility for Hannibal's actions. While the Romans were discussing with the Carthaginians the legal position of Hannibal, he took Saguntum, destroyed the city and sold the remaining inhabitants as slaves—a very serious blow to Roman prestige in Spain.

After wiping out Saguntum, Hannibal marched northwards, crossed the Pyrenees and disappeared into the then little-known country of southern France. The Romans were now alarmed, and with reason. The world had seen an adventurer flout the power of Rome. An army was despatched to the Po valley to meet Hannibal should he cross the Gulf of Genoa, but it was not a very strong force and a larger army was sent to Spain to attempt the difficult task of re-establishing Roman prestige there.

Hannibal meanwhile had vanished, but suddenly the news came through to Rome that he had descended from the Alps on to the plains of Lombardy. Hordes of savages had crossed the northern barrier of Italy in the past, but this was the first instance of a disciplined army with full equipment forcing its way through the Alps. As the Romans had expected no such thing, Hannibal's surprise was complete and the first Roman force he encountered was beaten, being probably too weak to oppose him successfully. Apart from this first success, however, Hannibal must have viewed with considerable apprehension the havoc caused in his army by the passage over the Alps. He had lost about two-thirds of his troops and could not have anticipated such heavy casualties. He set to work to repair the damage with characteristic energy and was soon in command of a large force of fresh warriors. The newly conquered territory in which he had arrived speedily revolted from Rome and, apart from the Roman colonies, the whole northern plain went over to him. With these Gauls, and with his previous African and Spanish troops now rested, he began to march down the Italian peninsula.

The Romans put their army under the command of Flaminius, the conqueror of the Gauls. He was full of confidence and had no proper estimate of Hannibal's genius as a general, any more than had the Romans as a whole. Hannibal, who possessed a most elaborate intelligence service all around the Mediterranean, knew his man and laid an ambush for Flaminius near Lake Trasimenus. The Carthaginian army concealed itself around the narrow pass which runs between the mountains and the lake and when the Romans had marched headlong in, each end of the pass was closed by powerful Carthaginian forces. The Romans were thus attacked on three sides with their backs to the lake.

Flaminius did all in his power to avert disaster and his troops fought with great courage, but there could be only one end. The bulk of the Roman force perished, so did Flaminius. A Gaul who had previously fought against him saw him in the midst of a body of Roman soldiers. Exclaiming that this was the enemy of his country and that he would add his spoils to his collection, he attacked and slew Flaminius.

Two results followed this battle. Hannibal resumed his march into the south of Italy where he expected to find fresh allies. The Romans were aroused to the need to make a really serious effort against him. An old general named Fabius came forward and was appointed dictator, a constitutional post held for only a few months among the Romans. His policy was to avoid battle with Hannibal, to waste his (Hannibal's) resources in small skirmishes, and to cut off his supplies. This line of conduct was so successful that Fabius was said to have restored the state by delaying, hence his title of 'Cunctator' and the term 'Fabian tactics'.

Unfortunately, Hannibal's genius was still not appreciated, ambushing methods being considered responsible for his success at Trasimenus. A sound judgement was prevented also by a political upheaval in Rome. The popular party demanded a more active front than was afforded by the slow efforts of Fabius and accused the senate of prolonging the war by failing to take sufficiently drastic measures. The consular elections were due and a representative of the popular party was returned, a man named Varro. His brother-consul was Paulus, a much more experienced man. Two consular armies were levied and the two consuls, with some eighty thousand men, marched out in search of Hannibal.

Hannibal had taken his army over to the Adriatic side of Italy, to the plains of Foggia. This is ideal ground for military manoeuvres, although it has little else to recommend it. As one emerges from the mountains on one's way to Foggia and Bari, one's eyes are at first pleased to see a wider view. If it is the end of winter there is the chance of some green plains, which are pleasant after the harsh mountains. Everywhere there are the small houses which were set up during the Fascist rule for the peasant farmers who were to develop agriculture and raise small flocks of sheep in the area. The little houses are scattered all over the plain and here and there are the civic centres, each with its own church, school and meeting-house, all very white and pleasant. Foggia was just one of these places, a trifle bigger, but the two curses of an Italian plain are mud in the wet winter and dust in the dry summer.

Still, Foggia plain was, and is, an admirable place for warfare, and on part of this plain Hannibal prepared to fight his greatest battle. He had about fifty thousand men, a heterogeneous collection of Gauls, Africans and Spaniards, men from the Balearics and Samnites. The nature of the country was such that no matter of ambushes, but military skill of a high degree was called for, and Hannibal needed a successful battle because no great city had as yet come over to him. The Romans should therefore have refused battle, contenting themselves with holding Hannibal in check whilst gradually cutting off his supplies. Paulus was in favour of this strategy, and for a while succeeded in restraining Varro, but the consuls were wont to command on alternate days and, after what must have seemed to him an unnecessary delay, Varro decided to fight. He wanted to go down in history as the people's candidate who had defeated Hannibal after two conservative generals had failed. No doubt he was also anxious to overthrow the invader of his country. At any rate, he gave Hannibal his opportunity.

The battle of Cannae which followed has become a military masterpiece. It figures in the training given at modern staff colleges, and during the 1939-45 war the Cannae method was used by both sides in securing their best results. The German victories in western Europe were won very largely by the use of the battle of Cannae tactics, and in Russia the method was very successfully applied by the invaders until the battle of Stalingrad, when the Russians turned the tables on their enemies. In the case of Stalingrad, incidentally, the German general was named Paulus.

Hannibal drew up his troops in a position where his flanks could not easily be turned, and with a narrow front on which the Romans would find it difficult to deploy their superior numbers. When the Romans attacked, Hannibal's centre gradually withdrew while his wings stood firm and his cavalry gathered round the Roman rear. At last the Roman force was surrounded, and in so small a space that the troops had not sufficient room in which to use their weapons with any effect. As a result, they were overwhelmed by the Carthaginians, except for a small body which cut its way through. By the end of the day the majority of the Roman army of eighty thousand lay dead, whereas Hannibal's losses were small. Paulus was one of the slain.

The events which crowded upon the victory of Cannae must have filled Hannibal with elation. Capua, at that time probably a richer city than Rome, went over to his side. The fickle inhabitants were soon to regret having invited such a guest inside their walls, but their example was followed by some of the other non-Italian communities of the south. Hannibal sent part of his spoils to Carthage, and the sight of a large collection of rings taken from dead Roman knights induced the government to believe that great profits might be obtained from the war, and they soon broke with Rome. Thus Hannibal found himself supported by his home government, possessed of a large city as a base, and with great prestige.

He had still a mighty task ahead of him. There had not been any mass movement of the allies of Rome over to his side. Varro had survived the battle and even been welcomed to Rome by the senate, which thanked him for not having despaired of the Republic. After the first great shock of the disaster the people rallied and took up the struggle with their accustomed tenacity; Fabius once more directed operations. Gradually, too, another good general appeared on the Roman side, Marcellus, who gained a few small victories against the Punic enemy and helped to restore the Romans' faith in themselves.

Hannibal used every ruse in his power to bring the Romans to battle, but they persisted in their cautious policy and at last, during one of his absences from Capua, they succeeded in surrounding the city. Hannibal tried hard to relieve it as it had more importance to him than simply as a base, inasmuch as failure to protect his ally would reflect badly on his prestige. He even marched on Rome itself in the hope of drawing away forces from Capua. The Romans knew that he was in no position to besiege Rome and refused to move any troops from before Capua. To show their defiance of him, they even put up for auction the land on which he camped.

Eventually, Capua fell to the Romans and the punishment they gave to it must have been a signal lesson to all who contemplated joining Hannibal. It is said that they degraded it from being the first municipality in Italy to being the first village. Like many places destroyed under the Republic, Capua was rebuilt under the Empire. It was now the turn of Hannibal to taste the bitterness of failure to protect an ally.

Nevertheless, the strain of the war was telling on Rome. Hannibal controlled most of Italy south of Capua and his army lived off the country, the produce of which was thus lost to Rome. The absence of the adult male population in the armies made agricultural work in Roman-controlled Italy very hard, and the cost of maintaining such huge forces (the nation was completely mobilised) weighed on a community which was not rich. The war had gone on for some twelve years and even some of Rome's Italian allies began to falter. Marcellus was killed in a skirmish. Hannibal's fertile brain continued to work against Rome. He maintained connections with every Mediterranean power hostile to Rome and the head of one of these, the king of Macedon, agreed to march into Italy from the northern Balkans and to make a co-ordinated attack on Rome. Although this threat was never carried out, the knowledge that it existed was an additional burden to the Romans.

Hannibal was unable to conquer Rome; Rome was unable to drive him from Italy. There was one source from which could come aid that would be decisive in tipping the scale. That source was Spain, where the armies of Rome and Carthage had battled with varying success since the beginning of the war. Hannibal's brother, Hasdrubal, did at last succeed in eluding the Roman army and marched with a large force for Italy. He crossed the Alps without great difficulty and advanced along the eastern coast of Italy.

Although Hannibal knew that his brother had set out he did not know how far away he was, nor was he destined to know. The messenger despatched by Hasdrubal to acquaint Hannibal of his arrival in Italy was captured by the Romans. Without waiting for the horror of these tidings to paralyse their actions, the Romans prepared to deal with Hasdrubal separately. Troops were brought together from every quarter, and by skilful manoeuvring some were even withdrawn from the front in the south, without this being revealed to Hannibal's reconnaissance.

The decisive battle of the war was fought near the Metaurus river (its name is now Metauro, so little does Italy change), and there the fate of Rome and Carthage was settled. Hasdrubal was slain, and his army destroyed. Hannibal's first intimation of the disaster was when his brother's head was thrown into his camp with an insulting message by a Roman patrol. As he gazed at the distorted features, Hannibal exclaimed sadly that now, indeed, Rome would rule the world. The Romans were thus enabled to pass to the offensive, but it was some time before they could defeat Hannibal. At last, they developed a young general of brilliant ability, one Scipio, who gained his spurs in Spain and was later sent to Africa to attack Hannibal's home base. This movement was successful and Hannibal finally evacuated Italy in order to defend his own country.

With defeat staring them in the face, the Carthaginians indulged in mutual recriminations instead of preparing to meet the common foe. The army was affected by this paralysis and, being disunited in itself could not, even under Hannibal's leadership, avert defeat at the hands of Scipio in 202 BC at the battle of Zama.

After a struggle of more than twenty years Rome had again defeated Carthage. The terms of surrender were now much more severe. All Carthaginian sway in Spain had to be renounced. A large part of the African dominions of Carthage became an independent kingdom, of Mauretania or Morocco, under Roman tutelage. The Carthaginian war fleet was reduced to ten vessels, a large indemnity had to be paid, and—perhaps the most important item in Roman eyes—Hannibal had to be surrendered to them.

He had tried to regenerate his country politically in the hope that by so doing he might prepare her for another and more successful struggle with Rome. Instead, the terms of peace demanded him, for a Roman triumph, to march behind the conqueror's chariot along the Sacred Way, to ascend the Capitoline Hill amid the shouts and insults of the Roman crowd, and finally to die miserably in the Tullianum prison at the foot of the Capitol.

There were men at Carthage who were willing to hand him over to Rome, but he spared them the shame of surrendering their country's greatest soldier. He fled his beloved city forever and for years he wandered in various countries. He could never settle long anywhere for Roman ambassadors always appeared to urge his extradition. Finally, the king of one country agreed to deliver him but, as always, Hannibal's spies had done their work well. Forewarned of the approach of the Romans, Hannibal said to his attendants: 'Let us relieve the Romans of their fear of an old man', and calmly took poison. When the eager soldiers arrived, they found the great Hannibal dead. He was sixty-four years of age and had fought Rome from his boyhood. Though he failed to destroy her in war, he left a decisive mark on the future of Rome.

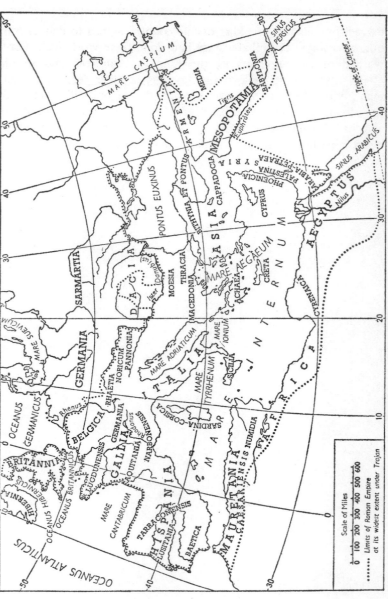

Map 5: The Roman Empire at its Greatest Extent

CHAPTER EIGHT

THE EXPANSION
OF THE ROMAN EMPIRE

FROM THE battle of Zama in 202 BC, and the defeat of Carthage, may be reckoned the origin of the Roman Empire. At the end of the second Punic War, Rome possessed the whole of Italy from the foot of the Alps to the Straits of Messina, the islands of Sicily, Corsica and Sardinia, and part of eastern Spain. She had not annexed any of the African dominion of Carthage, but had been content to set up so-called independent African states, which were really dependent on Rome and acted as checks on Carthage. A great deal of conquest lay in front of the Romans during the last two centuries of the Republic, and even under the rule of the Caesars considerable additions were to be made. The essential position was that after the defeat of Carthage in the second Punic War no adversary existed who could maintain a prolonged resistance to Rome; at least, not until the Roman legions had marched far from the shores of the Mediterranean.

For the two hundred years after Zama the Roman Empire was to expand. In the first century AD it was to attain its greatest size and remain more or less stable for some two centuries, then in the fourth century it would decline, and in the west at least, would fall into utter ruin by the end of the fifth century. For about seven hundred years after Zama, the story of the Mediterranean is the story of the vicissitudes of the Roman power.

The second Punic War was not only the struggle which caused Rome to become a certain candidate for world empire. It was also the era dividing an older and much simpler Rome from the Rome which was to become an empire. The second Punic War was the last of the classic wars of Rome. It is not impossible to imagine Cincinnatus summoned from his farm to become a commander after Cannae. Camillus would not have been out of place beside Marcellus. The old simple, hard and grim, but honest and pure Romans, who were represented by such men as Camillus and Cincinnatus, would have been in their element fighting against Hannibal, but one cannot imagine them fighting so easily with Marius, Sulla, Crassus, Julius Caesar, or even Scipio Africanus the Younger. Cato the Elder, whose favourite sentence was *Delenda est Carthago*, is an example of the survival of old Roman manners; though he is, we feel, an anachronism, and even in him there are modern elements which would have been out of place in the heroes of old. Roman strength of character had won the great wars of the older period, henceforward Roman military strength, Roman money, bribery, corruption and treachery were to have the biggest share in victory.

The Roman way of life had been changed almost completely by the war with Hannibal. Italy is not the most suitable of lands for an extensive agriculture because so much of it is covered by mountains, but previous to the second Punic War it had sufficed for the simple Italian way of life. The wars which had occurred had not involved the whole peninsula, but only small areas for short periods, while the first Punic War had been fought outside Italy. The presence of an enemy in the country for nearly twenty years had deranged the economy of Italy. Hannibal had done as much damage as possible to Rome and her allies. Large portions of southern Italy had been rendered waste, while even in the centre and the north, which Hannibal had not been able to occupy, the length of the war and the overall mobilisation required had taken away the normal cultivators of the soil. The women and children had often gone for safety into the walled towns, and at the end of the war a very large number of these country dwellers stayed on in the cities. Considerable numbers of farmers did not survive the war; many others had not the means to resettle on their farms and to pay for the necessary alterations and repairs. One result of this was that the wealthy Romans were able to buy up many of these smallholdings and to merge them into huge domains of their own. These new estates were not primarily agricultural; the vine was their main product. From the second century BC dates the appearance of the frequent complaints found in Latin literature of the ruin of the old free population and its replacement by slave labour. Slaves had been known at Rome, as in other parts of the ancient world, before the wars with Carthage, but the huge scale of the Hannibalite war produced very large numbers of captives. Human life was cheap. A great landed proprietor found the employment of slaves much more profitable than letting his farms to free men. The Big Business Man appeared in Rome, and flourished mightily; nor did he disappear until Rome itself crashed.

The free population which was thus dispossessed by the slaves and which had crowded into the towns, particularly into Rome, had still to be fed. Moreover, it possessed votes. The *cursus honorum*, or round of offices, which Romans with political ambitions coveted, was in the gift of the Roman people. The great Roman people, the terror of distant nations, might live in hovels or garrets, receiving its bread from the charitable hands of the state, but it was still sovereign and disposed by its franchise of the highest magistracies. The proud and wealthy, as their chariots rattled along the rough streets, must have been inwardly galled at the thought that the filthy crowd which jumped out of the chariot's path could make or mar them on election day. Only when a man had attained the highest office, that of consul, which carried with it membership of the senate, was he free of the people's votes. Even then he might need to canvass them on behalf of his friends. To woo this poor, dirty, supreme people was the way to office and, as office meant the opportunity to enrich oneself, many candidates were found. In Shakespeare's *Coriolanus* there is a very good example of a Roman electoral canvas.

It had been necessary to import corn from Sicily at the conclusion of the war, and soon food was brought in and distributed free to the Roman people. Bribery disdained some of its usual disguises and the lower magistrates prepared for their elevation to the higher ranks by a sedulous and corrupt wooing of the voters. It is, however, possible to exaggerate the extent of corruption, for there were, in fact, districts of Italy where the small freeholders maintained their land ownership for ages. Nor must it be supposed that at one bound the ancient honesty and simplicity of manners had given way to the corruption which was common enough at the time of Julius Caesar and Cicero. The fact remains, however, that the Roman state which had been poor, had emerged from the first of the Punic Wars with rich overseas possessions, and from the second with the dominion of the entire Mediterranean area in its grasp. The opportunities for the acquisition of wealth were provided and they were not neglected.

New arrangements in government had had to be made when Sicily was acquired. The consuls for the year were to go to these provinces on the expiration of their year of office and there reign as pro-consuls for a term. It can be imagined how this system would lead to abuse, especially when more distant provinces were added to the empire. The consul was allowed to take his wife, to add her rapacity to his own. He was responsible to the senate, but as long as the tribute was paid and no great disorder broke out he had little to fear. At the conclusion of his rule he could be prosecuted by the provincials he had wronged, but as he would be judged at Rome by his peers, who had mostly held similar positions, his sentence even when condemned was likely to be a light one. In the *Verrine Orations* of Cicero we have a not untypical picture of what a bad governor was like.

In the military sphere, the distant campaigns necessitated many changes in the old system of a conscript militia. Military service had of necessity to be prolonged in order to wage war overseas. Spain was the first country where the Romans experienced the need for something like a standing army. Generals also had to have their terms of command prolonged, and one of the results of these measures was to create a bond between the general and his army so that the troops looked to him rather than to the senate as the source of orders.

The last two centuries of the Roman Republic show us a gradual decadence and corruption in the Roman character, accompanied by a failure of the machinery of government to meet new needs. The Romans did not use the English system of voting by representation. They insisted that each voter should be present at

Rome in person to record his vote. In consequence, the bulk of the voters was supplied by the city rabble, which could not exercise any control over the senate. The rule of the senate became more and more the personal self-seeking of a crowd of plutocrats. Attempts at reform were, as we shall see, frustrated, until either the dissolution of the Republic or the substitution of one-man rule for that of the senate had become necessary.

The conquests achieved under the Republic have usually two features in common. There is first a period of muddling during which the Romans suffer defeats, followed by the complete conquest of the enemy when Rome applied her full vigour to the task. It is interesting to note, also, the number of cases in which a country later conquered by Rome was at first allied to her. For instance, the Mauretanian kingdom, which Rome had carved out of the domains of Carthage, was allied to her until the destruction of Carthage itself. Then the Mauretanian kings had attained their object and, having had enough of Rome, sought to make their independence real. A long and toilsome war resulted in the destruction of the Mauretanian monarchy and the creation of a Roman province of Africa.

It would take too long to trace in detail the course of Roman conquests, but some of the more characteristic wars may be selected. Between Zama and the assumption of supreme power by Augustus there are some two hundred years, and hardly one of these years was without warfare for the Romans. Spain was the scene of many Roman campaigns, and savage were the cruelties wreaked on the ancestors of the Conquistadors and Inquisitors. At length the country, which was useful to Rome for its wealth, was conquered. But whereas in Spain Romans were dealing with primitive tribes, in Greece they contacted a civilisation they were beginning to admire. They went there first as liberators of the Greeks from the Macedonian yoke.

Philip of Macedon, the foolish king who agreed to fight on Hannibal's side and then did not do so, had made himself memorable to the Romans. Eventually there was a series of Macedonian wars, the end of which was the destruction of Macedon as a separate state. The monarchy of Alexander the Great was led in

H

triumph behind a Roman general's car. The Greeks, who had always hated Macedon, welcomed the Romans at first, but the latter soon discovered that the liberation of Greece was much the easiest part of their task. Civil war broke out in Greece and the Romans found themselves involved. At length, Rome decided to make Greece a Roman province, and the glory that was Greece passed into oblivion in the title of Achaea, which the Romans chose for their new province. Never again would the famous cities of Greece be politically important. The culture of Greece was soon to be exported to Italy and to lead to a great new Latin literature and art. Greece did not give her conqueror more political trouble, perhaps because the fickle Greeks, with all their folly, realised that Rome was not to be treated with contempt. Corinth had rebelled and Corinth had been captured and destroyed.

The year (146 BC) which saw the fall of Corinth, saw also the end of the third Punic War and the destruction of Carthage. Whatever we may think of the Carthaginians, it must surely be admitted that the measures which Rome had taken after the second Punic War had deprived them of any chance of rivalling her. Nevertheless, the hatred aroused by Hannibal lasted on in Rome for fifty years, fanned by a very hard and bitter old man, Cato the Censor, whose practice it was to conclude every speech he made in the senate with the words: 'And I consider, Gentlemen, that Carthage should be destroyed'.

The commercial greatness of Carthage had soon revived and it may be that this, rather than memories of racial hatred, was responsible for the Roman attack on her. A quarrel was picked and the Romans set out seeking an easy conquest. Instead, the siege of Carthage lasted three or four years and great efforts were required before she was conquered. Multitudes of people were slain and the rest sold as slaves, the city was destroyed and the land sown with salt by the Romans, an act which symbolised in their opinion the complete devastation of the city.

In the eastern Mediterranean the Romans were not at first faced with any extensive wars. The king of Syria, who swayed the territory which the Seleucids had formed from the disintegrating empire of Alexander, challenged the power of Rome and quickly learned his mistake. Within a few years of defeating him the Romans were securely installed in the Levant.

According to the legend current among the Romans, the twin founders of their city, Romulus and Remus, had been exposed when helpless infants and had been suckled by a she-wolf. Not even the eagles which adorned the standards of the Roman army are as famous a Roman emblem as the she-wolf. Every visitor to Rome has seen hundreds of representations of the animal suckling the twins. All these representations are copies of the one original bronze group which stands to this day in the Palace of the Conservators on the Capitol, and which is over 2,500 years old. Other nations than the Roman might have thought with shame of the rapacity and bloodthirstiness which would surely be sucked in with the wolf's milk. Not so the Romans. The reputed site of this event was a shrine—the Lupercal—accounted one of the holiest places in Rome. The Romans may be excused their feelings of pride, for it has to be confessed that even modern visitors from far-distant lands, strangers 'from the northern isle sundered once from all the human race' feel some emotion as they view this ancient relic, so symbolic of the vanished greatness of a mighty people which, despite its fall, has yet left its lasting imprint on humanity.

The Lupercal was on the Palatine, one of the hills which overlook the Forum of Rome, but the image of the she-wolf stood on the ancient Capitol itself on the hill of that name, which looks right down the Forum to the Arch of Titus and beyond. (Picture, p 99.) The hill is crowned with buildings of the Renaissance period, but the rugged ascent necessarily remains. Up this same hill had wound the triumphal chariots of the Roman generals with their captives walking behind. The top of the hill, once gained, is purely of the style of 400 years ago, and the square was laid out by Michael Angelo as part of his multifarious labours. In the Palace of the Conservators on the Capitol are many beautiful rooms, but in, as it were, an inner shrine, is the famous bronze of the she-wolf, allowed to stand alone with no other ornament in the room, but with the lists of Roman consuls, the *Fasti Consulares* from Brutus to the emperors, on the walls. The bronze is, curiously enough, of

Etruscan work, wrought about 600 years before Christ at a time when Etruscan influence was strong in Rome; indeed this bronze must have been contemporary with the dynasty of Tarquin. The image had survived the mighty empire of which it was the symbol, and throughout the middle ages had stood in the anteroom of a Roman palace. At the Renaissance, some lover of antiquity had added the twins to the figure of the wolf. Strange that in antiquity the emblem of Rome had only partially commemorated the Roman legend, and that the cruel and rapacious animal had stood for the majesty of Rome without the humanising influence of the twins. Today the wolf stands once more upon the Capitol, after having survived in the empire for so many centuries in obscurity.

Certainly the wolf was a fitting emblem for the Romans, for it was difficult to appease the hunger of the she-wolf's breed. Spain, the South of France, the Balkans, Greece, Asia Minor, the Levant, Egypt and North Africa—all were conquered or came within the sphere of influence of Rome. In the eastern half of the Mediterranean this was often achieved by bloodless means. The king of Egypt, one of the house founded by Ptolemy, begged to be taken under the protection of Rome. This was graciously granted, the foreign policy of Egypt was controlled by Rome, a tribute was paid to her, and in return no other power dared to touch the she-wolf's booty. Some nations voluntarily rendered themselves into Rome's hands. Thus, the last king of Pergamum in Asia Minor made the Roman people his heir. By doing so no doubt he hoped to preserve his country from the horrors of conquest, but he none-theless brought it under the sway of rapacious officials from Rome.

By the beginning of the first century BC the framework of the empire was in being. Most of the coasts of the Mediterranean were in Roman hands. The work of the next two centuries, as far as conquest was concerned, was to fill in this framework, mostly in the directions of central and western Europe.

We are now at the beginning of the last century of the republic, which has been called the age of the adventurer-generals. The tendencies which had appeared in the life of Rome in the century following Zama were to be fully developed. Chief of these was the complete separation of the army from the main body of citizens, and the achievement by the generals of independence from the government. By the time that the empire was stabilised under Augustus, the army had become a professional force. All pretence of the *levée en masse* of Roman citizens had ceased. These professional soldiers then elevated their general to the position of supreme ruler of the state.

Various attempts at reform were made in the second century BC, the most celebrated being that associated with the names of the brothers Tiberius and Caius Gracchus. These leaders desired above all to secure agrarian reform and to revive the old farming life of Italy. Not unnaturally their proposed reforms ran counter to the wishes of the wealthy magnates who now constituted the senate, and with a violence which formed a sinister introduction to a century of civil wars the senate overthrew the Gracchi, both of whom lost their lives. One of them, before the arrival of his assassins, prayed that the Roman people might be slaves for ever since they had not courage to help themselves.

The senate had thus no other plan for the people of Rome than to reject reforms and to carry on the creaking machinery of government as long as it would produce profits for them. An age of violence was at hand in which the children of the wolf were to assault each other.

The first of the power-seeking generals was Marius, who became consul seven times. He rose to prominence in the African war, which destroyed Jugurtha, the last king of Morocco. Marius was a soldier of genius but no statesman, and he might never have left any mark on his country but for the approach of a menace which never failed to arouse extreme terror in the Romans—and with some reason since it was ultimately to destroy their empire.

From time immemorial there had appeared at intervals out of the little-known wilderness of central Europe hordes of wandering savages numbering sometimes between four and five hundred thousand, who travelled with their families and such scanty goods as they possessed in search of fertile lands. Such a horde had sacked Rome in 390 BC, when only the Capitol had been saved. The horror and shame of this memory had never been erased from the Roman mind, and it had needed only the threat of another such invasion to persuade the Romans to conquer the Plain of Lombardy. Now, in 100 BC, another horde composed of two nations known as the Cimbri and Teutones appeared from the great nowhere and steadily approached the frontiers of Italy through France. In their passage they destroyed more than one Roman army which had opposed them.

The Romans could not know the reasons for these wanderings, and it was not until several generations had passed that they were to learn vaguely of the existence of another great empire on the other side of the world. The Chinese had stabilised their frontiers earlier than the Romans and were for a long time successful in driving the barbarians away from their country. One wave of wanderers was in this way driven on to another until at last the movement reached the Roman frontiers. These periodic movements into Europe from central Asia did not cease until the fourteenth century AD, when the nomads succeeded in capturing both China and India.

Marius was carried to power by the terror of his countrymen. He was given full authority to remodel the army, which had obviously been found wanting. He swept away the last remnant of a property qualification and opened the army to anyone who wished to serve and to make it his profession. In this way a large number of men who had no stake in the country were brought into the forces. Having no settled ties, they looked to the military life as their all and to their general as the supreme chief. Marius was successful in his schemes, and in two great battles the Cimbri and Teutones, respectively, were annihilated. Rome breathed a sigh of relief. The senatorial party would now have liked to discard Marius and make the soldier retire, but he was re-elected consul by the people, who expected great reforms from him. His incompetence in the political sphere led him not to resign, but to endeavour to cover up his mistakes by the exile or murder of his opponents.

At length there appeared against him a champion of the senate, another general named Sulla, who had waged a successful campaign in Asia Minor against Mithridates, king of Pontus. The first of the civil wars of Rome began between Sulla and Marius, though the death of the latter prevented it from being as fiercely contested as the later struggles. Sulla then became dictator. His conception of a prosperous state was one in which the senate was supreme, and to restore this he worked with cruel consistency. He first brought into Roman life the horror of proscription, whereby the names of political opponents were put up for all to see as those of men who were outlaws and could be killed by anyone at pleasure. In this way thousands perished in Rome alone. Sulla later retired into private life, boasting that he had only to stamp his foot and one hundred thousand veterans would spring to arms throughout Italy. He had been more successful even than Marius in securing the allegiance of his troops to his person. He left his power to the senatorial party which he hoped he had revived, but nothing could make a successful and efficient government from a crowd of men whose sole idea in politics was to use the means of government to increase their own fortunes.

During this time of civil discord the state was faced with many external ills. The fierce old king of Pontus was only reduced by the efforts of three of Rome's best generals, and then not before he had massacred thousands of Romans. Mithridates was, like Hannibal, a man of political vision, and had very nearly succeeded in raising a coalition against Rome. The Italian allies also became so dissatisfied at the subordinate position they were expected to occupy vis-à-vis the Romans that they rose in rebellion, and it was only by great efforts, combined with the strategic advantages of Rome's position, that peace was restored.

In 73 BC there was a slave revolt under a runaway gladiator named Spartacus. The great increase in the numbers of slaves had led to the introduction of games for the people, who needed to be amused as well as fed, and as human flesh was now cheap, in the games men were set on to fight and kill each other for sport. Schools of gladiators were kept by various magnates and the origin of the rebellion of Spartacus was to be found in one of these schools. Eventually his revolt became so extensive that thousands of slaves and poor persons rallied to his standard and he succeeded in defeating several Roman armies before his own forces were destroyed by Crassus.

After the defeat of Spartacus the roads of southern Italy for many miles were lined by the crucified bodies of slaves who, in revolt, had been captured and condemned to death. When we think of the majesty of the Roman Empire and of its laws we are apt to forget the terrible price paid by the unprivileged classes for the amusements of their 'betters'. The death penalty inflicted upon these runaway slaves and gladiators was the normal one for criminals, and to the Romans the spectacles of the arena made the sight of a crucifixion seem little out of the ordinary. Perhaps there is nothing more horrible in the whole range of Roman remains than the presence, wherever one goes in the Roman world, of the amphitheatre. No major city or town was complete without one.

The amphitheatre at Pompeii is small and well preserved, despite the manner in which the city was destroyed. When one looks around it one thinks instinctively of the scene which Lord Lytton placed in it, Glaucus exposed to the lions in the *Last Days of Pompeii*—a recollection which only heightens the feeling one already has of the horrible tragedies which have taken place there. The amphitheatre now has a floor of grass instead of the sand which once covered it. The barrier is a solid wall well above the height of a man's head. (How did they keep the lions from leaping this barrier? Perhaps long ago there were iron railings on top of the wall; probably a deposit of earth has formed on the floor of the amphitheatre.) The amphitheatre is of oblong shape, and all the way round it are tiers and tiers of seats, the gradations nicely arranged as in a modern theatre with the best seats at the bottom of the tiers. At one end, opposite the gateway by which the victims entered, is what one might call the royal box, where the reigning Caesar or his deputy would sit. If the persons who entered were gladiators, they would march up to the front of the emperor's box and raise their swords, exclaiming, 'Hail, Caesar, those about to die salute thee.' *Ave, Caesar te morituri salutamus*. (Picture, p 100.)

When the Romans had such tastes in their sports and such punishments in their legal system, it is not to be wondered at that the enemies of law and order in the Roman state should have stopped at nothing. Thus, piracy on the high seas was rife, especially in the eastern Mediterranean, and a well-known incident in the life of Julius Caesar is his capture by, and subsequent ransom from, a band of pirates. It may not be so well known that Caesar, after his ransom, fitted out an expedition, captured the pirates and crucified them all. These pests of the seas were only overcome when a special force was sent out under Pompey to sweep the eastern Mediterranean.

Even in Rome itself, the state was only just saved from destruction by the prompt action of the consul Cicero (who afterwards figured in Latin literature as a most brilliant prose writer) in suppressing the conspiracy of Cataline. Cataline was a ruined aristocrat who had gathered around him some of the most desperate elements among the people, though whether he aimed at the establishment of some form of communism, or merely a reign of licence, it is impossible to say. Cicero destroyed those conspirators who were either in arms or definitely implicated, but although the evidence appeared to point against Julius Caesar, a debt-burdened patrician, nothing certain could be proved and he escaped.

The conspiracy of Cataline brings to light another element of the last age of the republic, the existence of patricians who, by speculations or luxurious living, had disposed of their estates and were therefore driven to the expedient of trying a *coup de main* against the state. One of the best ways of doing this was to pose as a champion of the people against the senate and so secure the office of consul, with command of the armies. After this, to an able and unscrupulous man, the rest would be easy.

The last fifty years of the republic resolve themselves into a duel for power between various persons. Cicero is a pathetic figure. His intelligence must have told him that the old republic which he revered was dead, yet his sentiments made him struggle to instil patriotic feelings into the selfish senatorial group. Then there was Pompey the Great, so surnamed from his earlier exploits when he carried the arms of Rome as far as the Caspian Sea and cleared the Mediterranean of pirates. His role in this drama was never quite clear. At one time he could have made himself master of the state, but apparently he did not want this. Yet one-man rule was to prove better than the hopeless confusion which prevailed at Rome. Another contender was Crassus, one of the richest men of Rome, who had advanced large sums of money to Julius Caesar, and was ambitious to secure high place for himself, yet lacked the ability to take the supreme position as pacifier and ruler of the Roman world.

More and more one man came to the front—Julius Caesar, representative of one of the oldest families among the Romans and credited with the usual patrician legend of descent from the gods. Until practically the age of forty he had given little sign of outstanding ability. He had been a typical man of fashion and by his luxury and extravagance had run through his own estate and acquired a vast collection of debts. He was given over not only to the usual forms of dissipation but to the peculiarly Roman variety described by Catullus. When he wished, he could exercise great charm over his fellows, but it is doubtful if he possessed any real feelings of friendship or affection. Once he had decided upon his ends he advanced towards them without consideration for any human being, without mercy and without fear of man or God. On the subject of religion he professed a complete scepticism. Thus his character had much that was repellent in it. Yet he became the idol of the Roman people, and of his troops. He was a consummate general, though his skill was sometimes displayed in his ability to escape from a situation into which he had carelessly blundered. He could describe his campaigns as well as fight them, and his rough notes or commentaries have ranked as a classic ever since they were first published. He was a very astute politician and man of business, a good orator and sufficiently learned in astronomy to arrange a reform of the calendar which lasted sixteen centuries. Last of all, he had the vision of a statesman and saw that the era of the republic was over.

Caesar became consul in 59 BC and there followed a year of rapid legislation. In 58 BC he set out as pro-consul to Gaul. There he spent seven years, during which he conquered the whole of modern France, besides making expeditions into Britain and Germany. So thoroughly was the work done in France that the Romans never fought another full-scale campaign in that country. At the end of this warfare Caesar had added a province to the empire, proved his ability as a general, and formed a powerful army devoted to himself. With this army he returned to Italy. His enemies had gained control of the senate and he was ordered to disband his troops. He refused, and by crossing the ancient boundary of Italy, the river Rubicon, declared war on the republic. Pompey became the leader of the senatorial opposition to Caesar and a civil war ensued between them.

In the end Caesar was victorious. Pompey was murdered, though not at his rival's instigation. The remaining section of his party which had been in arms was overthrown at Munda, in Spain, and Julius Caesar returned to Rome as sole ruler of the Roman world. The Romans surpassed themselves in bestowing titles on him and even that of King, the most abhorrent to a Roman ear, was said to have been offered to him. Julius Caesar did not live to test Roman reaction to his assumption of the kingly title; a party existed against him, composed of diverse elements, dissatisfied officers of his, jealous rivals and genuine patriots who hated him as a dictator. By a coalition of such persons he was murdered in 44 BC in the senate house at Rome.

Nothing could bring the dead republic back to life. Brutus and Cassius, the leaders against Caesar, were hunted down by a triumvirate of Octavius, Caesar's nephew, Mark Antony and Lepidus. This triumvirate then set itself to govern the empire. Antony secured the eastern portion and set up his court in Egypt, living with the Egyptian queen Cleopatra who had previously held Julius Caesar ensnared. She brought Antony completely under her control, with the result that he was in due course defeated by Octavius. Antony committed suicide, and Cleopatra did likewise when she found that Octavius was not to be another of her dupes. Lepidus had already been disposed of and in 29 BC Octavius became the successor of his uncle as ruler of Rome. He is known in history as Augustus Caesar, the first emperor of Rome.

CHAPTER NINE

THE PAX ROMANA

DURING THE commotions and upheavals of the last century of the republic it had really seemed that the Roman Empire would break up and dissolve, but now with the gathering, in Tacitus's phrase, of all power into the hands of one man, the whole Mediterranean world came under the control of a firm government.

In the long run this autocracy of the emperors was bound to harden into an iron despotism which would crush the life of Rome. Not that Republican Rome had been a democracy, but it had at least possessed the possibility of developing free institutions. Now, under the emperors, that possibility was taken away.

At first, however, the emperors were on the whole careful to conceal their power. The rich were the section of the community most opposed to the imperial power because they were exposed to spoliation, but for the bulk of the people the rule of the emperors meant peace and freedom from the evils of a weak government. The majority did not realise that in exchange for freedom from hunger and civil war the emperors had taken away their freedom to manage or mismanage their own affairs. For two centuries there was peace around the Mediterranean and that breathing space enabled the third great element in European civilisation to develop until it was nearly strong enough to take over whatever was good in the ancient world.

Augustus (Octavius Caesar, as he was originally named), the first emperor, was a very different man from his uncle and adopted father, Julius Caesar. Just as Charles II decided not to suffer his father's fate, so Augustus determined to rule whilst avoiding those matters by which Caesar had offended the innate prejudices of the Romans. Augustus never assumed the title of emperor or king. He styled himself the servant of the senate and the republic, and between him and the senate an elaborate comedy was enacted. Augustus professed to restore to the republic its original constitution, which had been damaged in the civil wars. The senate begged him to continue to afford his protection to the state. In reply, he could only agree to receive the commands of the senate and the Roman people, whose servant he was proud to be.

All this was very edifying and a tribute to the strong commonsense of Augustus. He lived a simple, unostentatious life. He did not tyrannise over his subjects, whom he preferred to call his fellow citizens. Yet everyone realised that his wishes would invariably prevail.

Apart from the semi-hypocritical comedy played between emperor and senate, worthy of the most compromising genius of England, there was a division of power between the two. The administration of the provinces was divided into an imperial and a senatorial section. The emperor was careful to see that in his section were those provinces which required the presence of an army, such as the frontiers on the north. The senatorial provinces, on the other hand, were always situated in the more peaceful portions of the empire and only in North Africa was there a military force under the command of the senate, and that consisted of but one legion. Thus the Roman dyarchy, though nominally an equal division of power, was most unequal in its division of military strength. Apart from being the chief of thirty legions to the senate's one, the emperor possessed a chosen bodyguard at Rome —the Praetorians—whereas the senators had not even a civil police under their control. The emperor was the paymaster of the legions. He had risen to power in the first instance by the support of the troops who had, of course, long ceased to be composed of responsible Romans though by entering the army they automatically became Roman citizens. If he were to hold his throne, it was necessary to maintain his grip on the army. Events were to show that the rulers of the empire were chosen not at Rome but by the armies on the frontier.

When Augustus was near the end of his reign he placed several monuments to his own life and work in various parts of the empire. This was not simply vanity, for he could reasonably claim that he had saved the Roman state. What he did say was that he had found Rome a city of brick and had left it one of marble. At Rome itself there can now be seen near the Tiber a restored version of one of these monuments. A brief study of it—especially when one realises that its statements are sober truth—is convincing proof that Augustus could have claimed to have rebuilt Rome in more senses than one.

The walk along the banks of the Tiber to reach the Monument of Augustus is a pleasant one, for the river is bordered by trees and boulevards which are delightful, especially in the spring. The Tiber is not a wide river, and the bridges across it are pleasant specimens of architecture. St Peter's, the Vatican and the Castle of St Angelo, lie on the bank of the river outside the city boundaries. The Castle of St Angelo is really the mausoleum of the emperor Hadrian, and in the middle ages was made into a powerful fortress. In it the Pope took refuge when the troops of the Constable de Bourbon sacked the city in the sixteenth century. The Bridge of St Angelo spans the river immediately in front of the castle. One is then on a bend of the Tiber and can just see the top of the Augusteum, that is the tomb of Augustus, near which is the monument. There is another bridge still between the Bridge of St Angelo and the Bridge of Cavour, which is just before the Augusteum.

Another quarter of an hour will bring one up to the tomb of Augustus, which served as the model for others of these pretentious structures, such as the tomb of Hadrian, which has just been passed. Today we have only the ruins of the original; apparently the last resting-place of Augustus did not find favour with the people of the Middle Ages in the same way as had that of Hadrian. Originally, it must have been a magnificent building, even if useless, but now it only serves to illustrate in the manner of copybook maxims the vanity of human greatness. Opposite the tomb is a large structure which represents what is left (and what has been restored) of the *Ara Pacis Augustae*—the Altar of the Augustan Peace. This was put up by the senate and Roman people after the death of Augustus, and commemorates his deeds in restoring peace and order to the Roman world.

There is no need to suppose that the Romans had their tongues in their cheeks in building this monument. They had been so harassed by civil war that they did genuinely revere the man who had brought them peace. As one looks at the monument, one can feel something of the sense of security which the ordinary Roman knew under the rule of Augustus. If mankind is ever to be forgiven the sin of apotheosis, it can perhaps be pardoned for deifying Augustus. The evils from which he rescued his country were real and horrible.

At the time of the defeat of Antony, when the Roman world acknowledged the rule of Augustus, a terrible civil war had raged for many years. The legions were withdrawn from the frontiers, which could hardly be said to exist so easily were they crossed by the barbarous hordes who delighted to find the firm rule of Rome relaxed. The military establishment was higher than it had ever been, but this force was used only in internal strife between rival generals. In the more settled days of the republic great public works had been completed, such as the roadways which covered Italy, and the aqueducts and drainage systems, to say nothing of temples and other public buildings. All this peaceful effort had ceased in the last days of the republic. The bonds of society were loosened, slaves and servants fled from their masters, estates went uncultivated and farms were abandoned, gang rule increased in the cities and brigandage in the country. Some Romans so much lost faith in the future that they committed suicide, while there were instances of Romans setting sail in search of the fabulous Fortunate Isles, to escape from a homeland of which they despaired. The Romans were the more unhappy in that they had no faith in religion with which to support themselves. Their gods, those personifications of the forces of nature, had formerly been real to them, but the spread of Greek culture and particularly the theories of Euhemerus—that the gods were merely heroes of the dim past who had been deified—had undermined the old religion until it was now regarded only as a useful check on the mob. No educated man believed in it and although some, like Cicero, tried to follow the

Platonic philosophy and reason themselves into a belief in one God, just and pure, and in a life to come, the majority abandoned themselves to their own appetites without thought of restraint. Divorce, adultery, prostitution and birth control rose to huge proportions and the sanctity of the Roman word was so weakened that it became little better than the old Punic faith.

From most of this misery Augustus rescued his countrymen. He had overthrown his chief rivals, but he declared an amnesty for the lesser fry who had fought against him. Men of character and ability such as Agrippa and Maecenas gathered round him. The number of the legions was halved, but the discharged soldiers instead of being turned loose were settled on lands taken from the more dangerous of Augustus's enemies. The frontiers were re-established, in most cases without bloodshed. In the east, where the Parthians had for many years ravaged the empire after defeating the army of Crassus, in 53 BC, peace was restored, and by skilful negotiation Augustus secured the restoration of the standards taken at Carrhae.

In the north-west of the empire, Augustus set out on a career of conquest designed to carry the imperial boundaries from the Rhine to the Elbe. This scheme, which would have brought western Germany under the rule of Rome, was ruined by a combination of several causes : bad Roman generalship, failure to use sufficient drive, and the violent resistance of the Germans, which culminated in the destruction of three legions in AD 9. A profound impression was created at Rome, and the numbers of the lost legions were never again used in the army list. This scheme of conquest had been the only instance in which Augustus had endeavoured to extend the bounds of the empire further than he had found them. Its failure seemed to him to vindicate the policy he had followed elsewhere and he left to his successors the maxim that they should not extend the empire.

Internally, Augustus reorganised the public services and rigorously repressed the gangsters and brigands. A powerful fleet based on Italy patrolled the Roman lake and prevented piracy. The provision of corn for Italy was made a first charge on Sicily, Africa and Egypt. As the last-named country had been a centre of trouble, it was placed under the rule of a Roman knight directly responsible

J

to the emperor. Augustus's main concern was to arrest and prevent the moral decay which loss of belief in the old religion had brought in its train. Like Louis XIV, Augustus commanded his people to be honest, chaste and good, but it is beyond the power even of an emperor to bring such results to pass. Realising that morals are inevitably connected with religion, Augustus endeavoured to revive the pagan faith. He initiated the restoration of many temples and built new ones. Under the republic, the *aediles*, who were responsible for the proper maintenance of the temples of the gods, were officers of government, but indifference on the part of the public and the upheavals of the civil wars had held up the necessary work of repair for many years. Horace pointed out the moral of this to the Romans, saying that as long as the cult of the gods was neglected so long would the Romans lose battles to their enemies.

Not only did Augustus give a great deal of attention to the restoration of the sacred buildings, but he also filled up the colleges of priests and gave solemn instructions that their duties were to be carried out properly. Festivals and sacred games were observed with all due ceremony, and the new cult of the emperor was greatly extended in the provinces. Augustus himself was not actually worshipped as a god during his lifetime, but he was deified after his death. Within a century, however, of the establishment of the empire, the reigning emperor was spoken of as 'our lord and god', and regarded as a deity during his life on earth.

Augustus possessed among his other gifts that of being fortunate. He could, no doubt, as master of the public purse, have secured the support of many venal writers, but it was his good fortune that there occurred during his reign a great flowering of Latin literature. Virgil, Horace, Ovid and Livy would have made any period distinguished, but unlike the great writers in the last age of the republic, such as Cicero and Lucretius, they were neither hostile nor indifferent to the ruling powers. All the great writers of the Augustan age perceived that Augustus had given the Roman state a fresh lease of life. Some of them, like Livy whom Augustus called a Pompeian, might regret the days of the republic, but they realised that these could not be restored and were thoroughly loyal to the new regime. In return for this support Augustus gave every en-

couragement to literary genius. It was due to his efforts that the
dying wishes of Virgil were disregarded and the *Aeneid* was
preserved for posterity. Horace found in Augustus a protector who
amply compensated him for the loss of his father's farm.

Apart from the failure to conquer western Germany, the reign of
Augustus was a success in the immediate objects which he set
himself to attain. In the long-range objectives, the restoration of
religion and morality, he was destined to failure. The loss of faith
in the gods was too far advanced to be overcome by any mere
revival of paganism. The Romans had been exposed for nearly two
centuries to the faith-destroying tendencies of the Greek philosophers, and although the direct influence was felt only by the
educated classes, indirectly the results were bound to work their
way down. The ignorant multitude could not fail to learn, or to be
impressed by learning, that the High Priest who stood before Jove's
altar and went through the various rites did not believe in the
value of what he was doing, but performed the ceremonies as a
matter of course, and in order to help keep the masses in their
proper social groove. The lack of a living faith meant a decay in
morality which the reforms of Augustus could not do more than
arrest for a time. The greatest man on earth cannot revive a dying
faith, especially when he himself does not believe in it.

Nevertheless, for the period of his own lifetime and, as it turned
out, for a long time after his death, Augustus restored the Roman
Empire and gave it a stability and peace it had never known
before. Gibbon has selected the age of the Antonines—the second-
century successors of Augustus—as the real golden age of mankind.
Certainly for the first two centuries of the Christian era the lands
around the Mediterranean enjoyed peace and a considerable
measure of prosperity, together with a fairly good legal administration. The barbarians were kept distant on the frontiers. Not only
were the territories of the empire as they existed at the death of
Augustus preserved intact, but new provinces were added: Britain
as far as the highlands of Scotland in the first century, and Dacia
on the Danube, plus many territories between Armenia and the
Persian Gulf conquered by the emperor Trajan at the beginning of
the second century. Internally, there was very little warfare, the

only serious case being the strife in 'the year of the four emperors', AD 69-70, after the death of the infamous Nero. In AD 70 occurred the Jewish War and the destruction of Jerusalem.

Considerable work was done in the erection of public buildings, temples, law courts, municipal buildings, aqueducts, roads, as well as luxurious palaces for the Caesars and amphitheatres for the cruel sports. In fact, old Republican Rome would have been obliterated by the buildings of the emperors, even without the effects of Nero's fire. In the city of Rome there is some difficulty in finding traces of the old Rome of the republic, although Imperial Rome is everywhere in evidence. Fortunately, no reforming genius has ever destroyed the 2,000-year-old bridge of Fabricius, which crosses the Tiber at the place where there is an island in the middle of the stream. The old bridge has two portions and the island forms a little community of its own with a church, shops and dwelling-places, all surrounded by a high wall which comes to the edge of the bridge on either side. Not far from the Pons Fabricius is a still more ancient structure, all that remains of an old bridge of the republican period. It is even whispered that part of it goes back to the bridge which Horatius 'kept in the brave days of old'. Let no vandal scholarship deprive us of this legend.

These traces of the oldest Rome are very few. The Colosseum was the work of the emperor Titus, the three triumphal arches are those of Titus, Constantine and Severus, all emperors. The palaces —Nero's golden house, or the Palatine palace—are imperial work. The Pantheon is a temple of the imperial period, the two mighty columns are those of Trajan and Marcus Aurelius, and the basilica of Maxentius is an imperial law court. The only real rival to the emperors in giving character to the city was the Papacy, and it seemed that the only way an imperial structure could be sure of keeping itself in a fit state of preservation was to become converted to the Church. The Pantheon is a splendid example of a pagan temple. The Christian ornaments appear incongruous, but if it had not been for the blessing of the Church the Pantheon would have been used as a quarry of material for the construction of other buildings.

It is quite clear, even if we were to allow the truth of Gibbon's description of the age of the Antonines, that such an age could not have been followed by the rapid decline and fall of Rome unless it had carried within itself the seeds of its own decay. Probably half the population of the empire was composed of slaves who possessed hardly any rights. Their position was ameliorated in the decline of the empire, but when we realise that the law's refusal to put to death every slave in a household following the master's un-explained death was regarded as an improvement, we can see that the slave had no easy time. The owning of human beings by other human beings has an effect at once brutalising and effeminate on the masters. While the manly qualities began to disappear in the Roman masters, cruelty and various odious vices began to assert themselves. At the same time the presence of so great a mass of slaves had a deleterious effect on the free population, who were in many industries undercut and ousted by the slaves. This was not-ably so with Italian agriculture. As we have seen, it became far more profitable for the Roman landlords to cultivate huge vine-yards by means of slave labour than to let out the same land to poor farmers for the raising of crops. Yet the poor farmers had been the strength of the Roman armies which had defeated Carth-age and founded the empire. When these poor freemen could no longer make a livelihood from the soil of Italy they flocked to the cities, especially to Rome. They no longer had votes to sell, but they could be a nuisance and a danger to the emperor, and to keep them quiet he gave them shows in the amphitheatres and doles of food (the bread and sports of the familiar quotation—*panem et circenses*) As Italy no longer grew sufficient corn to supply this dole, tribute had to be levied on Sicily, Egypt and North Africa. This was all very well from one point of view while the Roman world had one master, but in the times of disorder, which multi-plied rapidly after the death of Marcus Aurelius, the temporary masters of Rome's corn supply in Egypt and North Africa could cause immense suffering in Italy.

The disappearance of the hardy Roman population made it necessary to recruit the armies from the provinces outside Italy, and very soon from the barbarians who came from beyond the Rhine and Danube. If we can imagine the Gurkhas gradually taking the place of British troops all over the old British Empire and in the United Kingdom, we can form some idea of the de-Romanisation of the Roman armies. In theory, the emperor and the army were still servants of the senate. In practice, the emperor was elected by the consent of the armies, or at least had to be acceptable to the soldiers. The practice grew up of bestowing donatives on the troops at the accession of a prince, and a successful general could expect to become emperor. With the bulk of the troops barbarians from outside the empire, it became possible for a barbarian either to ascend the throne or to dictate the choice of emperor. As Roman citizenship was extended (until eventually it was granted to every free inhabitant of the empire) the emperors were more and more drawn from the provinces, but they were still officially Romans.

Augustus failed to solve the problem of his heir. He had no son of his own and he had to fall back on the legal fiction of adoption, which was liberally imitated by his successors. Even this failed, however, and by AD 70 the house of the Caesars expired. One dynasty succeeded another, never extending beyond three generations. The master of the legions had an uneasy life, and must have been one of the most unhappy men in the world. He never knew when some ambitious general might revolt.

The despotism established by Augustus may have been benevolent, but *qua* despotism it was a freakish thing dependent on the whims of individuals. The emperor was not only an absolute monarch, but in the course of time, a god on earth. He might be a good man, and Rome had an extraordinary run of good luck in the Antonine princes. More often he was weak or bad, but whatever his character he was ultimately controlled by his barbarian soldiers. Spaniards, Arabs, Syrians, Illyrians, and Africans occupied the imperial throne by grace of their troops. The last relics of Roman freedom passed away, the efficiency of government declined and it needed only a great movement in the lands of central Asia to precipitate hordes of warlike savages on to the weakening barriers of the empire.

It does not require a very deep sense of history, or a profound knowledge of the annals of Europe to realise that Rome is the

most hallowed city in Europe. The most historic place in the whole
continent, a place to stir emotions in anyone who cares for European culture, is the Palatine Mount; the vile Nero can be forgotten,
his palace grounds lead to the top of the hill where the pine trees
stir in the cool breeze before sunset. Below is the Forum of Rome,
the rays of the sun falling upon it. On the right is the Arch of Titus,
splendidly preserved, which he put up to commemorate his solution
of the Jewish problem—a monument which no Jew would pass
through until the restoration of the state of Israel (described in a
later chapter) was considered to have wiped out the disgrace of
Titus's capture of Jerusalem. Under the Arch the Sacred Way runs
through the Forum until it reaches the foot of the Capitoline Hill.
On the right of the Forum it passes the reputed tomb of Romulus,
and the certain site of the burning of Julius Caesar's body, outside
the senate house. All along the Way there are the remains of
temples and statues.

From the Palatine Mount, beyond the Arch of Titus can be seen
that of Constantine (the emperor who made the empire Christian)
and nearby is the huge bulk of the Colosseum where his predecessors had fed the Christians to the lions. During medieval times, the
floor of the Colosseum was used for the erection of prison cells so
that the full effect of the arena cannot be discerned as at Pompeii.
On the left from the Palatine stands the Arch of Severus. This
emperor has considerable interest for British people as he died at
York after a very severe campaign in Scotland. His reign is regarded
by Gibbon as the beginning of the decline of the Roman Empire.

The Capitoline Hill is crowned, as mentioned, with buildings
from the renewed classical ages, and contains the symbol of Rome.
On the Palatine Hill, legend placed the incident which that symbol
commemorates, the suckling of Romulus and Remus. The Capitol,
the Esquiline and the Palatinate were the hills which formed the
original Roman community. The Forum was the place of business
for the city, and its political meeting centre, like the agora of a
Greek city. Here the great events of Roman history had their
origins, here the sovereign people gave their vote for campaigns
which ended the freedom of kingdom after kingdom; here they
voted for the commission which sent Julius Caesar to conquer Gaul

and make it Latin for all time. Here Julius Caesar was cremated. Along the Sacred Way marched the armies of the republic and later of the empire in their triumphs. Then the ruins of the place, and its dilapidated appearance even after careful restoration, tell of the dark ages when the light of European civilisation flickered and nearly went out. For Rome was not only a conqueror, but had gathered round her, under her protection, the culture of the Mediterranean.

Yet even in the defeats and ruin of the fifth and sixth centuries, the fortune of Rome did not entirely desert her. Beside the Capitoline Hill is a church, and beneath this the evil Mamertine prison, where many Roman captives—the valiant Jugurtha of Morocco, and the heroic Vercingetorix, victim of Caesar—met their deaths. In that prison, now a place of hallowed visitation, were also imprisoned two obscure teachers who came to Rome in the first century AD and whose teachings were to give Rome a renewed life, despite all her material disasters. These men, St Peter and St Paul as they were afterwards canonised, might have passed unnoticed, had not the movement which they headed become entangled in the fierce politics of the end of Nero's reign. Instead, they were taken out from the Mamertime prison and martyred.

All around the monuments of ancient Rome are churches, often built on the site of old temples, or using the old edifices, but with Christ's figure substituted for that of Jupiter. From a mighty dome to the west, bells sound, recalling that the successor of the majesty of the Caesars is placed in the Vatican and St Peter's, swaying an empire far more durable in its extent and power because it is founded not on the basis of material conquest but on spiritual factors which persuade but do not force men's allegiance.

CHAPTER TEN

THE RISE OF CHRISTIANITY

THE IMMEDIATE successor of Augustus was Tiberius, a prince who is now in process of being represented as a good and wise ruler, possibly because it is thought necessary to upset Tacitus's verdict on him as a dark and jealous tyrant.

The character of Tiberius does not much concern us. His main importance in this abstract is that during his reign occurred the great events which founded the Christian religion. Jesus of Nazareth, known all over the world now as Jesus the Christ (the latter is the Greek form of the Hebrew Messiah or Anointed) lived and taught in Palestine in the reign of Tiberius, was crucified under the Roman governor of Judea, Pontius Pilate, about AD 29, was declared by His followers to have risen from the dead three days later. From this credence in the Resurrection the earliest Christians who made up the Church never wavered despite all the persecutions to which they were subjected. Today, nineteen centuries after the crucifixion, the belief that Christ rose from the dead and is a living person, the very and eternal Son of God, is the confession of all branches of the Christian Church.

Jesus was a Jew, a race subject to the Romans and about whom they possessed information sufficient only to make Jews odious in their eyes. If we may take a modern parallel, the Roman soldier or administrator who served in Palestine had towards the Jews much the same attitude as the Britons who during the war of 1939-45 and stationed abroad in North Africa, Malta or Egypt, had for the natives of those territories. Knowing little of them, puzzled by their habits, and often encountering their more unpleasant characteristics, such a person is apt to leave the particular country with a violent prejudice against its inhabitants and possessing only a garbled version of its history. This was the case with the Romans. Even a brilliant historian like Tacitus makes astounding misstatements about the Jews, their origin, history and religion. The Greek version of the Old Testament, the Septuagint, was available, so were the voluminous writings of Josephus, the Jewish historian, who wrote in Greek for the benefit of the Roman public. But Tacitus had been brought up in the society of the Roman ruling class to whom the Jews were obnoxious on account of their obstinate refusal to worship the emperor or even to permit his image inside their Holy City. This, to the Romans meaningless obstinacy, led to a bloody war, the result of which was the complete destruction of Jerusalem and the loss of political status by the Jews.

Alone among the nations of the empire the Jews refused to worship the emperor, though they paid him homage as their temporal sovereign. Other nations, though still worshipping their ancestral gods, added the Roman gods to their pantheon, thus according the emperor his meed of worship. In return, the Romans added the foreign deities to their own collection, or assimilated them to their Jupiter, Venus, Mars and other gods. They also sent gifts to the temples of these gods of Egypt, Syria, or Greece, and would have been willing to treat the Jews in the same way had they not vehemently declared that they had only one God who was the sole lord and ruler of the universe. Consequently they could not worship idols made with hands, the vanities of the nations, and would rather die than do so. Although they held this monotheistic belief, the Jews were not missionaries seeking to convert the polytheists from the errors of their ways, for they held just as strongly the belief that they were the chosen people of the one God, who was not particularly interested in any nation but their own. Their religion included blood sacrifices of animals conducted by a priesthood specially set apart. In the great Temple of Jerusalem and in the various Jewish synagogues or meeting-places there was no representation of the Deity, although worship was performed in a very solemn, and in the Temple, magnificent manner. Romans such as Pompey the Great, who forced their way into the Holy of Holies at Jerusalem, were astonished to find there no statue or image of the God of the Jews. Hence arose in the Gentile world the belief that the Jews were atheists and as such anti-social and enemies of humanity.

A Jewish synagogue of the present day is a large and well-constructed edifice, but inside there is hardly anything to see. The walls may have plaques bearing the names of members of the Jewish community who fought in both world wars, but except for the colouring of the borders of these memorial tablets the only ornaments in the building are at the end of the synagogue (in the place where one would expect the altar in a church to be) where, at the top of some steps are the heavily decorated Scrolls of the Law. These are rolls made in the manner of old papyrus books, and rolled around a stave which has a gold or silver top. The only other furniture in the place apart from some chairs for the worshippers is a rostrum for reading the Scriptures. In the vestry (as it might be termed), however, there may be some fine lamps inscribed with passages from the Old Testament.

This modern synagogue would, in essentials, bear a strong resemblance to those which have existed ever since the Jewish dispersion began. In the old temple at Jerusalem the Holy of Holies was bare, and this bareness of both Jewish and Mohammedan places of worship springs from the same cause—fear that a graven image will lead to idolatry, and that the one true God will be forgotten for the sake of a creature. But the Jews, at any rate, had not always been such determined monotheists and had only been educated to belief in the one Supreme Being by an extremely painful process.

The Old Testament and the Apocrypha are the record of Jewish history as written by the Jews. It is becoming increasingly easy to check these records by the results of archaeological discoveries and scholarly research and, in the main, the Old Testament record stands. The story of Israel as told therein may be summarised as follows.

Some 1,500 years BC the children of Israel, or Hebrews as they were then called, made their way under a leader named Moses from

Egyptian bondage into Palestine. Their national legends ascribed their origin to one Abraham, a native of Ur of the Chaldees, whence he had migrated to Palestine some centuries earlier. There he had lived for many years, as had his son Isaac and grandson Jacob, who had adopted the name of Israel and who had led his children and dependants down into Egypt at the invitation of the reigning Pharaoh. This incident is thought to have occurred during the reign of the Hyksos, or shepherd kings, foreign invaders who had conquered Egypt. On the expulsion of these foreigners the Hebrews found themselves sharing the detestation in which they had been held by the native Egyptians. Hence bitter bondage in Egypt and the appearance of a national leader who appealed to another powerful Hebrew belief that the Lord had promised Palestine to Abraham, Isaac and Jacob and their seed forever.

After some disturbances in Egypt, the people of the Hebrews, or Israelites as it is more convenient to call them, were led by Moses over the Red Sea into the peninsula of Sinai. Here, and in the adjacent wild country, they wandered for forty years, until they became a tough Bedouin race possessed of a code of law which included moral as well as legal and ritualistic commandments. As a nation they were to be faithful to God. They carried with them an ark of wood, in which God was thought to have a special presence.

Palestine was at this time possessed by various tribes related to the Israelites, except for the dwellers on the sea coast, the Philistines. Moses did not conduct the people into the Promised Land, but after his death his follower, Joshua, led the Israelites across the Jordan and conquered a large part of central Palestine. But the whole of the country was not subdued, and the three hundred years following Joshua's death were a period of intermittent oppression of the Israelites by the surrounding inhabitants of Canaan. These races possessed what the Israelites lacked, the central authority of a king. For some years, Samuel, the High Priest of the Lord, tried to use his position to weld the people together against the Philistines, but the Israelites at last insisted on electing their own king who should lead them in battle. Their choice fell upon Saul of the minor tribe of Benjamin. He proved a brave soldier and fought valiantly against the foes of his people, but his reign closed unsuccessfully in battle with the Philistines. Internally, his reign had been troubled by dissension with Samuel and the priests and the defection of his best general, David, who after Saul's death was acknowledged king by the bulk of the people and eventually by all Israel. David captured the strong city of Jerusalem, which he made his capital, the various oppressors of Israel were subdued or destroyed, and for the first time Israel assumed the status of a powerful nation.

David had risen from the position of a shepherd boy to be king of Israel and it was hardly to be expected that so spectacular an ascent could be accomplished without the creation of enemies, or that his kingdom should be firmly settled at his death. Nevertheless, Solomon, the son of David's favourite wife, succeeded to the throne without more than the usual minimum of disturbances incidental to the succession in an oriental monarchy. Solomon's reign was a reign of peace and great brilliance. He adorned Jerusalem with fine buildings, including a temple for the Lord which replaced the tent that had previously housed the Ark. He formed alliances with various great powers, marrying the Pharaoh of Egypt's daughter, securing supplies of cedar and the assistance of skilled workmen from Hiram, king of Tyre, and receiving a visit from the 'Queen of the South'. Sheba is said to have been attracted by the wisdom of Solomon, and he was certainly far advanced in various branches of ancient learning. Whatever the cause of the attraction, its result is held to be the Abyssinian monarchy, for Sheba reputedly came from that country. Sheba and Solomon were married and their son became 'King of the Kings of Ethiopia' (so runs tradition).

The peace and outward prosperity of Solomon's reign did not succeed in consolidating Israel, which had so lately been merely a collection of tribes. His great expenditure had sorely taxed the revenue of the new kingdom and on his death his son and successor, Rheoboam, was faced with the demand for lighter taxation and fewer government restrictions. Failing to receive satisfaction, ten of the tribes revolted from Rheoboam and chose as their king Jeroboam, who had been one of Solomon's officers. These ten tribes were henceforth known as the northern kingdom of Israel, while the two tribes which adhered to the house of David were known as Judah. For over two hundred years the two kingdoms continued their separate existence, sometimes in alliance with each other, more often in hostility, until in 722 BC Samaria, the capital of Israel, was captured by Sargon, king of Assyria, and a large number of the people carried away captive to the land of the two rivers. These deportees are the ten lost tribes whose modern descendants are variously located. Judah struggled on precariously until, in 586 BC, Jerusalem was captured by Nebuchadnezzar, king of Babylon. The city was destroyed, the monarchy of David overthrown, and the more important of the people carried captive to Babylon.

Such events were very common in the history of small nations which opposed great powers like Egypt, Assyria or Babylon, and they usually put an end to the history of the small country. Edom, Moab, Philistia, Tyre, Ammon, what are they but names in a history book to which the spade of the archaeologist now gives more interest? Thus it might have been with Israel, but:

'Now, in the first year of Cyrus, king of Persia, that the word of the Lord spoken by the mouth of Jeremiah might be accomplished, the Lord stirred up the spirit of Cyrus, king of Persia, that he made a proclamation throughout all his kingdom, and put it also in writing, saying—

' "Thus saith Cyrus, king of Persia, all the kingdoms of the earth hath the Lord God of heaven given me; and he hath charged me to build him an house in Jerusalem, which is in Judah. Who is there among you of all his people? The Lord God be with him and let him go up." ' (II Chronicles 36, verses 22-23.)

Whether Cyrus attributed his success to the Lord of Heaven or to Marduk, god of Babylon, he at least granted tolerance to the Israelites, and permitted those among them who wished, to return to Jerusalem. Many did not do so, and from the period of the captivity in Mesopotamia dates the 'Dispersion' of the Jews, the name by which it is now usual to speak of the Hebrews or Israelites. However, a number sufficient to rebuild Jerusalem and the Temple and to re-establish the Jewish way of life returned to Palestine.

For the two centuries of the Persian rule, the Jews dwelt peacefully in their own land, being reckoned among the most loyal subjects of the Great King, and the Jews of the Dispersion likewise received privileges. These latter Jews became more and more unfamiliar with the language of their ancestors, but they still kept up their religion and either went on pilgrimage to Jerusalem or sent gifts to the Temple. Among them the quality which has ever since distinguished the Jewish race became prominent, and powerful Jewish commercial communities arose throughout the Gentile world.

The Jews owed their continued existence after the disappearance of so many ancient nations to their belief that they were the chosen people of the one true God, and this belief they derived from the efforts, from the eighth century BC onwards, of the Prophets. These men, who are without parallel in the history of religion, were drawn from the most varied classes in the Jewish world. Some of them left written records of their preaching, others are mentioned only in the tradition (among them two very great names, those of Elijah and Elisha). Some were fairly successful in their lives, others apparently grim failures. Some preached throughout the whole of Palestine and beyond, others only in certain localities for short periods. Some appear to have foretold the future with fair exactitude (and thus earned for all the rest the popular meaning of the English word 'prophet'), others did no more in this direction than to make general predictions. But all agreed in preaching two great truths: there is only one personal God, the maker and ruler of the world; this God is, above all things, holy, and thus a moral power rules the universe. That Israel is the chosen people of God is also a doctrine of the Prophets, but it is also their doctrine that Israel is chosen for a specific purpose, that in it and through it all the nations of the earth may be blessed. There is much divergence of opinion among scholars as to the Messianic teaching of the Prophets, but it is clear that by the last century BC at least, the Jews had come to expect a saviour. Unfortunately for their own place in the development of mankind, their views of this deliverer were now narrowly nationalistic.

The teaching of the Prophets was reinforced by the tremendous disaster of the Captivity. A lesser nation would have lost faith in God, but Israel, after bowing its head before the reproof of the Prophets, received their comforting assurance that the Lord would lead them back to their own land.

Under the Persians, life was uneventful for Israel, but when Alexander the Great destroyed the empire the Jews approached a period of peril. True, Alexander granted peace to Jerusalem, but his successors were ambitious generals engaged primarily in furthering their own interests, and the Seleucid dynasty, which secured control of Syria and Palestine, attempted to impose Greek polytheism along with Greek culture on the Jews. The latter proved that they had learned the lesson of obedience to Jehovah, and under the noble leadership of the house of the Maccabees the Jews fought back successfully against the Seleucids. In the second century BC the Israelites once more became independent under their own kingly house (descended from the Maccabees). This independence was short lived. The Roman eagle was spreading its wings over the whole Mediterranean and Palestine could not escape. By the beginning of the Christian era the Jews were under the rule of an Idumean, Herod, who has somehow acquired the title of Great and who was the liegeman of the Romans. It was during his reign that Christ was born. In the first thirty years of the first century AD Palestine gradually passed from the sons of Herod to direct Roman rule, and it was therefore necessary for the Jews to secure the condemnation of Christ by the Roman governor of Judea before He could be put to death.

From the time of their return from captivity the Jews possessed no prophetic voices. The great succession of the Prophets had ceased and in their places were scribes and interpreters of the Law. Sects arose such as the Pharisees and Sadducees, the principal difference between them being that the former believed in a future resurrection which the latter did not accept. These sects claimed to have their own special marks of holiness above the ordinary people. Though the feasts and temple services were celebrated with ever greater magnificence, the normal place of worship for the Jews was the synagogue in their local town or village. Here the Law was read, exhortations given, and prayers said. Sacrifices could be celebrated only in one place, the Temple at Jerusalem.

Among the Jews of the Dispersion the synagogue had naturally great importance. These Jews had acquired the Greek language as the most convenient for their commercial purposes, and with it they learned something of Greek culture. Most of the literature of the Apocrypha (written between the Old and New Testament) was in Greek and emanated from the Alexandrian Jews. Many Jewish beliefs which appear in the New Testament—above all, the belief in immortality—are first set out clearly in the Apocrypha. The Jews of the Dispersion were somewhat more liberal in their attitude towards the Gentiles. Philo, the great Jewish philosopher of Alexandria, went to considerable pains to reconcile Platonic thought with the Old Testament.

Despite all this, the Jewish mind was still centred upon Jerusalem. All Jews endeavoured to visit the Holy City once at least for the Passover, and Jewish nationalism had by no means abandoned the hope of a return of the kingdom to Israel, but rather looked more passionately than ever for the Saviour. Thus, at the beginning of the Christian era, the Mediterranean world was dominated politically by the rule of Rome, while Greek culture was universal among the educated classes of the Roman Empire. The law and discipline of Rome were combining with the science and arts of Greece to provide an important element in the future culture of Europe. Another element, in the shape of a universal religion, was to come from a third Mediterranean country.

Jesus Christ, the Founder of the Christian religion, Whose Deity is the main doctrine of that religion, was born in Palestine in the reign of the emperor Augustus. From the date of His birth is reckoned the beginning of the Christian era, AD. The traditional site of the birthplace of Christ at Bethlehem will surely retain the reverence of mankind whatever the future has in store for the various religious bodies, unless the Marxian philosophy comes to overshadow everything else.

Jesus had worked as a carpenter at Nazareth, but He set out to preach the Gospel of the Kingdom of Heaven, the Good News of God. His ethical teaching demanded of men a tremendous effort of self-abnegation and of love towards each other as common child-

K

ren of the one Father in Heaven. He claimed in His own name to
alter or abrogate the Law of Moses and it was precisely this claim
to do what none of the prophets, His predecessors, had dared to do,
which provoked against Him the hostility of the Pharisees and the
High Priests with their council of the Sanhedrin. This calm claim
to alter the most sacred features of the Jewish past could only be
construed by His disciples to mean that He claimed to be the
Messiah, the chosen one of Israel, a view of Christ in which they
were confirmed by the daily life and actions of their Master which
they regarded as miraculous. Their faith was to receive a very
severe testing. Jesus began to speak to them of His rejection by
the Jewish people and His death at their hands. Such ideas were
strange and unacceptable to the disciples who were dominated by
the current Messianic ideas, and although Jesus spoke of His ultimate triumph in the form of His resurrection from the dead, for
the most part the disciples dismissed the revolting thought of His
sufferings from their minds and, until the very end of their
Master's last journey to Jerusalem, hoped against hope that He
would assume the role of a new Maccabeus against the Romans.
But when the opposition against Him became formidable, when He
was seized and condemned to death by the Roman governor at the
insistence of the Jews, and when finally He was crucified like the
commonest malefactor (indeed He suffered in the company of two
such), and died on the Cross—the disciples collapsed completely.
For a few days they lingered about Jerusalem in terror of their
lives. One of them had indeed sunk so low as to betray the Master,
and with the rest in a state of pitiful cowardice it appeared on any
rational consideration that Jesus's movement had died with Him.

Yet a few weeks later the disciples were proving themselves a
curse to the Sanhedrin by preaching all over Jerusalem the tidings
that the crucified one was indeed the Messiah and that He had
risen from the dead. No amount of persecution could shake the
Apostles, as the chief disciples were now called. They insisted that
Jesus had risen from the dead three days after His death and after
a period of forty days with them had ascended into Heaven to
abide with God until He came again in Judgment.

Perhaps there is no place that so plainly tells us of the difference

between the mood of the disciples at about the time of the crucifixion and a period some six weeks later than the Garden of
Gethsemane. It is on the Mount of Olives, and just near the
traditional garden a church has stood for many centuries. A
rebuilt version of this ancient church was erected as late as 1920
and this fine modern building is known as the Church of All
Nations because it was built with funds supplied by all Christian
races and exists specifically for the performance of services on
behalf of the whole world. The garden has been laid out as a
flower garden, but there are certain ancient olive trees there which
help to recall the Agony of Christ. The garden is enclosed, but by
stretching over the railings some of the brilliant trailing bougain-
villea can be reached. The atmosphere of the place is one of profound peace. Sadness is there, but it is not prominent. The Agony
was the necessary trial of One who was to prove the conqueror.
Those who have written off the Gospel as the story of a man who
lived and died—just that—one thousand nine hundred years ago,
should visit Gethsemane. To them no doubt it would mean the
place of torment of One who failed, but that is not the feeling it
normally conveys. Nowhere can a greater sense of peace be felt.

The movement of the twelve Apostles gathered a following of
some thousands, but despite the universal implications of Christ's
teaching the Christian body might have remained as a sect of
devout Jews but for the spur of persecution. There were always at
Jerusalem members of the Dispersion, the more liberal-minded
Jews who spoke Greek. It became necessary for the Apostles on
the multiplication of their followers to appoint seven deacons, who
should be responsible for the business of administration of the
little community which had started on communistic lines by having all things for general use. One of these seven was Stephen, a
man of wider sympathies, who in the strength of converting zeal
carried the war into the enemy camp and uncompromisingly
denounced the Jews as people who had always resisted the promp-
tings of the Holy Spirit and who had now filled up the measure of
their iniquity by crucifying the Messiah.

Stephen became the first Christian martyr and there was an
outbreak of Jewish fanaticism. The leader in this was a man who

himself belonged to the bigger world of Greek Judaism, Saul of Tarsus; he had been educated at Jerusalem in the rabbinical lore of his fathers, but he possessed a knowledge of the world and the Greek tongue unknown to the rabbis of Jerusalem. He could even quote Greek poets and knew well how to address himself to Gentile audiences. He had been born a Roman citizen—a fact he never failed to bring home on any suitable occasion—so that in his own person he united the faith of a Pharisee, the knowledge of a Greek, and the political consciousness of a Roman.

Saul started his public career as a fierce persecutor of the wretched Christians. He put many of them in prison in Jerusalem and then, hearing that the vile heresy had spread to Damascus, he betook himself thither armed with letters from the High Priest. On the road to Damascus occurred the incident known in Christian annals as the Conversion of St Paul. There Saul had an experience which he always declared to have been a vision of Jesus Christ, in which he received from Christ a commandment to preach the Gospel. A very different man entered Damascus from the fiery spirit who had left Jerusalem. A few days later he was baptised in the name of Jesus and from then on until his death he preached the Gospel. He has passed into history as St Paul, the greatest man in the whole record of the Christian Church. Not only was he a great missionary who spread the Gospel as far as Italy and perhaps to Spain; not only was he, with St John, the founder of Christian theology without whom no Augustine, Aquinas, or Calvin could have worked as they did; not only did he lay down administrative rules still carried out by the Christian Church, but his supreme title to fame is that he was responsible for the separation of the Christian from the Jewish Church. He saw and boldly stated that the Gospel was a thing of the spirit and therefore that the old law of Moses was abrogated by the death of Christ, so that the Jewish Law was not incumbent on Christians. Others such as Stephen had perceived the truth, and the persecution following Stephen's death had dispersed the Christian missionaries with the result that first Samaritans and then Gentiles were converted and entered the Church, but it was St Paul who insisted on the freedom of the Gentile converts from the tedious restrictions of the Mosaic Law.

It is not difficult to follow St Paul in the way of his journeys round the Mediterranean, and his itineraries have often been worked out. Jerusalem, Corinth, Athens, Malta, Rome, each one of them preserves mementos of the Apostle of the Gentiles, but often the reminder lies not in some creation in marble or stone but, to the discerning eye, in the present-day characteristics of each place. In the narrow streets of the old city of Jerusalem and at the Wailing Wall it is possible to picture the fierce scenes when St Paul, it was alleged, had introduced Gentiles into the Temple. The Wailing Wall is the only surviving relic of the Temple destroyed in AD 70, and derives its name from the Jewish custom of wailing beside it.

Then Athens, where St Paul was laughed out of court by the easy-going, unbelieving Greeks; well, today, despite the large numbers of churches and the devotion of the people before their icons, Athens does not give the impression of being a very religious city, or one where men would get excited about creeds or dogmas. The most prominent building in the city is the Acropolis, and there the ruins of the most lovely temple of the old paganism dominate the scene.

At Malta, the Apostle was almost worshipped by the ignorant natives as a god, because he had wrought one or two wonders among them. No country is as religious as Malta, and in no place are the Apostles (not only St Paul but also the rest of the apostolic band) referred to in more familiar yet pious tones.

Finally, at Rome, where Paul experienced first the protecting power of Roman justice and then, later, the cruelty of Roman legal murder, we find the apotheosis of Paul. Although he died the death of a condemned man, although he was inferior in ecclesiastical theory to St Peter, yet the practical Roman nature could not fail to be impressed by his importance. Very soon St Paul was coupled with St Peter, not only because both were believed to have been martyred on the same day, but also because they were linked in importance as the twin Apostles, one of the Jews, the other of the Gentiles. So they have a joint feast day in the Latin calendar and Rome rejoices that she possesses the tombs of both of them. St Paul's tomb stands in the church of his name known as that 'outside the walls' of Rome, a church dark and heavy with columns taken from ruined temples, and with a floor of polished marble. As at St Peter's, the Altar of the Confession, which stands above the Saint's tomb, is in front of the High Altar. (Picture, p 199.)

It was through the heroic life and equally courageous death of St Paul that the Christian Church was now able to enter fairly upon its career as a universal religion. In its first stages it had to face the active opposition of the Jewish official body and for a while the Roman authorities appeared in the guise of friendly protectors. Yet in spite of the work of St Paul, the influence of the Hebraic element in the Church could have continued to be a drag but for an event of outstanding importance in the year AD 70. This was the total destruction of Jerusalem and of the magnificent Temple, and the cessation, continuing up to the present day, of the age-old Hebrew system of priesthood and sacrifice according to Mosaic Law. The hill of Zion, the great object of Jewish pilgrimage and aspiration to which multitudes of Jews were wont to journey for the great Passover festivals, was no more. It became a Roman camp and so remained for sixty years. The emperor Hadrian then allowed a city to be built there, but even this city was a Roman colony barred to the Jews. Ever since the capture of Jerusalem by Nebuchadnezzar, the Jews had been dispersed about the world, but now their expulsion from the Holy Land was carried much further, and was eventually to result in the total loss of their homeland following another unsuccessful rebellion by them in the second century under Bar-Cochba.

After the ruin of Jerusalem in AD 70, a tax was laid on the Jews which went towards the upkeep of the Temple of Jupiter on the Capitol at Rome. This same year was also to have very considerable significance for the whole of the Roman world. Four years earlier there had occurred the fire of Rome, in which a great many places of outstanding interest to Roman patriots were devastated. Popular opinion assigned the responsibility for this conflagration to Nero, who was supposed to have been fiddling while the city burned, and to have caused the fire to be started in order that he might rebuild Rome to his own design. Aware of this widespread opinion, Nero tried to divert suspicion from himself towards some body of persons who could then be made the victims of his and the popular wrath. Lighting upon the Christians of Rome, he accused them of many crimes of a particularly anti-social nature, including that of setting fire to the city. The feelings of the people were thus turned against the Christians and in this, the first of the ten persecutions of the Church, St Peter and St Paul perished, the former by cruci-fixion, the latter, being a Roman citizen, by the axe. Along with them died some thousands of Christians—according to the Latin historian Tacitus, as many as 7,000. Their deaths were accompanied by such excruciating tortures that the bitterness felt against them at first by the Romans later turned to pity for their appalling sufferings. Tacitus is also the first of the pagan writers to mention Christ, whom he calls Chrestus, and states that He suffered in the reign of the emperor Tiberius.

Nero's actions were only temporarily successful in turning the hostility of the populace away from himself. Murderer of his wife and his mother, with whom he was supposed to have committed incest, Nero succeeded in making himself an object of dislike and presently of hatred in the official circles of the Roman world. He was destined to be the last of the Caesarian house. Revolt started against him, and when he found that he could no longer command allegiance, he contemplated suicide. He had to be helped to this final step, having the dagger more or less thrust into his hand. Despite his excesses, it is possible to feel some pity for him, since he was, in fact, a third-rate artist who, had he not been born to power, might have been happily occupied as a mediocre singer and actor. Many worse men have disgraced imperial positions, but he has none the less acquired a horrible reputation, and indeed has the doubtful distinction of being the original of the Beast in the *Revelation* of St John. All sorts of persons, including Napoleon, have been identified with this figure of prophecy by the tortuous skill of misguided commentators, but it is true that in Hebrew the name *Neron Kaisar* has the numerical value of 666 which is, of course, the number mentioned in the 13th chapter of the *Revelation*. Certainly his monstrous cruelties towards the early Christians of Rome and his many crimes epitomised the vile character of the Beast, and like other emperors he did accept the flattery and incense of godhead, so that the prophetic writer was not far out in describing him as setting himself up as a god.

Following on the death of Nero, there came the most terrible year the Romans had known since the battle of Actium and the peace which Augustus had given to the world. They were not to experience anything like it again until the third century. The year 69-70 became known as the year of the four emperors, these being Nero, Galba, Otho and Vitellius, all four of whom met violent deaths. Also a new and sinister situation had arisen in the Roman Empire through the determination of the provincial armies to put up their own candidates for the purple. Galba came from Gaul; Otho had besides the Praetorians the support of the Spanish legions; Vitellius was put forward by the most powerful and important of all the legionary forces, the armies of Germany. Galba was murdered, but when Otho replaced him, it was only to meet death at his own hand, after his legions had been beaten by those of Vitellius. The fighting took place in Italy, a terrible renewal of the troubles from which Augustus had delivered Rome.

During this violent period there was raging in Judea a most bloody insurrection, in which the Jews succeeded in defeating the troops under the Roman governor and in clearing the Romans out of Jerusalem and most of the Holy Land. The hatred felt for Rome by its Jewish subjects had boiled over, and fanaticism ran riot. The Roman governor of Syria took measures to deal with the Jewish revolt, and under the generalship of Vespasian the Romans began the reconquest of Palestine. Steadily they reduced the Jewish forces, until they approached Jerusalem. Then Vespasian found himself proclaimed emperor at Alexandria in July 69. Vitellius was deserted and in the ensuing disturbances the Capitol was burned and Vitellius murdered.

Vespasian handed over the conclusion of the Jewish campaign to his son Titus who was a keen soldier, ardent for military glory, and himself returned to Rome to restore order. Probably, the Romans were so preoccupied with the new emperor that they scarcely concerned themselves with the end of the Jewish revolt, until Titus later came to Rome for his triumph. The affairs of the year 70 were to have consequences, however, far beyond the smaller sphere of Roman politics.

With an adequate force of four legions and auxiliaries supplied from the eastern sub-kings who were clients of Rome, Titus drew a ring round Jerusalem. The city was thronged, for it was the time of the Passover and, despite the war, immense crowds had come for the sacred festival. In addition, a very large number of Jews had taken refuge in the city. The non-scriptural writers, Tacitus and Josephus, the latter a Jew who had gone over to the Romans, are full of the portents which accompanied the doomed city's last agonies. They are also mentioned in Suetonius's *Lives of the Twelve Caesars*. The small Christian Church in Jerusalem, comprised of Jewish Christians, had fled in good time from the city before the siege lines tightened around it. The earliest of the Gospels, that of St Mark, agreed by all critics to have been written at latest by 65 AD, contains this prophetic warning: 'Those who are in Judea must take to the hills ... For those days will bring distress such as never has been until now since the beginning of the world ... and will never be again' (ch 13, v 15-20). Referring to the Temple in all its magnificence in AD 29, Christ had said 'You see these great buildings? Not one stone will be left upon another, all will be thrown down' (*ibidem*, v 2).

In the event, this came true to the letter. One million persons perished in the siege of Jerusalem, and even cannibalism was practised by the besieged before the end. The captives were sold at the rate of ninety Jews for a talent. The most desperate of the rebels held out in a few strongly fortified places, like the rock of Masada near the Dead Sea, but the revolt was completely crushed. Titus set up the Arch in Rome, to which reference has been made, and all seemed over for the Jews.

A great historian has written: 'The demolition of Jerusalem which lay in ruins as Carthage and Corinth had once, lain, deprived the Jewish nation of a centre. The high priesthood and the Sanhedrin were abolished and the Israelites were left without a head'. (*A History of the Roman Empire* by Prof J. B. Bury, 1893, p 372). The Temple of Onias near Memphis in Egypt, which was a sanctuary of the Egyptian Jews, was closed. The Xth Legion pitched camp on the site of Jerusalem, and Emmaus received a colony of Roman veterans. Sichem, the chief town of Samaria and so famous in St John's Gospel, was reorganised under the name of Flavia Neapolis. Eventually the whole of Palestine became part of the province of Syria.

With the woes of the Jews we are not for the moment concerned, they will be dealt with in a later chapter. Suffice to say that the ills inflicted on this martyred people have never turned them from their belief in God, and most astonishing of all, after nineteen centuries, they once more possess their own state in their ancient homeland.

It is to the events of the year 70 in so far as they affected the course of European civilisation that attention must be given. The third ingredient of that civilisation, the ideas derived from Jewish sources and so powerful in the spiritual and ethical spheres, entered into the composition of our culture through the Christian faith which, of course, is purely Jewish in its origin. The severance between Jew and Gentile resulting from the destruction of the Jewish polity in AD 70 also caused the end of specifically Jewish Christianity. A small, little-known, dwindling remnant of a sect struggled on to the second or possibly third century in regions to the east of Jordan, but the Christian Church was no longer under its influence. Without this severance from Judaistic scruples the third element in European civilisation would probably never have established itself. By the end of the first century the Apostles and the first generation of Christians who had known Jesus Christ were dead, leaving behind them the twenty-seven books of the New Testament. The extraordinarily minute scrutiny of the German critics of the last 150 years has shown that of these books perhaps one—the Second Epistle under the name of St Peter—is a writing of the second century. The rest were written well within the first century and, as mentioned above, the earliest of the Gospels is considered to be that of St Mark and to date from not later than AD 65.

Reading the New Testament in conjunction with the non-Christian writers, Tacitus, Suetonius and Josephus, it is possible to see the deeper significance of the year of the four emperors, coupled with the complete winding-up of the Jewish Dispensation.

For Jewish moral and spiritual ideas to find a wider sphere and to become of value to the future civilisation, the peculiarly Jewish polity had to die. A new Dispensation then came into being and the best commentary on this is to be found in the book mentioned once above, the *Revelation of St John*, a work that is usually misunderstood and has been the plaything of many cranks. The error arises from dating the book as late as the reign of Domitian, when it ceases to have any meaning. The whole burden of the work is that it relates to and is a warning of events shortly to take place. The use of the word 'seven' in many parts of the work, and the reference to a city on seven hills, unfortunately led commentators to suppose that Rome was meant, but as the great city whose destruction is prophesied in the eleventh chapter is definitely described as the place of Christ's crucifixion, this seems unnecessary. Rome, it need hardly be added, never has been destroyed despite many sacks and convulsions—hence its title of the Eternal City. Jerusalem, in its destruction in AD 70, does fit the bill and the matter is clenched by the identification of the Beast whose number is 666, with Nero. The book is actually quoted in other parts of the New Testament, eg, St Paul refers in his Letter to the Galatians to Jerusalem which is above, and to Jerusalem which now is; clearly a reference to the new Jerusalem of *Revelation*.

The *Revelation* is a profoundly Hebraic work, steeped in the imagery of the Old Testament, whose constant warnings against Jerusalem culminate in its pages. It shows the winding up of one Dispensation and the opening of another. Jerusalem, we are told in the Gospels, is to be trodden down by the Gentiles (ie, the nations) until the times of the Gentiles are fulfilled. So far from being destroyed, Rome became the head of the Christian world, but Jerusalem has only just emerged from the down-treading of the nations, and only just been restored to the Jews.

The new Dispensation of Christ's teaching was now manifestly free from the cradle of Judaism in which it had been reared. The Church took over the Jewish Scriptures as her own, but gradually discriminated from the bulk of early Christian writings those which were the product of the Apostles and apostolic men. These were formed into the Canon of the New Testament. By the end of the first century of the Christian era the Church Catholic (or universal, to distinguish it from heretical sects) had spread around the Mediterranean, being most powerful in the great cities such as Rome, Alexandria, Antioch and Carthage. The Church was organised on the same pattern everywhere, with two sections of the one body, clergy and laity. The clergy were divided into bishops, priests and deacons. The bishop presided over the particular church, assisted by his priests and deacons.

The Church of Rome had the pre-eminence, not only because of its secular renown as capital of the empire, but as being the place of martyrdom of the two chief Apostles. Although the Church at Rome had existed from a short while after the day of Pentecost and had not been founded by an Apostle in person, the two martyrs, SS Peter and Paul, were regarded as co-founders of the Roman Church, and their joint feast is still kept on 29 June. The different churches which were considered to be of apostolic foundation or founded by followers of the Apostles (Ephesus by St John the Evangelist or Alexandria by St Mark the Evangelist and follower of St Peter) reckoned the succession of their bishops from the founder. The first three Roman bishops after St Peter are listed as Linus, Cletus and Clement, the last being the author of 'An Epistle to the Corinthians', the first instance of pastoral care exercised by Rome over another church. Another instance occurred about 190 when Victor, then Roman Bishop, excommunicated the Asian churches because they kept Easter at a time different from the Roman practice. Eventually in this as in other controversies up to the fifth and sixth century, the views and practices of the Bishop of Rome prevailed.

The Church regarded itself as the Body of Christ and in consequence Christians were members one of another. The Christians of the early ages showed a happy spirit of unity irrespective of colour and race in the one brotherhood of Christ. The moral teaching of the Church was strict, but it was accepted by multitudes who were weary of the bestialities, cruelties and uncertainties of the old pagan world. For the most part the Christians were pacifists and were obedient to the imperial power, but there was one element in the state system which the Christian could not endure. He refused to worship the emperor or the state gods. Although tolerant, Rome would not condone anything which implied sedition against the state, and the Christians came to be looked on as atheists, communists, haters of God and man. As such, they were subjected to a series of persecutions, often by the best of the emperors who were the more concerned that a large body of their subjects should hold themselves aloof from the state religion and appear to form a self-contained community within the all-embracing state.

In the second century the Church grew from the sect which Tacitus had deigned to notice as an offscouring of the Jews into a body large enough to alarm the provincial governors of Marcus Aurelius, the last of the Antonine princes. The letters of Pliny to the emperor contain a very interesting picture of the Christian community written by an outsider. During the course of the third century the Church continued to expand, and at the end of that century came the final effort by the state under the emperor Diocletian to stamp it out.

CHAPTER ELEVEN

THE FALL OF WESTERN ROME

FOR SIX HUNDRED years one power was paramount in the Mediterranean world, and for about four hundred years all the coastlands around that sea were in the direct possession of the same power. This was the first (and it was to be the only) time that such a thing had happened in the Mediterranean area. When the Roman Empire crashed it was a calamity for mankind, but its direct rule lasted long enough to develop culture and institutions which, when sheltered by the Christian Church, produced the civilisation of Europe.

The house of the Caesars, who claimed by descent or adoption to be of the lineage of Julius, failed with the death of Nero. After the year of anarchy 69-70, the Flavian dynasty took over, itself giving place in 96 to Nerva, the first of the five Antonine princes, the line which ended in 180. Thus for two centuries, from Augustus to Commodus, the dissolute son of Marcus Aurelius, the empire enjoyed peace and apparent prosperity, except for the Jewish war of 70 and the outbursts of Caligula, Nero and Domitian, which affected mainly the nobles of Rome.

The factors which were to be the cause of the empire's subsequent decline were gathering force in the first and second centuries. The most serious was the great decay in the numbers of the Italian population, which had originally supplied recruits for the legions. Soldiers had to be found, and more and more the areas of recruitment began to recede from Italy. Declining population was seconded by an unwillingness on the part of the citizens in countries like Gaul and Britain to fight and troops in sufficient numbers could only be obtained from the prolific barbarian tribes beyond the imperial boundaries. The armies of Rome were thus more and more composed of Germanic troops, who were not Roman citizens, had only a smattering of Latin, and possessed no sympathy for Roman culture. The slave population of the empire was a problem. A large proportion of the people had no real rights and their very existence caused a brutalisation of the Roman character and prejudiced the position of free labour.

With a great decline in the number of citizens and the available free labour it became more than ever difficult to meet the demands of taxation, and this may have been reflected in the comparatively small armies raised by the imperial power. One estimate of the population of the empire in the time of Constantine at the beginning of the fourth century places it at seventy millions; yet the Roman army with its auxiliaries did not exceed six or seven hundred thousand men.

Another great difficulty, perhaps the greatest, was the lack of a living unitive faith in the empire. The old polytheism had lost all hold over the educated classes, philosophy had failed as usual to be a substitute for religion and in its stead various oriental religions were offered to the Roman world. The majority were mystery cults. The worship of Isis, the Egyptian goddess, or of Mithras, the soldiers' god from the east, for example, agreed in being 'mysteries', that is, in possessing rites which purported to set the individual free from sin and misery. The great difference on a speedy view between Christianity and the mysterious religions was that Christians possessed a jealous God who allowed no one to share His worship and who demanded holiness from His worshippers.

Christianity eventually triumphed over its rivals. It was adopted by the emperor early in the fourth century, and within a lifetime it had become the exclusive religion of the empire. By the sixth century the old paganism and the mystery religions had nearly died out, but the triumph of Christianity came too late to avert the fall of Rome by infusing fresh faith and hope into the citizens. Besides, soon after the triumph of the Church it became distracted by disputes on doctrine, and one of the most unfortunate results of this was the conversion of the barbarians in the west to heretical

Page 165 The Pyramid of Caius Cestius in Rome

Page 166 (*above*) The Crater Lake of Averno, Campania; (*below*) the
Tomb of Cecilia Metella, Rome

forms of Christianity so that a barrier was at once formed between them and the Catholic Christians of the empire. It was only in the course of three or four centuries that this was removed by the conversion of the western barbarians to Catholic Christianity.

Many people doubt the stories of corruption in the Roman world, but a visit to Herculaneum or Pompeii ought to dispel any illusions on this score. At Herculaneum there are preserved some of the wall paintings of the houses, and if anyone can imagine such drawings appearing on the wallpaper or wall designs of any fashionable home in England he will then be able to say that we are as the Romans and that there is no such thing as moral progress. It was quite normal to represent the god Priapus or his male worshippers with their bodies naked except for hats and having their distinctively male organs in a most aggressive attitude. This sort of ornamentation to a fashionable lady's drawing-room or nursery was quite the thing in the polite Roman society of these pleasant resorts on the Campanian coast, Pompeii and Herculaneum. Naturally, the brothels which existed in these cities were not extraordinary in being brothels (such institutions do exist in modern cities) but they were remarkable in the amount of ornamentation they possessed. The chief brothel at Pompeii has been preserved. Inside it there were a number of cells where the assignations took place, and over the doorway of each cell were paintings illustrating the particular mode of behaviour, the Spanish way, the Italian way, etc.

Such scenes must have been nauseating to a healthy man, yet they were accepted as quite normal in old Rome, and no one frowned on the existence of brothels or corruption of every kind. To make matters worse, at the same time that corruption grew within the state, pressures on the northern frontiers of the empire became greater owing to events on the other side of the world. As we have seen the empires of Rome and China flourished in almost complete ignorance of one another, despite an occasional exchange of embassies and the silk trade of China with the west, which was conducted through the intermediate empire of Parthia. The two empires did, however, have problems in common. The Chinese were assailed by barbarians who came out of the deserts of central

L

Asia, and for a long time Chinese territory was subject to their ravages. But at last a powerful dynasty arose, that of the Han, which unified China and drove out the barbarians or subdued them; the Great Wall of China, a huge fortification, beside which the Roman frontier lines appear trivial, was put up to keep the wandering savages away.

The unification of China under the first real emperor and its continuance under his successors of the Han dynasty was contemporary with the period of Roman history extending from the Punic Wars to the age of the Antonines. Although the Han dynasty fell, China did not suffer a decline and fall similar to that of Rome. The history of China for more than two thousand years is the record of the rise and fall of dynasties, while all the time the patient Chinese people refused to be effaced. Between the dynasties there would be periods of great upheaval, but when the country was again centralised under a firm government, the civilisation of China was found to have endured. Sometimes the foreign invaders would subjugate China and their kings would found new dynasties of emperors, but these always ended by becoming as Chinese in outlook as their subjects. It was perhaps due to the innate respect for the wisdom of their ancestors that the Chinese were able to subjugate each of their conquerors in their turn. To advance civilisation to a certain height, then to maintain it stubbornly there, is possibly the best recipe for continuance.

Be that as it may, the vigour of the dynasties which ruled China during the period of 200 BC-AD 400 was responsible, in conjunction with the climatic changes of central Asia and Europe, for the impulsion of hordes of savages on to the Roman Empire. The events which occurred on the far-distant frontiers of China were the originating cause of the break-up of the unified Mediterranean world. After the age of the Antonines the Roman world was to know only fitful periods of peace. Occasionally, an Aurelian, Diocletian or Constantine by dint of hard fighting and supreme ability would unify the Roman world for a short time, but seldom did twenty or thirty years pass from the third century AD onwards without usurpers springing up against the occupant of the throne, and often there were several rulers dividing the empire between them.

The end really came when Constantine the Great transferred the capital of the empire from Rome to his new city of Constantinople, which he had built on the confines of Asia and Europe. His object in doing this was to preserve, not to destroy, the empire. The barbarian invaders were coming across not only the Rhine but the Danube as well, and Constantine decided to establish a seat of government more suitable for dealing with this menace. In this action, as in many others, Constantine altered the course of history. While the Mediterranean was a Roman lake, Rome was the most suitable place for a capital, but when the tribes from the north forced their way on to the Inland Sea, Rome was too distantly placed to afford quick defence to the Balkans, which were the great danger spot. The placing of an impregnable city at Constantinople meant that there was a nucleus of empire which for many ages withstood pressure from the wilds of Russia and Germany, and also from the East. In consequence, the peoples of the Balkans and Russia were brought under European civilisation and, just as important, the Arabs, Saracens and Turks were prevented from entering Europe by its eastern door until the fifteenth and sixteenth centuries, by which time Europe was rising to its full stature.

Various men are described as epoch-making, or as having been responsible for changes affecting the life of millions, but Constantine was certainly one such. His recognition of Christianity and practical establishment of the Church has set the pattern for the relation of Church and State ever since. He was responsible for the existence of the nominal Christian, owing to the practice of mass conversion which he set in motion, and by his removal of the seat of empire he also helped the Papacy to emerge as the ecclesiastical head of the western Church.

The change of the imperial capital had happier results and was the main cause of the continuance of Graeco-Roman civilisation in the eastern Mediterranean for a thousand years after the complete ruin of the western half of the empire. When the eastern or Byzantine Empire eventually went down before the Turks, it had done its work by bringing Christianity and civilisation to the

Balkans and to Russia, and by protecting the west of Europe as it struggled out of barbarism.

The second half of the fourth century is the period when the barbarian invasions reached the point at which no emperor, however great his genius, could do more than check them for a time. From the heart of Asia came the Mongolian horsemen known as the Huns. Their impact on the western peoples caused the Goths to cross the Danube and invade the empire. The emperor Valens, with most of his army, was destroyed in battle with the Goths at Adrianople in 378, and although the situation was temporarily repaired by Theodosius the Great, the various peoples who were moved by the Huns and by hunger—Franks, Goths (of the west and the east), Vandals—began to move in and out of the Roman boundaries with an alarming degree of freedom. The outer provinces of the empire were abandoned and the Roman troops recalled for the defence of Italy. Thus Britain was left to its own devices, whereupon it was promptly invaded from the north by the savages of Caledonia and ravaged by the Saxon pirates from the eastern side of the North Sea. In 410, Alaric, king of the Goths, captured Rome, the first time in eight hundred years that a foreign foe had taken the Eternal City. To most Roman citizens it seemed that the end of the world was at hand, and it was to refute allegations that the misfortunes of the empire were due to Christianity that St Augustine wrote his *City of God*, in which he outlined a philosophy of history which was to guide European thought for a millenium.

St Augustine was Bishop of Hippo, a small seaport on the Algerian coast of very little importance until he gave it fame by writing his famous works there. Under its modern name of Bone it has had little further fame since but its church can still boast the possession of some relics of the great Augustine.

St Augustine may well have concluded that the world was about to end, and though it did not but merely continued to grow more wretched, the system which represented civilised life to Augustine was indeed ending. Gaul was under the rule of the Visigoths, then of the Franks who founded the French monarchy. Spain became another barbarian province and the Vandals spread thence over the sea, becoming a sea power, seizing Corsica, Sardinia and North Africa, and thus robbing the empire of its great corn supplies. The Ostrogoths secured Italy and Sicily. Half of the empire had passed under barbarian sway. Most of these barbarian kings professed to be lieutenants of the emperor, so great was the prestige of Rome, and when the Huns under the leadership of Attila threatened the whole of southern Europe, Franks, Visigoths and Romans fought against and defeated them at Chalons in 451. For a time the shadowy figure of the Roman Empire lingered in the west, but in 476 a harmless youth, the last Roman emperor, was deposed by the Gothic king of Italy. This poor boy was called, ironically enough, 'Romulus Augustulus'.

In the sixth century a great effort was made by the eastern emperor Justinian to recover the western provinces. Under the brilliant generalship of Belisarius and Narses, small Roman armies did re-establish Roman rule in Italy, North Africa, the islands and on the coast of Spain, but the power which Justinian could bring to bear was inadequate to sustain such wide conquests, and at the end of his reign his empire was weakened in the east by his efforts in the west. These latter were in any event precarious and were disputed by fresh hordes of barbarians pouring out of the apparently inexhaustible centre of Europe and Asia.

Thus by the year 500 the Mediterranean Sea was bordered, as it had been seven hundred years earlier, by various nations having no particular connection with each other save vague affinities of speech, race and religion. None of these states was predominant over the others and none was likely to become so, although the eastern empire still contained Greece and the Balkans, Asia Minor, Syria and Egypt, but was no longer aggressive and much of its territory was precariously held.

The Christian Church was now established not only in the official sense in which Constantine had established it in the empire, but it had spread far beyond the old imperial boundaries into central Europe, Persia, Arabia and Abyssinia. Many of its conquests among the barbarians were won by the Arian heretics who taught a doctrine of the deity of Christ at variance with that of the Catholic Church. Gradually, the barbarians were won over to the faith of the more cultured Romans, but for two or three centuries in half-a-dozen countries there was an Asian ruling caste in the midst of a subjugated Catholic population. Rifts were coming in the unity of the Catholic Church itself. The rival pretensions of the Bishops of Rome and Constantinople foreshadowed the days when the western and eastern Churches would part company, ostensibly on a question of doctrine but in reality through the intolerance of rival ecclesiastical rulers and the incompatibilities of the Latin and Greek temperaments.

In the eastern empire, something of the Greek spirit continued along with the Greek language, literature, philosophy and science. In the west, the end of the empire and its substitution by a medley of barbarian kingdoms led to a great decline in culture. Despite the destruction wrought by the barbarians, much that was Roman continued: schools, law courts, aqueducts, roads, villas; but now there was no central power to look after these things. Everything was left to individual effort and under the Roman Empire individualism had not always been encouraged. Some things, such as literature, could hardly be fostered by rare individuals living in the midst of a barbarous society.

Fortunately there was an institution which could conserve something from the wreck. That institution was the western Church, which not only absorbed the Arian heretics and converted the savages of northern Europe, but also saved a good deal of the Graeco-Roman culture. The use of Latin as the language of the Church ensured the survival of some Latin literature, and the fact that the rulers were barbarous and ignorant made them more dependent upon the only educated men, who were the clerics. As these latter were versed in the relics of the old Roman culture, they were able to bring the influence of the older civilisation, reinforced by the Christian revelation, to bear upon their kings and nobles.

Nevertheless, to anyone looking at the western world in the sixth century, it must have seemed that the legacy of Rome was likely to be lost. Justinian's attempt to restore Roman rule had failed. Another effort to unify the Mediterranean area was to come from a totally unexpected quarter, and it was to make the Mediterranean again a great factor in the exchanges of West and East.

Strangely enough it was in the period of Justinian's failure to restore Roman rule over the western portions of the empire that he achieved the work which, more than anything else, has succeeded in making Roman influence a living factor to this day in Europe. Justinian codified the Roman law and by so doing made it a powerful influence on the legal codes of all European nations. Even in England where the law is not built on Roman law, it has nevertheless been greatly influenced by the Code of Justinian. To witness the perpetual fecundity of Roman law it is only necessary to visit the lecture rooms of the Inns of Court in London during term, and there see hundreds of young men—not only from England or the white dominions, but from India, West Africa, China, Egypt—all intently studying the Institutes of Justinian. So, not only has the work done by Justinian in gathering the laws of Rome into one comprehensive code been influencing the world ever since, but the fact that it is studied by English law students also means that it is likely to influence regions Caesar never knew and to spread throughout the whole of those Asiatic and African countries with which England has been associated.

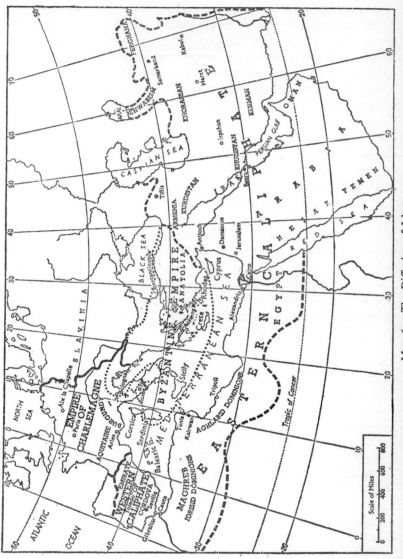

Map 6: The Diffusion of Islam

CHAPTER TWELVE

ISLAM

A STORY IS told concerning Alexander the Great and the Arabs which is too good not to be repeated. When Alexander had returned from India he was acknowledged as King of the World by nations far and near, yet the sheikhs of the Arabian desert sent no embassy and no tribute. Alexander was wroth and an army and a fleet were prepared, the one to advance over the Syrian desert into Arabia heading for the Gulf of Aden, the other to round the peninsula of Arabia from the Persian Gulf. Their combined operations were to bring the insolent Arabs to submission.

But Alexander died and the Arabs were left in their solitude for another thousand years. So they might have remained for three thousand years as far as the other races of the world were concerned, for Arabia is a peculiarly inaccessible sandy, rocky peninsula. It was the Arabs' own initiative, or rather their initiative when awakened by one man, which brought them before the world at a time when the other Semitic peoples had either been destroyed or reduced to political impotence. Phoenicia and Carthage were memories and the Jews were dispersed about the world, when the Arabs—that mighty rearguard of the Semites, as Sir Edward Creasy called them—suddenly appeared from their solitude in the year 633, and within one hundred and twenty years had acquired an empire which extended from Afghanistan to the Atlantic, embracing all the southern shore of the Mediterranean, Spain, part of southern France, the islands of the western Mediterranean, and Syria. What was the cause of this mighty change?

Arabia was not wholly desert, over which tribes of savages wan-

dered. Such was the greater part of the peninsula, the north and
the centre, which were well placed to defend the fertile and
settled portion on the west and south, now known as the Hejaz
and the Aden Protectorate. In olden days this area was described
as Arabia Felix and was reputed to possess vast wealth owing to
the fact that the few caravans which reached Syria from thence
carried articles such as spices and perfumes for which the Romans
were prepared to pay large sums. Readers of Horace will remember the adjectives which he applies to the Arabians, expressive of
happiness and wealth.

In reality, the cities of western and southern Arabia were small
and were mostly the result of colonies which had grown up around
oases and wells where the soil promised some return for cultiva-
tion. From a distant period a Jewish colony had been settled in the
Yemen and had founded a kingdom. The Jewish king exercised
considerable power, including the *jus primae noctis* over the brides
of his Arabian subjects. With the exception, however, of this one
Jewish colony, the Arab cities were inhabited by people of the
same race. They were independent and sometimes at war with each
other but they had, like the ancient Greeks, a common religion,
the worship of many gods, and their religious festivals served as
peaceful reunions where worship was conducted, social and business relations were renewed, and where poetic and athletic contests
took place.

Among the hundreds of idols worshipped by the Arabs, the
Black Stone or Caaba, reputed to have been associated with Abraham, gave to the town of Mecca, where it reposed, a peculiar
sanctity. A place of pilgrimage long before the birth of Mohammed, Mecca was ruled by an aristocracy known as the Koreish and
to one of these families Mohammed belonged. His early condition
was poor; he had been left an orphan and brought up by an uncle.
Unable to read or write, he was at a youthful age apprenticed in
the service of the wealthy widow Khadijah, whose merchandise
he took on camel-back to the great fairs of Syria where the
Arabians sold their goods and bought such things as they needed.
Medina, some one hundred and twenty miles from Mecca, was
the starting place of these caravans and as such the rival of the

holy city. Khadijah had been unfortunate in her previous stewards and the honesty of young Mohammed, together with his business ability and pleasing appearance, made an impression on the widow's heart. She proposed to him, and when they married Mohammed retired from active business to live as a respected citizen with his good wife at Mecca.

During his journeys he had seen something of the world, had met some Nestorian Christians, and had also had relations with the Jews of Syria and of his own country. A serious and thoughtful man, his very lack of learning threw him back on the resources of his own mind so that the universe and the Power behind the universe could make itself felt upon him. Gradually his own reflections, aided by what he had heard from the Jews and heretical Christians and stimulated by the inner voice, brought him to the conviction that the gods of his countrymen could not represent the maker of the universe. The mighty truth that there is but one God dawned upon his mind. Having made such an advance and utterly rejected the polytheism of his upbringing and ancestry, it was too much to expect that he could rise completely above his early prejudices—and repudiate all veneration of the Caaba, and so to this day the Black Stone remains the object of pilgrimage for the devout Moslem. Later, Mohammed was to modify his teaching, but he never swerved from his proclamation of the unity of God.

His first attempts to communicate the truths he had learned were to his intimates. His wife, his slave, his cousin Ali and his friend Abu Bekr were converted. His revelations began at the age of forty, and even by the time he was fifty his disciples numbered only a few scores. His public preaching was resisted by the Koreish, and Mohammed was to experience the truth of Christ's saying, 'No prophet is without honour save among his own people'. Although he could not convert the Meccans, his words were eagerly heard by visitors to Mecca, and when hostility made it wise for him and his disciples to flee that city he was invited by the people of Medina to reign over their city. Accompanied only by Abu Bekr, he escaped the pursuit of the Koreish and reached Medina. From this year, AD 622, the Mohammedans date their era, the Hegira, or Flight, as it is called.

From this period there also dates a coarsening in Mohammed's character and methods. At first he had looked upon himself as a messenger of God sent to call his countrymen to repentance; now the opposition he had met and the temporal power put into his hands by the people of Medina persuaded him to the belief that he was not only a prophet, but the sole prophet of God. There had been others before, Abraham, Moses, Jesus, and these were to be revered, but he, Mohammed, now produced the final authoritative revelation, the last word on heaven and earth. As Gibbon says, the creed of Mohammed—There is but one God and Mohammed is His prophet—contains an eternal truth and a necessary fiction. Whereas he had preached tolerance and gentleness, he now organised raids against the caravans of Mecca and fought battles with the Koreish. When victorious, he sometimes executed his enemies; when defeated, he cursed them heartily. As his sphere of power widened, he made convenient concessions to his new subjects. The time came when the Koreish could no longer resist, Mecca opened its gates and the adversaries of Mohammed were at his feet. Sparing them, he destroyed their idols, but the Caaba was kept and the faithful were to venerate it.

In his theological and moral system Mohammed showed the nice shrewdness of a statesman rather than the idealism of a visionary or a saint. There are no sublime passages in the Koran, as in the Sermon on the Mount. Mohammedanism is not an easy religion (what real religion can be easy?), but it presents its followers with none of the heart-searching challenges of the Gospel. The teachings of Mohammed may be summarised thus : There is but one God who has created all things. He has revealed Himself to men in previous ages, but these revelations—notably the Jewish and Christian—have become corrupt, and it was therefore necessary for a new (and final) Prophet to appear, who is Mohammed. All men are called upon to repent and to submit (Islam) to the will of God. The duties of a Moslem in this life are prayer (five times a day), abstention from wine and other strong drink, almsgiving, pilgrimage to Mecca, and fasting, particularly during the month of Ramazan. The true believer is permitted four wives, but incest and adultery, also fornication, are forbidden. All Moslems are to be brothers, irrespective of race, colour or class. The true religion is to be propagated by all means and it is to be defended by the sword. The world will eventually be judged by God at the last day. Unbelievers and the unrighteous will fall into the abyss of hell, but the righteous believers will follow the Prophet into the Paradise of God, where the meanest of the blessed will be attended by seventy houris or dark-eyed maidens who will bring them flowing goblets as they recline in green meadows beside the gently running waters.

In his lifetime Mohammed's teaching was oral, though his disciples copied down the precious words. No collection of these suras or chapters was made until after his death, when the whole was brought together in the Koran. This ranks among the Bibles of the world, and to the Moslems it is the book of books. To read it is one of the occupations of a pious Moslem. All these suras were believed to have come down from God by the mediation of the Angel Gabriel. Wide freedom was, according to this belief, given to the Prophet from the rigour of his own laws, and he was permitted to enjoy fourteen wives after the death of his loving and loyal Khadijah. Most of these women were middle-aged or elderly and were taken under Mohammed's protection. Only one child, a daughter, Fatima, lived beyond infancy, to be productive of trouble in the Islamic world later on.

After his establishment at Mecca, Mohammed sent out messengers to the various potentates of whom he knew, calling on them to repent and to embrace Islam. These envoys were dismissed with pity or scorn, but the world surrounding Arabia was soon to find the error of its ways. Mohammed died at the age of sixty-three before he could actively direct the work of evangelisation, but his successor (or Caliph) Abu Bekr began to send out armies against the powers of Syria and Persia. The enterprise was not quite as desperate as it appeared. The Roman Empire had been vastly weakened by the loss of all its western provinces and the constant wars in the east with Persia. The re-establishment by Justinian of Roman authority in Italy, Africa and Spain did not extend much beyond the coastline, and in the first quarter of the seventh century the struggle between Rome and Persia, which had been going on for some seven hundred years, reached a stage when it seemed that the Persian monarch would accomplish in the east what the barbarians had achieved in the west.

At last, there was a reaction. The emperor Heraclius defeated the Persians in one battle after another, restored the Euphrates as the Roman frontier and recovered his lost provinces, but the long war between the two empires had enfeebled both. The Persian monarchy was discredited and a succession of pretenders and usurpers appeared on the throne. Rome had proved the victor at the cost of exhausting most of her reserves and, in addition, she was afflicted with the curse of internal strife. The disputes concerning the being of Christ, which had first become public at the council of Nicaea in 325, had in three centuries become more refined in speculation and more savage in controversy. The effort of theological thought on the relationship between God and man in Jesus Christ was supplemented by the enthusiasm of the populace, and the fury which they showed towards their adversaries. Arianism, Nestorianism, Eutychianism, the Monothelite controversy—to name only the more prominent—waxed and waned. The faith of the Catholic or universal orthodox Church was defined in a succession of councils, the decisions of which were ratified by emperors who proceeded to enforce these decrees by the power of the state. Large minorities of Christians did not see eye to eye with the ruling power which tried to make them conform by force to what were considered orthodox views. This was the case in Egypt, Syria and Asia Minor, with the result that the emperor's own bigotry had created in the dominions nearest to the Arab onslaught a large class of disaffected subjects.

So it was that when the Arab armies emerged from their deserts they came upon a Persia weak and distracted by rival claimants for its throne; an eastern Roman Empire weakened and racked in its eastern provinces by religious discord, the most rancorous and embittering of strifes; and the remnants of a western empire precariously held by the Romans and degenerate barbarians. Against such foes the Arabs brought the force of enthusiasm. Religious fanaticism, which preferred death in battle to surrender because it brought paradise to the slain believer, was united with a thirst for plunder. Everything was new to the Arabs, and they were ready to

attempt anything. Although they had not previously experienced
great battles, they brought against Greek and Roman science the
force of cavalry, and none knew better than the Arabs the management of the horse, both in peace and war. Roman armies had
never been properly provided with cavalry, the arm in which the
Arabs were overwhelmingly superior. Even when faced with the
difficulties of besieging cities, in which they were as yet inexperienced, the Arabs usually succeeded through sheer persever-
ance, starving the besieged into surrender or opening a breach in
the city walls by some desperate feat of arms.

Thus the new power, within a few years of the death of Mohammed, had conquered Syria and Palestine and Persia. The Romans
were defeated in several pitched battles and driven behind the
Taurus range into Asia Minor. In many of the cities the Christians
were able to make a concordat with the Moslem conquerors who
were not sorry to acquire tribute-paying subjects. This was notably
so at Jerusalem, which was sacred to Moslems as well as to
Christians and Jews. Persia was completely conquered as far as
the borders of Afghanistan and India. The last heirs of the King of
Kings were driven into exile, and eventually extinction in the court
of China. The old fire worship of the Persians was largely abandoned for the profession of Islam and the Persians contributed a
mystical and poetic strain to their new faith.

The turn of Egypt followed and here was the most decisive
proof of the previous folly of the Roman emperors in persecuting
their subjects for theological subtleties. The native Copts went over
to the Moslems on condition that they were given religious toleration. The Greek and Roman officials, with their families and re-
tainers, withdrew from Egypt, and despite two expeditions against
Alexandria, Egypt with its corn supply was for ever lost to the
empire.

It was a natural progress from Egypt along the coast of Libya
and North Africa. Not only was there no political body capable of
resisting the Moslems, but the spiritual forces, too, were exhausted.
The Church had been divided by fierce, bloody disputes for several
centuries, while outside the great cities and the Roman hinterland
the tribes of the Atlas and the desert remained pagan. Now these

people were converted to Islam.

Islam in North Africa differs radically from Islam in other countries, though outwardly there are many of the signs of the Mohammedan religion. Apart from the large mosques in the towns, there are many hundreds of marabouts or local shrines in every district. These marabouts are little white dome-shaped buildings which are, for the most part, set on the tops of hills or mountains. They cover the bones of Moslem saints and seen from a distance on the tops of hills or across intervening valleys they have an attractive appearance. They are, however, usually very dirty, being frequently used as places for physical deposit by the Arabs, who seem to have the same notion as medieval Europeans as to the affinity between piety and dirt.

The difference between the picturesque appearance of these little chapels and their interiors is also symbolic of the discrepancy between the nominal Islam of these countries—Algeria, Tunisia, and Morocco—and their real faith. The Berber has survived so much, so many empires and religions, that he is tolerant of them all. Often a countryman in Africa will kneel down to prayer at one of the appointed times while his co-religionists standing by him are engaged in conversation or laughing at jokes. This sort of thing does not happen in the Indian Moslem community, or in Egypt.

When first brought over to Islam, however, the Berbers were apparently enthusiastic, and became willing partners in future wars. These soon came. In 711 the Moslems invaded Spain. The Visigothic kingdom was in decay and the Moslems had been invited by a great noble who had cause for enmity against Roderick, the last king. Roderick was defeated and disappeared in a battle. Spain was overrun with remarkable speed and a flourishing Moslem community founded there. The Pyrenees did not prove a more difficult barrier to the Arabs than to other invaders, and by the year 732 (one hundred years after the Prophet's death) they had penetrated as far as Tours, in central France. At the other end of the Mediterranean the Moslem power had spread through Asia Minor and in 668 and 716 they besieged Constantinople. Once having reached the shores of the inland sea, the Arabs had become a sea power. Their navies voyaged in the Aegean, in the central and western Mediterranean. Malta was captured by them, they invaded Sicily, Sardinia and southern Italy, and Rome was subjected to a sack. It appeared that the Mediterranean world would once again be ruled by one power and become an Arab instead of a Roman lake. Moreover, this new power possessed much more energy than old Rome and was ready for far-flung adventures in central Europe.

The plight of Europe was grim. The poor remnant of the eastern Empire in Greece and the Balkans was menaced with the loss of its great principal city. Italy was threatened as far as Rome, Spain was gone, and in France, England and central Euorpe barbarian kingdoms were only very gradually climbing out of the chaos which had followed the fall of Rome. The north of Europe, Scandinavia and Germany was still pagan and Scandinavia was soon to pour forth on distracted Christendom the fierce pagan Vikings. Across Russia from central Asia there came hordes of savages, of whom the Magyars of Hungary are a survival. The horns of the vast pincer movement of Islam in France and at Constantinople had only to continue their previous progress and Christendom would be destroyed in its infancy. But the horns were broken in each instance. The more celebrated defeat of the Moslems was at Tours when the leader of the Franks, Charles Martel, the grandfather of Charlemagne, in a battle of seven days beat the Moslems and drove them back into Spain. They never invaded France again. Less celebrated, but equally decisive, was the failure of the Moslems to capture Constantinople. The Greek Empire fought back successfully, and it was not for another seven centuries that the Moslems were able to invade Europe from the east.

One of the greatest weapons used by the Christian power against the Moslems was that known as the Greek fire. This was an early form of chemical warfare and was used with great success by the Greeks in the sieges of Constantinople. The formula was a closely-guarded secret and consequently it is not possible to describe Greek fire exactly. It is generally thought to have been a compound of sulphur, petroleum and quicklime, a mixture which has the property of igniting when coming into contact with water. It is said to have been known in China in early times. In the Greek Empire the invention of Greek fire was ascribed to an architect named

M

Callinicus, who had fled to Constantinople from Syria in the seventh century. It was used against the Saracens in 673 and set their fleet on fire. Despite precautions in keeping this valuable compound a secret, knowledge of it was gained by the Saracens, who used it against the Crusaders. In the seventh century the Greeks discharged it by means of syphons and hoses.

By the time (1453) modern Europe had been born, the Moslems had been driven from most of southern Europe, and the vast resources of the Americas were nearly within Europe's grasp. The attempt to rebuild the Roman Empire into an Arab shape had failed, but the possession of more than half the Mediterranean coastline by the Moslem power had a very great influence on the future of Europe. Under Roman rule the Mediterranean had been a lake in the midst of an empire embracing the temperate regions. Between the Roman Empire and the wealthy countries of India and the Far East there had been only the empire of Persia and the disunited tribes of Arabia. Trade with the Far East had been possible either by the caravan routes across Asia, or by ship up the Red Sea and across the Indian Ocean, and a considerable amount of intercourse had taken place by these means. After the Moslem conquests, the weakened and besieged Europe of the early Middle Ages found itself largely cut off from the Mediterranean and from access to the East by a hostile power. This was to lead to huge efforts to break out of the narrow confines of western Europe, efforts which were to bring about great discoveries in geography and navigation.

The unity of the Moslem world did not long endure. Although Mohammed had been careful to repress, as far as he could, disputes on strictly theological tenets, the rancour of religious controversy, which seems inseparable from all religion, reared up in Islam over what one might call a point of administration. The first three Caliphs, Abu Bekr, Omar and Othman, had been elected by the votes of the faithful, but there were those who thought that the son-in-law of the Prophet, Ali, should have been elected. Two great sects then arose in Islam, the Shiites or separators—who added to the simple creed a third article that Ali is the Vicar of the Prophet of God and who are represented mainly by the Persians—and the Sunnites or orthodox. The Shiites do not accept the succession of the first three Caliphs, claiming that Ali should have succeeded his father-in-law. Ali did become the fourth Caliph, but the faction which was opposed to him then rose in revolt. He was murdered and was succeeded by Moawiyah, of the family of Ommiyah. As time went on, fresh divisions were added to the Moslem world. The Ommiades were driven from their thrones and destroyed by the Abbasides, or descendants of Abbas the Prophet's uncle. One member of the family of Ommiyah, a youth named Abdalrahman, escaped to Spain where some governors averse to the ruling power welcomed him. At Cordova he set up the Spanish or Moorish Caliphate and reigned in power and splendour untouched by the Abbaside Caliph at Baghdad. In addition, there appeared in Tunisia a Fatimite Caliph, reputed to be descended from the Prophet's sole surviving child, who had married Ali.

Thus by the close of the eighth century, the Moslems were divided among themselves and no doubt these discords contributed to the safety of Christendom, which was thus given the chance to grow up and become strong. The internal strife of Islam did not alter the fact that the coasts of the Mediterranean from the Pyrenees southwards and eastwards to Asia Minor were in the hands of peoples hostile to the Christian inheritors of Graeco-Roman culture. Many of the principal Mediterranean islands were also for long periods in Moslem hands. Islam formed a solid barrier between East and West and, except at the pleasure of the Moslem nations, Europeans could not trade with India or the Far East but were confined in north-western Europe on the edge of the known world. There were only three ways in which this obstacle could be overcome. One was to find a way across the Atlantic to the Far East, but this possibility was not seriously entertained in Europe until the fifteenth century. Another was an overland route across central Asia to China, which had been proved possible by Marco Polo. He had had many followers who thus maintained a measure of intercourse between Europe and China, but the vast distances and the slow methods of transport involved made this route hardly practicable. The third course was to break through the Moslem barrier by the sword, but before this could happen in the Crusades, Europe had to rise out of the Dark Ages. In large measure the

creations of the Middle Ages in Europe were a reaction to the spur
of Islam.

It has often been observed that the period of five hundred years
following the fall of Rome, which in European histories is known
as the Dark Ages, was a very brilliant epoch in the history of the
Moslems. The first half-dozen or so generations of the Arabs after
the settlement of the Ommiade dynasty were, excluding the nations
of the Far East and the Greeks of the eastern Roman Empire, the
leaders in science, and in civilisation. Baghdad, Cairo and Cordova
were the great cities of the Arabs, and they had no counterpart in
Christian Europe save Constantinople, which was known to the
wondering nations of the early Middle Ages as Micklegarth. Not
only were these Moslem cities possessed of splendid buildings, great
wealth and large populations, but the sciences founded by the
Greeks were studied there and some progress made. Great libraries
were collected, the Greek and Latin classics were translated into
Arabic, mathematics progressed, and algebra was either invented
by or owed its development to the Arabs. They also discovered and
used the astrolabe. Thus they not only appropriated Graeco-Roman
knowledge, but added to it. The stimulus of their progress came
clearly though from the previous Graeco-Roman culture, and when
they had added their own contribution they were able to return to
the West the culture which it should have inherited intact, but had
received only in imperfect preservation from the monks. The effect
of Islam upon the West is misunderstood if it is thought of as the
reaction of an oriental civilisation upon Europe. The religion of
Islam is a truncated Christianity with one new article added, the
position of Mohammed as Prophet. It is closely allied with Christianity and Judaism, and in any book on Comparative Religion these
three will rank as the family of monotheistic faiths. Islam has only
to be compared with one of the religions of India or China—
Buddhism, Hindooism or Confucianism—to realise how western it
is and how strong its affinities with Christianity and Judaism.

Similarly, the brilliant culture of Islam in Europe's Dark Ages
was produced by the effect on fresh and receptive minds of the
culture of Greece and Rome. The Greek Empire at Constantinople
preserved the language and literature of ancient Greece, but this

did not spread to the barbarian countries of the West. In western Europe the only civilising influence was the Church, which had kept Latin as its language and preserved something of Latin culture. The knowledge of Greek came to be very rare in the West, and thus the remnants of the Greek classics were known only in garbled Latin versions. The Arabs obtained better translations of the Greek masterpieces, especially the works of Aristotle, and these found their way into Christian Europe through the medium of the Moslem universities of Spain and Italy. They created a great new intellectual ferment in the European mind, and in the eleventh century western Europe had passed out of the Dark Ages and was ready to contend with Islam for mastery in the Mediterranean.

The light of Arab genius did not last long. There is an Islamic saying 'What use of Arabs, without the Prophet and angelic aid', and not even the most enthusiastic admirer of the modern Arab can really say that he would expect them to have invented the astrolabe. It is not hard in North Africa to witness an Arab funeral: a horrible droning dirge is heard, and six men can be seen carrying on their shoulders a board, with a body under a white covering. Closer inspection reveals the man's feet sticking out from under the sheet. When the body is buried, the last resting place will not be secure, for the grave, usually in poor rocky soil, is soon uncovered by the winter rains. 'To what base uses we may return', not only as individuals, but as nations, if such persons are the descendants and representatives of the cultured Arabs of Spain who advanced science in the Middle Ages and before whom the Christian princes had trembled.

It was in the long centuries of the Arab and later Turkish domination of North Africa that the city of Algiers was founded (in the tenth century). It was not until the sixteenth century that it became the centre of piracy, whence sailed out the dreaded corsairs to despoil and enslave the inhabitants of the south of Europe. The name of Algiers is derived from the island which lies off the harbour and which was later joined to the mainland in the defences of a fort. Its possession was long contested by the Spaniards, but in spite of several attacks upon it, Algiers continued to be a pirates' haunt until the French took it over in 1830.

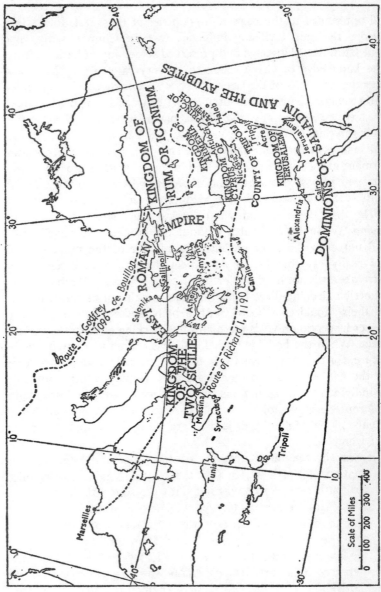

Map 7: The Latin Kingdoms of the Holy Land and the Crusaders' Routes

CHAPTER THIRTEEN

EUROPE AND THE INFIDEL

AT THE END of the eleventh century, Europe, though still far behind what should be the norm of a civilised state, had emerged from the chaos, weakness and ignorance of the Dark Ages. The siege of Europe had ended. The Moslems were held all along the Mediterranean, and in Spain the Christian kingdoms of the north were beginning to push back the Moors. The Scandinavian peoples had been converted to Christianity, their piratical raids had ceased, and from them had descended the Normans, a brave, skilful race devoted to the Church's service. In eastern Europe the fierce savages of the steppes were being broken-in to Christianity and some form of civilisation. In Poland and Hungary this was the work of the Latin Church, but in Bulgaria and Russia the glory belonged to the Greek Church and the empire at Constantinople. Orderly governments were the rule rather than the exception in western Europe now. The settlement of England after the Norman conquest was a case in point. Although after 1066 there were intervals of disorder, the strong central monarchy established by William the Conqueror saved the country from further invasions, gave it a chance of internal development and ultimately led to it becoming the nucleus of a powerful empire.

The interests of the Church were in favour of orderly lay government and in the eighth and ninth centuries a strenuous effort had been made to revive the Roman Empire in the west in the person of the Carolingian monarchs who had put away the Merovingian kings of France descended from Clovis. Charles Martel, the victor of Tours, was nominally servant to the captive Merovingian king;

his son, Pepin, was rewarded by the Pope for his aid against the
Lombards by the bestowal of the French crown. Charles the Great,
Charlemagne, Pepin's son, was again summoned across the Alps
to help the Pope and to receive a higher reward. On Christmas Day
in old St Peter's, Rome, in the year 800, the Pope placed on the
head of Charlemagne an imperial crown and hailed him as Emperor
of the Romans.

The right of the Pope to revive and bestow the Roman Empire
rested upon a pious fraud and a fact. In the period of the Church's
weakness in the Dark Ages, when her lands and her rights were at
the mercy of savage lay lords, some ecclesiastics fell back on the
weapon of forgery and fraud. One of these compositions, which
were written with great skill and easily escaped detection in an
unscholarly age, were the Forged Decretals, allegedly letters of
early Popes which laid claim to great reaches of jurisdiction over
the Church. The bishops, when these Decretals were universally
accepted as genuine, had a claim to appeal to Rome over the heads
of their own monarchs.

The Donation of Constantine was an even more imposing fraud,
and purported to be a grant of the western empire to the Pope
of the time from Constantine on his removal to Constantinople.
According to this, the western empire was in the gift of the Pope
and he was within his rights in giving it to Charlemagne. Under the
aegis of this tremendous forgery the Papacy endeavoured to control
the princes of the Middle Ages, overthrew the dynasty of the
Hohenstaufen and bestowed, by the hand of the only Englishman
who was ever Pope, the land of Ireland upon Henry II and his heirs.
The forgery of the Donation was not discovered until the fifteenth
century, but by then its work had been done.

Behind the so-called revival of the Roman Empire lay the growing
hostility between the Latin and the Greek Church. For several
centuries the Greek emperors had been no more than the nominal
sovereigns of the countries north and west of Italy. They had not
exercised any effective control or been able to protect the West
from the barbarians. They wished to control the Pope as they controlled the Patriarch of Constantinople, but the former repudiated
the claim, more especially since some of the eastern emperors were

tainted with heresy in destroying the images of Christ, the Virgin and the saints, which were now part of the equipment of the Catholic Church. The rift between East and West was not absolute until 1054, but before this date there were long periods of break in communion. The bestowal of the revived empire upon Charlemagne did not please the Greek emperors, but the Popes had obtained their wish and the new emperors were in a position to smile at the remonstrances of the rulers of Constantinople.

This new Roman Empire is known as the Holy Roman Empire. It is easy to repeat the cheap gibe that it was neither Holy, nor Roman, nor an Empire, and to represent it as a corrupting influence in European history, but in reality, in the early Middle Ages, it served as a stabilising factor and brought, especially under the Hohenstaufen holders of the title, large tracts of central Europe under its control.

In the ecclesiastical sphere the monastic life became purer and more influential. It had been founded, as far as the West was concerned, by St Benedict, at Cassino in Italy, and had provided nearly all the light and culture of the Dark Ages. The Celtic monasticism of Iona and Ireland was also very fruitful, and produced in Scotus Eriugena one of the world's original thinkers who possessed in the midst of almost universal ignorance a knowledge of Greek, and who showed that the chain of philosophical thought in Europe was never broken even in the worst period. The Benedictine and Celtic monastic systems, like all the western monastic orders, were very practical, and in addition to purely religious work contributed to the life of the countryside in agriculture, in building, and many other arts. The Celtic system also sent forth many missionaries to England, Germany and the countries of the north.

The history of western monasticism is one of alternate progress and decay. When the first thrill of enthusiasm had passed away it was easy for the monks to fall back into routine work and then into sloth. Against this a new enthusiast would rebel and would lead his followers to a fresh attempt at the conquest of human nature. Thus there arose in the tenth century the Cluniac foundations which were to provide the Church with some of her best leaders. With this revival in the monastic life the Church was strengthened and the Popes were able to launch their crusade for the celibacy of the clergy and the total independence of the state ecclesiastical.

Learning also flourished in numerous schools and in the institutions which later developed into the universities of Europe. St Anselm, who was Archbishop of Canterbury in the reigns of Rufus and Henry I (about 1100), has been called the last of the Fathers of the Church and the first of the schoolmen, as the new race of theologians and philosophers were termed. The romantic figure of Abelard is perhaps more representative of the new age. He had a thirst for knowledge and did not in the least mind where his speculations led him. The new knowledge that was coming in from the Jews and Moors of Spain, with the fresh Latin translations of Aristotle, set the mind of Europe on seeking new answers to old questions about the universe and human life.

This intellectual movement in western Europe was to lead to a great development in the universities, to the enormous growth of scholasticism with its giant intellects in Albertus Magnus and St Thomas Aquinas, and to the growth of European poetry in Dante and Petrarch, Chaucer and Langland. For the purposes of our narrative, however, we are concerned principally with the military reactions of Europe at the end of the eleventh century, when the era of the Crusades opens. Before the beginning of the eleventh century, western Europe could not have undertaken a concerted movement against Asia. Charlemagne had crossed the Pyrenees into Spain and his retreat, after an unsuccessful attempt to overcome the Moors, has been immortalised in the great poem of the Song of Roland. After Charlemagne's death his empire was divided among his sons, none of whom equalled or approached him in ability or resources. The revived western empire existed only as a name or a series of kingdoms until it was restored by the Saxon emperor, Otto I. The real invigoration of the west came from the martial Normans. Wherever these warriors went, whether with many or with few, from Ireland to Syria, they conquered. They united the fierce vigour of their Viking ancestors with the polish they had so quickly acquired from the revival of Graeco-Roman culture. They

were law givers and zealous members of the Church. The combination of intellectual and moral ability with physical courage
gave them the advantage everywhere.

For long periods after the Islamic conquests in the Near East,
the Christian subjects of the Arabs were left in possession of their
liberties, and pilgrims from the West were able to visit the holy
places of Palestine, probably without much molestation. The
ascendancy of the Arabs in Islam did not, however, endure, but was
replaced by that of the Seljukian Turks, a fierce race from central
Asia who were not softened by their conversion to Islam. The
pilgrims to the Holy Land were then not only robbed, but in many
cases murdered, while the native Christians were subjected to
heavier tributes and ignominious laws. Their sufferings roused the
compassion and the anger of a western visitor, Peter the Hermit,
who repaired to the Vatican where he found an eager listener in
Pope Urban II. The great reforming Pope Hildebrand (Gregory
VII) had desired to launch a holy war against the infidels and his
successor, Urban, embraced the opportunity given him by Peter.

At the Council of Clermont, Urban made an impassioned speech
which moved his thousands of hearers to exclaim, 'Deus vult',
'God wills it', of the crusade to which the Pope called them. The
reports of Urban's speech were carried throughout the western
world, already inflamed by the preaching of Peter the Hermit.
Hundreds of thousands took the Cross and set out for the crusade
without waiting for guidance or direction. Religious enthusiasm
was not the only motive-force; to many persons the idea of life in
a new setting made a great appeal, while others were desirous of
escaping from creditors and unpleasant surroundings. Naturally,
many of this first promiscuous multitude were poor peasants who
had not the vaguest conception of what lay ahead. They marched
(if such a dignified term can be applied to their movements) through
Hungary and Bulgaria into the dominions of the Greek emperor.
The Hungarians had been lately converted to Christianity and
might have been expected to give some succour to the wanderers,
but the differences of language and outlook were so great that
enmity was easily aroused and the Hungarians attacked and plundered many of the crusaders. With their numbers diminished by

this and the hardships of the route, they reached the neighbourhood of Constantinople. Here they received help from the Greeks
which, in their ignorance, they badly repaid, so that the emperor
lost no time in getting them across the Straits into Asia Minor. The
crusaders were then fairly launched into the area where they
would meet the Turks and their fate at the hands of the latter was
only too certain. Very few of them lived, with Peter, to see the
West again.

The crusade had been proclaimed by Urban in 1095, but it was
not until some eighteen months later that the real military power
of the West arrived in the Greek Empire. None of the great
sovereigns of Europe was present, but there were numerous brave
and skilful Norman knights at the head of the host, who were
probably more capable than the kings and princes of waging a
fierce war in Asia. The chiefs were Tancred, Bohemond, son of
Robert Guiscard, Raymond of Toulouse, and Godfrey de Bouillon,
with a large number of knights and men-at-arms. The backbone of
the host were the Normans, but there were adventurous spirits
from many countries who were fired not only with zeal for the
faith but with the hope of carving for themselves in the East the
possessions they lacked in the West. This disciplined and well-
armed body, the real crusade from a military point of view, was,
however, little better equipped in knowledge of the geography,
climate, and characteristics of the enemy it had to meet than
were the followers of Peter the Hermit.

The crusaders were divided into three bodies which made a juncture at Constantinople. Godfrey de Bouillon, who was destined to
be the ultimate deliverer of Jerusalem, led an army along the route
of Peter the Hermit, overland through Hungary to Constantinople.
Raymond of Toulouse with the Papal commissary, Bishop
Adhemar, led the crusaders of southern France down the Illyrian
coast and then due east across the Balkans to the imperial capital.
Yet another band, mostly of Normans, went by sea to Durazzo
and then by land to Constantinople. Robert of Normandy wintered
at Bari and crossed over to the rendezvous before the end of 1096.

When the Greek emperor saw this new powerful body of assist-
ants, which his own appeals to the West for protection against the

Turks had unexpectedly helped to produce, he realised that any mismanagement on his part might well result in the overthrow of his own kingdom. The western army was no longer composed of footmen, for the Normans had mastered the art of cavalry warfare. A special breed of powerful horses was used to mount the knights who were armed with heavy lances and with swords, battle-axes or maces. Each knight was attended by a squire and men-at-arms. The defensive armour of the Normans was a helmet and a coat of mail, and though this was hot enough for wear in eastern countries, it had not at the time of the First Crusade become as inhibitive of movement and so tiring to wear as later armour was to be. In effect, the more lightly armed Saracen cavalry were faced with new tactics, the charge of a long line of lances, not yet heavy enough to be too cumbersome, but sufficiently heavy to overwhelm anything more lightly armed which stood in its path.

Passage to Asia Minor was facilitated for the new host and the crusaders moved down into northern Syria. Despite difficulties of climate and terrain, which caused them many casualties, they overthrew the Moslems in several engagements and at length captured the important city of Antioch. Here it seemed that the term of their progress and their lives had been reached, for the Saracen hosts gathered around the city and straitly besieged it. No more succours from Europe or the Greek Empire were forthcoming and the crusaders were in a most difficult position. From it they were delivered by the discovery in the great church at Antioch of the Holy Lance or spear which pierced the side of Christ, an event which has been described as a miracle or a fraud according to the outlook of historians.* Whatever the truth, the discovery of this lance renewed the enthusiasm of the host, which issued from the gates of Antioch and destroyed the besieging army in a pitched battle.

---

*See *Anonymi Gesta Francorum et Aliorum Hierosolymitanorum*. Edited by Beatrice A. Lees, MA. This work is the account by an eye-witness, a knight of southern Italy, of the First Crusade. When the crusaders were in dire straits at Antioch, one of their priests had a vision in which Christ appeared, saying that if they dug up the ground before the high altar of the great church, they would find the means of deliverance. The vision was obeyed and the Roman spear which pierced the side of Christ was found.

It was now possible for the crusaders to follow up their success by marching on Jerusalem. One can imagine faintly the enthusiasm and transports of joy with which they panted up the last remaining heights to reach the top of the Mount of Olives and gaze across to Jerusalem. Zion! Goal of their pilgrimage! An almost mythical city of which their priests and teachers had been able to tell them much less than any well-informed Sunday-School child knows today. Here was the Holy City towards which they had journeyed through such difficulties and for whose sake they had surmounted so many hazards. Little wonder that they fell on their knees weeping.

Can we picture at all what they saw? From the Mount of Olives today one sees a sight which would have been strange to most of the early generations of pilgrims, or indeed any before 1918. Right in front is the old Jerusalem on its several (some think seven) hills surrounded by the Turkish walls of Saladin. Around these hills runs a deep valley—the valley of the sons of Hinnom, as it is called in the Old Testament—and from this valley rises the group of which the Mount of Olives is one. Today, these hills are covered in most places with fine modern buildings, such as the former Commissioner's House, the Hebrew University, St George's English Cathedral, and many private residences. In fact, a new Jerusalem has been built there and so great has been the development that it is difficult to realise that, during most of the historic events with which Jerusalem is associated, the only buildings standing were those on the site of the old city itself.

What would a crusader have seen? The walls and towers much as they are now, and right in the main view, the Dome of the Rock —the Mosque of Omar—which stands on the site of the old Jewish Temple of Jerusalem and is the traditional place of Abraham's sacrifice. No Christian symbol would have been visible in the city, for it was then under Moslem rule and in general appearance it would still have remained very much as it had looked to the legionaries of Titus, or even earlier to the Assyrians, except that before AD 70, the dominating building was not the Mosque of Omar but the Temple of the Jews. To the Moslems, Jerusalem is, unfortunately for the peace of Palestine, almost as sacred as it is to the

Jews and Christians, for did not Mohammed alight on the Rock after his nocturnal journey, and in any case was not Abraham the prophet of God?

The mood of the crusaders soon changed. On the walls and towers still flew the Crescent of Islam. There was work to do and the tools were largely lacking. After a fierce, toilsome effort in the construction of siege-engines, the army, now under the command of Godfrey de Bouillon, moved up to the assault. The strong Moslem garrison strenuously resisted but the city was taken. In the aftermath of victory, the Moslem inhabitants—seventy thousand in number—were slaughtered, and when this blood-bath was over the crusaders knelt, again 'weeping with excess of joy' at the traditional site of the Redeemer's sepulchre. The object of the crusade was attained.

The aspirations of Christendom were satisfied by the recovery of the Holy Land from the infidels. The Greek Empire was strengthened by the removal of the Saracenic pressure on Asia Minor. Europe was extended overseas and the Greek Empire had a fresh bulwark in the array of Latin kingdoms extending from Syria to the south of Palestine. A wedge had been driven into the solid block of Islam and possibilities were opened for the recovery of the old Roman grip on the area from Egypt and Sinai to the Syrian desert, which would enable western Europe to trade uninterruptedly with India and the Far East.

Such were the bright hopes excited by the victory of the First Crusade, but they were not fulfilled. By the close of the twelfth century Islam had regained Jerusalem and most of the crusaders' conquests. By the end of the thirteenth century the Moslems had driven the last remnant of the Latins from western Asia, and a new and formidable Turkish power confronted the eastern empire from the Asiatic provinces which the Greeks had lost. Various causes accounted for the loss of the gains won in the First Crusade. A vast host of western warriors might be moved by a mixture of religious zeal and cupidity to journey to the Holy Land and conquer it, but when this had been achieved not very many were willing to stay as garrison troops in Palestine and Syria. Consequently, the Latin kingdoms were always afflicted by a shortage of manpower. On the one side were the vast hordes of Moslems of western Asia driven on partly by Mongol pressure from central Asia, on the other the scanty Latin garrisons reinforced by passing bodies of crusaders from Europe. The expedient was tried of creating religious bodies of military monks, the Templars, the Knights of St John and the Teutonic Knights. But these were insufficient in number, and as corruptions crept into their strict rule they were more inclined to seek lands and possessions in Europe than battles in the East. The climate also had its effect in wearing out the western soldiers, for instead of adapting themselves and their equipment to it, they added even heavier armour, just as their brethren in the West were doing.

Perhaps the most serious cause of the failure of the crusades was the abuse of the whole movement by the Papacy. When the results of the First Crusade were found to be in jeopardy Europe was roused again by the Church under the influence of St Bernard, and the monarchs of France and Germany set out for the great adventure which ended in as great a failure. The Third Crusade was undertaken by some of the most powerful monarchs in Europe, including Richard Coeur de Lion of England, but it also failed in its objective, although part of the coast of Palestine was temporarily regained. The total number of crusades to capture Jerusalem is usually reckoned as seven, but the remainder need not be detailed as they were all failures, except the crusade, if such it can be called, of Frederick II, although they had important consequences for the history of Europe and the world.

The Popes, having once realised that by preaching a crusade or holy war they could raise large armies to carry out their wishes, began to proclaim crusades in various parts of Europe and for various purposes. Crusades were organised against heretics, such as the Albigenses in the south of France, against the pagans of Lithuania (indeed the whole effort of the crusading order of the Teutonic Knights was transferred to the eastern Baltic area and led to the foundation of East Prussia), and against kings who had incurred the Pope's displeasure. Pope Innocent III preached a crusade against King John of England which the king of France was induced to undertake, but when John submitted the Pope

Page 199   (*above*) The Mosque of Omar in Jerusalem; (*below*) the interior of
St Paul's Church in Rome

Page 200   (*above*) The Walls of Constantinople; (*below*) the Castle of
Krak des Chevaliers in Syria

endeavoured to call off the crusade, and thus not unnaturally fell foul of the French who had already invaded England.

Bound up with the raising of crusades were the powers of interdiction, deposition of kings, and the granting of indulgences. As the Pope claimed to be head of the Church on earth and to possess the right of disposing of earthly kingdoms according to his pleasure, he claimed the right to depose a recalcitrant monarch and give his kingdom to another. To accomplish his aims he used various measures: the interdict, whereby he prohibited all religious services in a country, thus, in the Ages of Faith, striking a deadly blow at a religious people; the crusade, which gave him the army he would not otherwise have possessed for the enforcement of his orders; the indulgence, whereby in return for certain acts of penitence (such as undertaking a crusade) he claimed to remit the sins of the faithful. All these powers came to be bound up with financial arrangements, for the Popes needed large revenues. After the first enthusiasm of the crusades had passed, the dangers and difficulties of the enterprise had become apparent. At the same time the Popes had learned to harness the crusades to various ends other than the capture of the Holy Sepulchre, and the whole crusading movement was prostituted. It was not only the Popes who learned the lesson of applying organised force; the crusaders themselves were quick to learn the same lesson. Thus the Fourth Crusade, which had been organised by the great Pope Innocent III, turned aside from its objective and captured Constantinople from the Greeks, in the year 1204. The eastern empire held out in Asia Minor and the Greek dynasty returned after sixty years to its throne in Constantinople, but Europe's bulwark on the east against Islam had been badly weakened by this scandalous exploit; and although the Greek Empire remained for two or more centuries, it never again possessed the same strength. Innocent III protested strongly against this action of the crusaders, but so much had the crusading spirit declined that the Latin knights persisted in their partition of the Greek Empire and ignored their original vow to proceed to Jerusalem.

Crusading zeal flared up again in spirits like St Louis of France, who in the Sixth and Seventh Crusades strove to subvert the

N

Moslem power in Africa in order to take Jerusalem more easily. But the enterprise of this pure and sainted king failed dismally and led to the loss of his army, and to his own death.

The indecent depths to which the crusading movement had descended were seen in the performance of the celebrated emperor Frederick II, the *Stupor Mundi*. He had in his youth taken the crusader's vow, but his long delay in carrying out his promise provoked the hostility of the Pope who, for this and other reasons, pronounced him excommunicate, unfit to rule, and preached a crusade against him. Whilst his dominions in Italy and Germany were the object of attack by the Pope's forces, the emperor at last set out for the Holy Land. He did no fighting but made a business arrangement with his friend the sultan which enabled him to visit the Holy Sepulchre and to reach an agreement whereby Christians were allowed unmolested passage to Jerusalem. To Frederick, all religions were equal, in so far as he did not believe in any of them; but he may well have thought that Islam was more simple and more of a man's religion.

After two hundred years of effort the net result of the crusades was that the Moslem powers remained in possession of the Holy Land and were, in fact, in a stronger position to attack Europe owing to the weakening of the eastern empire at the hands of the later crusaders. Europe was more firmly cut off from sea or land passage across the Mediterranean to the east at the end of the crusades than she had been at the beginning. Despite the conquests made in Spain, Italy and the islands, the Mediterranean for the last two centuries of the Middle Ages was largely a Moslem sea, in which the chief fleets were those of the Moslem rulers of Spain, Africa and western Asia. It is true, as we shall see later, that Venice and Genoa had become great maritime powers, but they did not seek to overthrow Islam, rather to trade with it for their own advantage.

Some of the crusaders had formed sage schemes to strike at the heart of Islam by going down the Red Sea and overland to the holy cities of Mecca and Medina. Many other crusaders had been attracted by the plunder of the pilgrims and rich caravans on the way to Mecca, and had set up strong castles in the desert to interfere with this stream of wealth. But all alike were destined to failure in their aims with the general failure of the crusades. Europe was flung back on itself, as the small western portion of the great land mass of Europe-Asia-Africa, with the Moslem power in the dominating central position. New ways had to be found to circumvent Islam.

What was the legacy of the crusades to the after-ages, apart from affording Asia a firmer grip on Europe? Very little in outward show, despite the facility with which writers sometimes ascribe everything in the later Middle Ages, from heraldry to scholasticism, the decay of the feudal system and the growth of towns, to the influence of the crusades. To the traveller, however, there are many interesting vestiges of the crusaders still to be found in two continents. The crusaders were great builders, and fine specimens of their work in Jerusalem and other parts of the Holy Land have been brought to light in recent years. Many fine churches in Jerusalem, for example, are now shown to have had a crusading foundation, and the work is both beautiful and enduring. There remain, too, such specimens of the work of the knights as their castles—like Krak des Chevaliers in the desert east of the Dead Sea—mighty fortifications which could house one thousand men-at-arms and their horses. (Picture, p 200.) There is little in the lands of western Europe to compare with such fortresses as these, which make one realise that writers like Sir Walter Scott were only following the path of fact in the boldest of their fictions.

These mighty castles were part of a definite military policy to use very strong fortifications in order to overcome the shortage of manpower which was a permanent weakness of the Latin kingdom. Seldom if ever did the Moslem hosts succeed in taking the crusader castles by assault; only by long-drawn-out sieges and ensuing famine for the besieged, or by treachery.

CHAPTER FOURTEEN

THE EASTERN DOOR CLOSED

AT THE END of the crusading epoch, in 1300, the Mediterranean remained a sea still in dispute but with the dispute much inclining in favour of the Moslem powers. A large part of Spain yet remained in Moslem hands; the whole of the southern and eastern shores were theirs while the islands of the sea were exposed to the depredations of the African and Turkish pirates. The land power of the revived Greek Empire was weak and subject to renewed attacks from Asia Minor.

The Moslems did not voyage without opposition in the Mediterranean. One of the orders of crusading monks, that of St John of Jerusalem, when it was expelled from the mainland of Asia in the general ruin of the crusading cause, took up its station in Rhodes and there maintained its fight against the Moslems. When it was expelled from Rhodes, the order went to Malta, which it was given by the emperor Charles V and where it remained until the capture of that island by Napoleon in 1798. The Order of St John fought against the Moslems at every opportunity and checked their progress into the western Mediterranean. It also rescued many Christian galley slaves.

To this day the island of Malta is full of the presence of the Knights of St John. Valetta was the knight's capital city, a city built by gentlemen for gentlemen, and is still the main city of the Maltese archipelago though the actual capital is the old Medina Rabat which, as its name denotes, dates back to the days of Arab rule over Malta. Medina Rabat is a walled city of narrow streets standing high above the rocky countryside of Malta, possessed of

many magnificent churches and, above all, an atmosphere power-
fully reminiscent of the medieval city.

Malta's history goes back long before the connection with the
Knights, and the island is full of historical remains, many of which
far antedate the Christian era. (See Note, p 214.) The bulk of the
people are a race apart, as is their language which is described as
Phoenician Maltese. (The Phoenicians settled and used the island,
followed by the Greeks). Several ruling races have controlled
Malta, beginning with the Carthaginians. The native inhabitants
have always had a character and independence of their own. They
gave up the island to the Romans who, with their usual commonsense, allowed the natives a considerable measure of autonomy
and brought prosperity to Malta. Malta is the Melita (the Greek
name) of the Acts of the Apostles, where St Paul was shipwrecked
while on his way to Rome. The chief man of the island, Publius,
mentioned in the narrative of the Acts, is reputed traditionally to
have been the first bishop of Malta, and from an early period the
Maltese have been, as they are now, zealous Catholics. Malta came
into the sphere of the eastern section at the time (395) of the
division of the Roman Empire, but the Arabs captured it in 870.
Their dominion was neither long-enduring nor deeply impressive
upon the Maltese, and Malta was one of the first Mediterranean
lands to be liberated from the Moslems. This was accomplished by
Count Roger the Norman who came from Sicily, drove out the
Arabs and exterminated any who were left. From the Normans,
Malta passed under the rule of the kingdom of Aragon, one of the
constituent parts of the Spanish monarchy—which explains how
it was that Charles V was able to bestow Malta upon the Knights
of St John of Jerusalem.

The greatest event before the twentieth century in Malta's history was the famous siege in 1565, when the Turks tried to capture
Malta as they had taken Rhodes. The forces of the Knights did not
much exceed 9,000, while the Turkish soldiers are estimated as
upwards of 40,000. From May to September the Christian forces
under the leadership of La Valette, the Grand Master from whom
Valetta is named, withstood the fiercest attacks until the Turks
were driven to their ships in total defeat. Had the Order done

nothing else in its history, this successful defence should have earned it the gratitude of Christian Europe. With the defeat of the Turks at Lepanto six years later, the tide of Moslem aggression was rolled back from the western Mediterranean.

During the rest of the sixteenth and through the seventeenth and eighteenth centuries the Knights continued their work of opposing and harassing the Turks and of delivering Christian captives. They became unpopular with their Maltese subjects and, towards the end of the eighteenth century, they began to decline in efficiency so that Napoleon on his way to Egypt in 1798 was easily able to capture the island. (See Chapter Sixteen for this and the subsequent history of Malta.)

Another great opponent of the advancing Turk was the republic of Venice, which was founded in the fifth century. Wordsworth in his famous sonnet, and Ruskin in his *Stones of Venice*, have commemorated her greatness, but it is hard for us today to realise the importance of Venice in the Middle Ages. From very early times the small islands of the lagoon had been peopled by fisher folk, and these were later augmented by refugees from the successive invasions of Lombardy, that of Attila the Hun being one of the worst. Only on the lagoons and marshes of the Venetian coast could these unhappy people, who had fled from the splendid cities of the Roman province of Venetia, feel secure, and it was from these humble and inauspicious beginnings that a great state emerged.

Gradually, the scattered people of the shallow lagoons had coalesced into large communities and one great city arose on the collection of islands. Of the western empire, either prolonged or revived, Venice was independent. She was nominally subject to the emperor of Constantinople, but in reality was in a position to dictate terms to her suzerain.

The enemies of Venice were the architects of the republic. Pepin the Frank, the father of Charlemagne, tried to conquer the Venetians from the sea, and his defeat led to the concentration of the Venetians at Rialto. The first of the doges of Venice to be elected there was Angelo Particiaco, and during his reign the first church of St Mark was begun and the body of the saint brought from

Alexandria to Venice. In the course of the next two centuries the community increased in wealth and power, and the seal was set upon Venetian supremacy in the Adriatic by the attacks of the Libirnian pirates from the Dalmatian coast.

It became necessary for Venice to build a fleet, and in the year 1000 the doge Pietro Orseolo II attacked and crushed the pirates in their strongholds. The doge assumed the title of Duke of Dalmatia and in commemoration of his victory there took place the annual ceremony on Ascension Day in which the doge solemnly wedded Venice to the sea. For Venice was now supreme in the Adriatic and for the next 500 years was to enjoy a lucrative position as the carrier and go-between of Europe with the east. The crusades proved most profitable to Venice, for armies coming from north-western Europe to be transported across the Mediterranean had to use ships provided by the republic.

The constitution of Venice as it gradually developed to its final form in the twelfth and thirteenth centuries was that of an oligarchy, the rule of the noble families. Indeed the term 'Venetian oligarchy' has become the description of any society ruled by the few, and Disraeli applied it to the rulers of England in the period from 1688-1832, when the British aristocracy were the governing class. The suffrage in Venice belonged only to the patrician caste whose ancestors had sat in the council. Above them came the senate which discussed, deliberated and legislated; but from about 1310 onwards there was parallel with the senate, the Council of Ten, an executive body concerned with public safety and possessing great power. Above both senate and council came the Collegio, or cabinet, which handled all affairs of state. At the last, above all others, was the doge and his council. This intricate structure had been evolved to prevent the development of either democracy or absolutism; by distributing power among a number of wealthy citizens the prosperity of the state was to be assured.

The securing of supremacy in the Adriatic, followed in the twelfth century by the crusades, gave the Venetians their greatest opportunity. As the Levant was opened to Christian powers, Venice secured valuable rights in the cities of the coasts, trading rights and special quarters. The Venetians began to claim for themselves the exclusive right to trade in the eastern Mediterranean.

They were not without rivals. On the western side of Italy was the republic of Genoa, a state which had arisen from obscure beginnings in struggles against the Moslems. It was associated at first with another state, Pisa, but fell out later with this ally, which was crushed by the Genoese in 1284. Sardinia had been retaken from the Moslems ere this, and seaports in Spain were also won back from the infidel. Genoese trade expanded into the Levant and the Black Sea. Just as with the East India Company in India, both Genoese and Venetians were constrained to build forts and equip fleets to protect their trading-posts in these distant areas. Like Venice, Genoa earned great profits from the crusades.

It was inevitable that these two powers should come into conflict, and for over 130 years there was a succession of wars between them. These conflicts were undertaken purely for economic reasons—they are classic wars in the terms of economic materialism. They were fought only for trade and no other consideration entered into them. More than once Genoa nearly overwhelmed Venice. In 1299 at Curzola, in the Adriatic, Venice was signally defeated. The Visconti ruler of Milan acted as peacemaker. Again in 1354 the Venetians were beaten at Sapienza, losing their entire fleet, but the Genoese did not press their victory to the destruction of Venice. Then in the final struggle in 1380 the Genoese, under their admiral Luciano Doria, sailed into the Adriatic and defeated the Venetian navy in its home waters. The Venetians chose Vettor Pisani as their admiral and he succeeded in blocking the Genoese in their turn and compelling them to surrender. The contest between Venice and Genoa has a similarity to that of Rome and Carthage, for Venice, like Rome, could endure for a final battle, whereas her enemy was exhausted by her own victories.

Genoa never recovered from the defeat of 1380, and although she remained a wealthy state right down to the French Revolution, she never again seriously rivalled Venice. The latter had, however, to contend from the fifteenth century onward with a much more dangerous enemy, the Ottoman Turks. The course of events which led up to this encounter was as follows.

The Venetians (and Genoese) were bankers, brokers and carriers for Europe. The Third Crusade, the first of these expeditions to go by sea, was carried in ships hired from the Italian maritime republics. For such transactions the creditors, like modern banks, required lodgement of securities, and in the absence of money, other possessions, such as crown jewels and estates, were pawned to the Venetians. The greatest 'job' of this type successfully put over by Venice was the infamous Fourth Crusade. Not only was the whole crusading body shipped overseas by Venice, but the expedition was conducted as a business transaction. The eastern empire was subverted and a Latin empire set up in its place. The Venetians secured at one stroke a huge profit as well as substantial territorial gains. The islands of the Aegean, with Crete and Rhodes, became Venetian possessions, and Venice had a powerful hold on Constantinople and various places on the mainland of Greece. This was in 1204, and Venice maintained her place as a first-class Mediterranean power until the end of the sixteenth century. Pope Innocent III who had launched for the recovery of the Holy Land this enterprise, which had become an orgy of vice and plundering, robbery and murder, tried to punish the evil-doers, but the Venetian principle of business first, last and always triumphed. The Venetians found the Turks too useful as business men to desire a real crusade against them and their influence was decisive in destroying the crusading movement.

There was a great outcry in Europe against the Venetians for having dealt with the Turks, and they were soon to discover that those who made agreements with the Turks would need the proverbial long spoon. The later centuries of Venetian history are occupied with two disastrous policies: the decision to become a land power on the Italian mainland and to engage in warfare with the Turks. The Venetian government could plead necessity for both policies. To prevent a blockade it was necessary to have possession of part of the mainland, but other Italian states, like Milan, were jealous of Venice. In any event the maintenance of large forces in Italy overstrained the state's resources, and even more serious were the four Turkish wars between 1499 and 1716. Cyprus came into possession of Venice in 1488, when the Christian Lusignan dynasty ended, and was retained for nearly a century until it fell to the

Turks. In *Othello*, the alarms of Turkish attack which sent him to Cyprus are extremely topical.

As a result of the Turkish wars the Venetians were gradually driven from their stations in the Levant and enfeebled by the loss of these and the discovery of new trade routes to the Far East and India. Even so, up to 1571 the Venetians were able to put forward a powerful fleet and in that year they took part in the defeat of the Turkish navy at Lepanto by Don Juan of Austria. By this victory the Turks were prevented from controlling the whole western Mediterranean, but they could still make the passage of merchant shipping to the Levant an extremely hazardous business. From 1453 onwards, when they captured Constantinople, the Turks drove on into the Balkans, and in 1529 they had penetrated as far as Vienna. Here they were halted, and from the half-century, which saw a successful resistance to them on land in eastern Europe and the destruction of their fleet at Lepanto, dates the resurgence of Europe to a position of dominance. The door to the East, which the crusaders had sought to force, the Venetians to negotiate, and the Polos to open by a land route to China through centrol Asia, was at last opened, or rather another door was found.

After the failure of the crusades, it was in the natural swing of the pendulum that the Moslems should return to the attack against Europe, but it was not until the fifteenth and sixteenth centuries that the Turkish menace became most acute. The Moslems had surged into Europe right up to the Pyrenees in the eighth century, but after that the tide had gradually receded in the West, while in the East the eastern Roman Empire had kept the Moslems away from entry into Europe at the other extremity. The wicked Fourth Crusade weakened the eastern empire beyond recovery and as a result the Turks pressed into Europe. The fall of Constantinople was only the last act of the tragedy and thereafter the Turkish armies forced their way deeper and deeper into the Balkans. In 1521, Solyman the Magnificent took Belgrade. In 1526 at the battle of Mohacz, Solyman destroyed the Hungarian army and killed their king. He then marched on and besieged Vienna, but was driven back and it was not until 1682 that the Turks again made an attack upon Vienna, or went so far into Europe. In 1683 they were beaten decisively by John Sobieski and from then on the Turkish power steadily declined.

In the Mediterranean, however, the Turkish ruler Solyman did great damage to European trade and to European peoples. In 1516 the Amir of Algiers invited two brothers, Arouj and Khair-ed-din, later known to history as the Barbarossas or 'red beards', to assist him in getting rid of the Spanish garrison which held the original island of Algiers. The brothers drove out the Spaniards, but as they were only concerned with their own interests they soon killed the amir and took charge of the town. Khair-ed-din was the founder of the Pashalik or Deylik of Algiers. Barbarossa made his homage to the Sultan of Constantinople and was by him appointed Admiral and Regent of Algiers. At first the piracy which was conducted from Algiers was levied upon the vessels of the emperor Charles V, who at war with the sultan. But when Barbarossa was succeeded by Dragut and the alliance which had existed between the French and the Turks was ended, the pirates of Algiers attacked any and every vessel they encountered on the seas. The cargoes were divided between the state, the shipowners, the captains and the crews, while the sailors and passengers on the captured ships were reduced to slavery.

The emperor Charles V endeavoured to take Algiers, but his fleet and army were dispersed and his attempt failed in 1541. From then on the centre of the Barbary pirates was Algiers and, despite all opposition, they continued to range the Mediterranean and to be a menace to shipping. Several times the fleets of the European nations bombarded Algiers and partially destroyed it, but on each occasion the pirate nest was rebuilt. One of the most famous of these attacks was by a British squadron under Lord Exmouth in 1816, but it was not until 1830 that the piracy of Algiers was at last put down by the French conquest which was to lead to the occupation of the whole of Algeria, Morocco and Tunisia by France. The country behind Algiers was, of course, completely neglected as regards agriculture, and the net result of the occupation of North Africa by the Moslems was the ruin of the granary of Rome, as it had once been called by the ancients.

Here it is perhaps not out of place briefly to describe the occupation of North Africa by the French. Between 1830 and 1920 the French occupied Algeria outright and established protectorates over Morocco and Tunisia. There was considerable fighting in the conquest of Algeria, but at the end of it the province was more thoroughly under the control of Europeans than any territory in Asia or Africa. Out of the population of seven millions, one million were well-established French men and women, while the natives possessed only the most backward and miserable parts of the country. The former pirate haunt became one of the few really large cities in Africa, with a population predominantly European.

The native quarter of Algiers during the French regime was almost indescribably filthy, yet in this same Casbah it is easy to find some magnificent palaces of the pashas of Algiers. A gloomy gateway admits to a really fine house with spacious halls and magnificently tiled floors. The ornamentation of the tiles and the Moorish arches is in the flowered style of the Moslems. The prohibition against depicting either human or animal form has nearly always impeded the Moslem artist, but he has thereby been forced to resort to some very lovely flower designs or to using the beautiful Arabic script of the Koran to decorate his palaces and Mosques.

The thieves' kitchen, which was Algiers for some four centuries, was in the habit of electing a pasha, or chief robber, but as may be imagined he did not live easily or long and, in fact, only one of the pashas was able to retire from office and live comfortably on the proceeds of his industry. In some of the palaces a slight depression in the floor was used to catch the blood of a pasha murdered there in pre-French days. In the old native city are the palaces of the various temporary monarchs and their chief henchmen or rivals. Proceeding across the top of the hill from the Casbah—incidentally, the view of the bay of Algiers from the heights is far superior to that of the bay of Naples—one comes upon some lovely villas which are still in use and where one can see some fine examples of the old Turkish work. The Turks were, of course, great believers in hot baths, and in these old villas one sees the Turkish-style bath which is very deep and narrow so that the man must have stood up in it while water was poured down on him. From the roof of a villa high above Algiers one can command on a fine moonlight night a splendid view of the city, and as one looks over it the marvel grows that so fine a sight can even at the present day cover so much that is sordid and brutal, almost as much of filth and horror as in the not-so-distant past when the corsairs ruled. The endeavour of the French was to make the natives into Frenchmen or rather into French citizens, and so Algeria was part of France in a legal and political sense. Morocco and Tunisia were not in the same position, but were protectorates and contained a much smaller number of French settlers.

European control existed over most of the southern shores of the Mediterranean just as it did during the earlier part of our story, for in 1911 Italy gained control over Tripoli, or Libya as it was afterwards called, and when Egypt was under British suzerainty the whole of the African coast was once more ruled by the heirs of Roman civilisation.

NOTE : The prehistoric remains in Malta, going back to the neolithic and bronze ages, are of the greatest interest. The most important are referred to as sanctuaries or temples, and there are about fifteen in Malta and two in the neighbouring island of Gozo. They are described as Megalithic buildings meant for religious worship and dating to the 3rd millennium BC, in short they are relics of a belief older than any of the world's leading religions. The sanctuary at Hal Tarxien in Malta has been the most thoroughly excavated and is some 40ft below the ground, hence its name of Hypogeum. Some of the stairs in the descent are not easy—almost as though designed to bring about a fall; perhaps the ancient worshippers used the sanctuary as a place in which to store treasure and were therefore anxious to preserve its secrets. In the centre of the place is an altar, with a stoup to catch the victim's blood; there are rings at the side of the chamber where the victims—human or animal?— had been fastened before the sacrifice. At the sides of the chamber are holes through which the guardians of the place could watch anyone who was in the chamber. Easy to muse in such a place upon the strange mystery of the martyrdom of man; the tragedies of unknown beings slain in the vast anteroom to written records which we call pre-history; easy to imagine in such a place, half lit by feeble electric lamps, the slow appearance of some gloomy face of a man-devil obsessed with the worship of his forgotten deity.

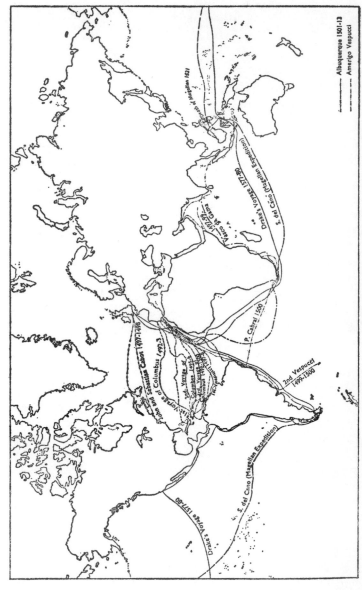

Map 8: Voyages of the European Explorers (15th-16th centuries)

CHAPTER FIFTEEN

THE DOOR OPENED

THE PORTUGUESE were the first nation to smash the deadlock created by the European failure to break through the Near East. Portugal was freed from the Moors and united earlier than Spain and was thus enabled to turn her attention to affairs outside her own territory. This she needed to do for her soil was poor and, her whole seaboard being outside the Mediterranean, she could hardly trade with the East without the good graces of the Genoese and the Venetians, unless another way to the riches of Cathay could be found. To that end a great part of Portuguese brain and energy was directed. Early in the fifteenth century the Portuguese discovered and annexed the Canary Islands and began the exploration of the West African coast. This work was pushed forward greatly by a distinguished member of the Portuguese royal house, Prince Henry the Navigator. Expeditions to explore the Atlantic and the African coast became a regular feature of Portuguese life. Madeira, the Azores and the Cape Verde Islands were discovered and before the Prince died in 1460 the explorers had reached the Gulf of Guinea. A system of leasing out the African trade to merchants was instituted on condition that they explored another hundred miles of coast each year. In 1487, Bartholomew Diaz rounded the Cape of Good Hope and sailed into the Indian Ocean, but was compelled by his crew to turn back and leave the glory of reaching India in 1487 to Vasco da Gama, whose exploits are commemorated by Camoens in the great Portuguese national epic, *The Lusiad*.

Thus an alternative route by sea to India had been discovered and two great monopolies were endangered. The Venetians saw

P

themselves faced by total ruin with the loss of their position as middlemen between East and West. Similarly, the Arabs were threatened by the appearance of the Portuguese in the Indian Ocean where they had for long held a monopoly of the carrying trade. Immediately European exploration of the world involved the European powers in war. Portugal sent fleets to support her traders and found it necessary to annex territories right round the huge stretch of coastline from their homeland, along the African coasts to the Persian Gulf, India and even to Maçao in China. For some one hundred and fifty years Portugal was thus the world's leading power and her remaining colonies in Africa and Asia show the former extent of her empire.

The ruin of the Venetians, which Portugal had begun, was completed by the Genoese, although the latter did not launch great expeditions themselves. One of the seamen of Genoa, Christopher Columbus, after being turned down by Portugal, persuaded the king and queen of Spain, a country recently united by the conquest of the last Moors in the kingdom of Granada, to finance an expedition across the Atlantic. It was now known by geographers that the world was round and there had been conjectures as to the possibility of sailing across the western ocean to India. In 1492 Columbus crossed the Atlantic and claimed the Bahamas for Spain. He thought he had reached India, hence the term West Indies and Indians. It had not occurred to him or to anyone else that a huge unknown continent lay between Europe and Asia. It was on his third voyage that he reached the mainland of central America, though even then he still considered himself to be in Asia, and only after many further explorations by other men was the true geographical position realised. Magellan, a Portuguese in the Spanish service, led an expedition which was the first circumnavigation of the globe; he himself was killed in the Philippines, but he had found the way, through the straits now bearing his name, into the Pacific, and his subordinates sailed home to Spain round the Cape of Good Hope.

Some other Genoese, John and Sebastian Cabot, in the pay of Henry VII of England, sailed from Bristol in 1496 to North America and Newfoundland. Nearly another century, however, was to pass before the English began to turn to account their own discoveries in this New World. With their rivalry with the Spaniards, and with Drake's voyage round the world. we have no more to do here than with the Spanish discovery and conquests of Mexico and Peru. Suffice to say that the centre of world interest had passed from the Mediterranean to the Atlantic. The nations which bordered on the western ocean had in the Middle Ages either been comparatively unimportant or wasted their strength in endeavours to reach the centre of interest, the Inland Sea. Now their attention was turned to the great New World with its apparently inexhaustible wealth and its openings for people of energetic character who were tired of Europe. First, Portugal entered the new domain and obtained a huge prize in the shape of Brazil, but she was soon overwhelmed by Spain and for sixty years was herself actually annexed to the Spanish crown. The Spaniards were not left in peace. Their possessions were harried by English and Dutch privateers and these nations together with the French, Danes and Swedes spread into the dominions which the Pope had allotted to Spain and Portugal. (See Note, p 224.) The Spanish expansion into North America was checked and many of the West Indian islands were torn from Spain to become colonies of Britain and France. The British, French and Dutch even succeeded in penetrating to the mainland of Central and South America and establishing colonies there. Two great western European nations took no part in this scramble for the Americas. Italy and Germany were disunited or absorbed by religious strife, and it was not until several centuries later that they would be able to enter the colonial market.

With the Venetian monopoly ended, Venice slowly declined and trade with the Levant became a second or third-rate interest. The Indian trade was conducted round the Cape without the help or hindrance of Arab or Venetian. The main issue in the Indian Ocean, as in the Atlantic and Caribbean, was between the Europeans themselves. Portugal was outstripped by Holland, another example of a small country which for a time led the world. Then the principal rivals in the east, as in the west, became France and Britain.

These rivalries of the European nations were rendered far worse by the break-up of the old religious unity of Europe. When the

Pope divided the New World between Spain and Portugal and
ignored the claims of England, France and Holland, he seemed to
anticipate the days when these nations would exhibit heretical
tendencies, whereas a fervent orthodoxy was one of the outstanding characteristics of both Spain and Portugal. In the twenties of
the sixteenth century the Reformation movement was begun by
Luther in Germany, from which arose Protestant as opposed to
Catholic Christianity. It was not until 1648 that the Treaty of
Westphalia ended the armed conflicts of Europe and stabilised the
boundaries of Catholic and Protestant states. By that time the unity
of European men had been completely broken and instead of
Christendom there emerged the Great Power system whereby
Europe and (through Europe's extension overseas) the rest of the
world has suffered a great war at intervals of every fifty years or
less. European men no longer thought of themselves as members
one of another but as rivals in trade and war. They contrived to
look down on the coloured races of the world and to regard the
European as in his own right a superior being, even though this
feeling did not lead them to unite with their fellow Europeans.

After the fall of the western Roman Empire, the Christian
Church, the sole institution surviving from the early centuries AD,
had been compelled to undertake the civilising of the nations of
western Europe. Most of the Church's great thinkers and statesmen,
lay as well as ecclesiastic, had been dominated by ideas not of
nationality, but of empire and commonwealth. The Roman Empire
had never really died, hence the effort to perpetuate it in the Holy
Roman Empire to which, in theory, all the nations of Europe owed
homage. The empire was to control the secular sphere and to
ensure law and good government all under the tutelage of the
Church which was the supreme goverment and society. The end of
man was not in this world. He had been created a son of God and
was destined to eternal life. The purpose of the Church was the
salvation of souls, and the state existed to further that supreme
activity by making conditions suitable for the best growth of the
Christian life.

As the barbarian nations of the west grew up into the Christendom of the early Middle Ages two tendencies appeared which were

mutually opposed. The one to which most of the greatest minds of
the eleventh, twelfth and thirteenth centuries inclined was towards the idea of internationalism, of a League of Nations, in short,
of Christendom. The other tendency was to accentuate the differences among Europeans and thus to lead towards the separate
nationalisms which eventually split up Christendom into the Great
Powers. The second tendency triumphed, but it was not before the
former had produced some very great achievements.

In the thirteenth century the Papacy reached the height of its
power. Innocent III is perhaps the only man who can claim to have
ruled western Europe, for one after another of its monarchs were,
in turn, humbled before him, in countries as distant from each
other as England, Portugal and Sweden. The Pope was the arbiter
of Europe and although the crusading movement no longer evoked
its previous enthusiasm, crusades were still launched by the Pope
with formidable results, as the Albigenses, the Greek emperor, and
Frederick II could testify. There was thus in Europe a proper conception of international law, an institution to administer it and
occasionally an army to enforce it.

In other spheres we may note the great development of Gothic
architecture as seen in the cathedrals, castles and guildhalls; the
poetry of Dante in which the whole life of man and of this world
was shown in relation to eternity; the stupendous all-embracing
synthesis of thought in the work of the philosopher, St Thomas
Aquinas; the great religious orders of Francis of Assisi and of
Dominic; the growth of parliamentary institutions; and the use of
Latin as a *lingua franca* among the educated in every country. But
the unitive tendency was fighting a losing battle against the separat-
ist movement towards nationalism. The barbarous tribes had
gradually coalesced into nations, and were now filled with a
healthy, vigorous national spirit which manifested itself not least
in the development of the vernacular tongues. For all his ideas of
universal monarchy, Dante had furthered the cause of nationalism
by choosing the Italian rather than the Latin as the language of his
great epic. In the fourteenth century he found imitators not only
in Italy but in other European countries. Chaucer in England
ensured the dominance of English over French and Latin. National

characteristics were hardened and in the fourteenth and fifteenth centuries it became increasingly common for nations to adhere to a national policy in clear defiance of the wishes of the Pope. The disastrous Hundred Years' War of England against France was opposed by both Pope and emperor, but it continued none the less. At its inception it was a case of French-speaking seigneurs on either side fighting out in tournament style their quarrels over certain lands. Before its close it had become a struggle between Englishmen and Frenchmen, and Shakespeare's *Henry V* is by no means anachronistic in portraying typical English troops (the king and his nobles as much as the archers) fighting on a foreign field.

It is quite obvious that in the opening years of the sixteenth century the European nations had come to full stature as we know them now. Although they still professed the same religion, they were no longer capable of concerted action as Christians, and the riches of the New World had added immeasurably to the rivalries already existing among them. Had there been no Reformation and no split in Latin Christendom the Europeans would perhaps have scrambled less violently for the Americas and the East, but there is no reason to suppose that they would have been more capable of united action than the Roman Catholic nations of today.

The Reformation happened, however, and the evil of religious differences was added to national hatreds. The whole scheme of Christendom was ruined. Furthermore, any pretence at a spiritual basis for western civilisation was progressively abandoned. In the Middle Ages, European society had been based on the conception of the Christian life with this world as merely the preparation for the next. In practice, there were, of course, many persons of purely materialistic outlook, but such people were compelled to pay lip homage to the prevailing ideas. With the division into Protestantism and Catholicism the power of the Church was greatly weakened. The separate churches into which Protestantism was at once divided made for further weakness; in combination with the vast increase in physical scientific knowledge and its application, this weakness led to a reduction in the Christian doctrine of the spiritual life so that by the time western influences in full force were exerted upon India and the Far East, the westerners appeared to the inhabitants of the ancient civilisations of India, China and Japan to be materialists, pure and simple.

These great consequences followed on the discovery of the New World. For the purpose of our survey it might be said that the Mediterranean had ceased to be one of the major important trade routes of the world, but more than that was involved. No longer was the Mediterranean world the home of empires, or the meeting-place of ideas. The secret of building great states had been discovered by the Atlantic nations. From the end of the sixteenth century to the end of the eighteenth the Mediterranean was really a backwater. To see it may have been, as Johnson said, the great object of travel, but the empires which he mentioned as being round its shores were dead empires. It was not until a world power (in the sense that no previous power had ever been) became interested in the Mediterranean as a highway to the East that its importance again revived.

During the eighteenth century the Mediterranean was an area which cultured Europeans loved to visit, providing that they did not stray into areas dominated by the Grand Turk. They loved to dig up Roman and Greek remains, to collect coins and statues, to pride themselves on having escaped the curse of medievalism with its barbaric outlook, and they really thought that they were living in a truly polished age, a worthy successor and reviver of the classic period of the Antonine princes. It is almost amusing to see this idea in possession of people as widely different as Gibbon the historian, the younger Pitt and Edmund Burke, all on the eve of the French Revolution, or in the early struggles with it.

People of taste in the eighteenth century were not content to admire classic remains, they also liked to restore them and even to build imitations of them, so that the modern builder with his run-up 'Tudor Grange' is only following a two-hundred-year-old precedent. For instance, at Rome in the Pincian gardens—which offers one of the loveliest views of Rome at eventide—or rather in the gardens of the Villa Borghese, which run on from the Pincian, there is a charming little lake and on the shore of the lake a temple to Aesculapius, the god of healing. These little buildings are charming to look at and seem to fit in well with their surroundings, but

they are too good to be true in the sense that we know that they
cannot really be ancient because they are too well preserved. And
when we realise their true age, they give to the scene a 'pretty-
pretty' effect, as though we were looking at stage scenery.

That was how the Mediterranean area appeared to tourists two
hundred years ago—a time when no one thought that it would
ever again be an area where the destinies of nations would be
decided. The northern shores were picturesque and culturally
delightful, whereas the southern shores were in the hands of
barbarians, such as the emperor of Morocco, whom Gibbon
stigmatises.

NOTE: The Bulls of Pope Alexander VI of 3 and 4 May 1493 are
here referred to. 'A Papal Bull granted to Spain all lands that lay
west, to Portugal all lands that lay east of a line drawn 100 leagues
towards the west and south from the Azores and Cape Verde
Islands.' (*The Expansion of Britain* by W. R. Kermack, 1925, p 10.)
The Bull became the basis of the Treaty of Tordesillas between
Portugal and Spain 'by which the Castilian and Portuguese governments determined the boundary line of their respective discoveries;
a line that secured the vast empire of Brazil to the latter, which
from priority of occupation should have belonged to their rivals'
(W. H. Prescott, *Conquest of Mexico*, ch VII note). 'By the Treaty
of Tordesillas (1494) this line was moved 370 leagues west of the
same point, which carried it through the Bahamas. Therefore when
the Portuguese admiral, Cabral, driven westward out of his intended
course on the Cape route to India, discovered the eastern angle of
South America where it juts out nearest to the Old World, forty
degrees east of the line of demarcation, Brazil became a Portuguese
possession. With this single exception, however, the effect of the
Papal Bull was to create a monopoly for Spain in the whole of the
mighty continent which, in the geographical ideas of the day,
stretched from pole to pole across the path of Europe in its
westward expansion.' (Kermack, *op cit*, p 10.)

According to Prescott, the basic idea behind this division of the
new lands was that they could be claimed by the Holy See, and
could then be bestowed upon any temporal potentate who would
undertake the work of conquest. This was more or less the view
advanced by the priest who accompanied Pizarro to Peru, and who
expounded it, via an interpreter, to the Inca, who thus learned with
astonishment that the Pope had bestowed his dominions upon the
king of Spain.

The idea behind the papal claims to apportionment of territory had a long pedigree. It probably went back to the alleged Donation of Constantine.

'These lofty pretentions of the successors of the humble fishermen of Galilee, far from being nominal, were acknowledged and appealed to as conclusive in controversies between nations' (Prescott, *ibidem*). Had the Reformation never come to split the unity of Christendom the position of the Pope as universal arbitor would presumably have endured, to assist, eg in the nineteenth century, partition of Africa. Some adjustment would have had to be made to allow for English claims to new countries. The Treaty of Tordesillas covers only Spain and Portugal because they were then the only European maritime powers. Other Catholic nations were not excluded because of heretical tendencies—the Lutheran outburst was nearly a generation away—but because they did not count as explorers and navigators. England was only just beginning to recover from the Wars of the Roses and her maritime expansion must have seemed very unlikely. Still the king of France, on hearing of the Pope's allocation of the New World to Spain and Portugal, remarked that he would like to see a copy of Adam's will.

Of the papal bulls, Bishop Creighton remarked: 'The Pope's solution of the difficulties likely to arise between Spain and Portugal was sufficiently accurate for the knowledge of his age.' (*History of the Papacy*, vol 3, p 171.) Also G. M. Thomson wrote: 'In the circumstances Pope Alexander's demarcation can only be considered an impressive exercise of level-headed and imaginative statesmanship.' (*Sir Francis Drake*, 1972, p 2.)

CHAPTER SIXTEEN

BRITAIN
ENTERS THE MEDITERRANEAN

THE FIRST effective entry of Britain into the Inland Sea was in the time of Cromwell, under whose rule she attained for a while the position of the first European military and naval power. In his zeal for the protection of English merchants and European Protestants generally, Cromwell interfered with the exactions of various potentates, such as the Bey of Tunis and the Grand Duke of Tuscany. The cruelties of the bloody Piedmontese towards the Protestants of Savoy, so unforgettably described in Milton's famous sonnet, were checked, as many other horrors have been, by the action of the British Navy off the coasts of the offenders. The appearance of Admiral Blake's squadron in the Mediterranean was a surprise to several exalted highnesses of the countries on its shores, and Blake proceeded to administer an even greater shock, for he was the first, in Clarendon's words, 'to teach ships of war to contemn castles on shore'. The Bey of Tunis, for one, found his castles and towns subjected to a naval bombardment, and hastened to give satisfaction to the government of England.

Robert Blake, parliamentarian and 'sea-soldier' (1599-1657) won fame by many bitter and successful battles with the Dutch. He hunted down and destroyed Prince Rupert's royalist ships, but the exploit which earned him Clarendon's commendation was his entry into the bay of Santa Cruz, in Teneriffe, to destroy the Spanish plate fleet under the guns of the shore batteries.

The defeat of the Spanish Armada and Cromwell's interference in

European affairs are the chief manifestations that England* had attained a foremost place not only in Europe but in the world generally. Yet it would be too much to speak, after Blake's expedition, of the British Mediterranean fleet, for Britain possessed no bases in the Mediterranean until 1704 when Gibraltar was taken from Spain in the War of the Spanish Succession. Ever since, Gibraltar has remained a British possession and although the Italians boasted that its defences would not stand up against air attack, in World War II 'The Rock' proved a thorn in the side of Italy and Germany. Gibraltar is, of course, the smaller of the Pillars of Hercules, but while its fellow is still left to the possession of goats and vagrants, Gibraltar has a large civilian population as well as its garrison. At the foot of the Rock clusters Spanish Town, with some twenty thousand inhabitants in ordinary times.

The British Empire was the largest of all the imperial systems known to history. In 1939 it included one quarter of the world's land surface, and probably more than a quarter of the human race. It is almost terrifying to contemplate what its power and resources could have been had the promise of 1763 been fulfilled and the whole of North America remained British. Yet this vast dominion was the latest in time of the European empires, as well as being the greatest. It was preceded by Portuguese, Spanish, French and Dutch possessions and inherited some of the territories formerly owned by each of these nations. The Portuguese and Dutch dropped out of the race for world power owing to the poverty of their natural resources, and small populations. The considerable remains of the Portuguese empire owe their continuance to the dominance of British sea power in the nineteenth century and to the British government's lack of aggression during that period. The Spaniards were first foiled in their progress toward universal empire by England, and the gradual decay of their power overseas, and its final

---

*England, not Britain, for the Scots did not begin to contribute to the British Empire until the fourth quarter of the eighteenth century, after the departure of what may well be termed England's greatest child, the United States. Even the term 'Great Britain' dates only from the Treaty of Union in 1707. For convenience both terms, Britain and England, are used in this chapter.

extinction, can be traced to the influence of their absolutist policy in church and state. Nevertheless, Spain, though deprived by her own folly of her colonies, has left an indelible mark on the world in the numerous Spanish-speaking communities which owe their origin to her.

France is the European power which has suffered most from England's acquisition of empire. Her colonial possessions as they were in 1939 were acquired mostly in the nineteenth century, but they could not compare in wealth with those which she lost— Canada and India—at the conclusion of the Seven Years' War in 1763.

After contests with Holland and Spain, England's principal antagonist was France. Spain was often the more or less unwilling ally of France, and it was to prevent a juncture of the Spanish Atlantic and Mediterranean fleets and the exit of the French Mediterranean fleet into the Atlantic, that Gibraltar was retained. Gibraltar was not sufficient, however, as a base to control the movement of shipping in the Mediterranean and to protect British trade with Italy, Egypt and the Levant. Other bases were required and during most of the eighteenth century, when a 'ding-dong' struggle was waged with France, England possessed Minorca in the Balearic Islands, where Port Mahon gave her a fine base for operations against the French fleet in the Mediterranean.

'Minorca was the Malta of the 18th century. The island represented to England all that Malta represents now, to France it represented much more, for she was not at that time accustomed to our presence in the Mediterranean. Tangier, indeed, we had held and given up, and Gibraltar had already been English ground for four years when Minorca was captured. These places were only at the gates of the Mediterranean, whereas the possession of Minorca meant that England was becoming a Mediterranean power, a consummation that France was resolved to hinder if possible.' (*The Lost Possessions of England*, by W. F. Lord, 1898, p 98.) Minorca was captured by the British in 1708 in the War of the Spanish Succession, and like Gibraltar was retained at the Peace of Utrecht.

In 1756 at the beginning of the Seven Years' War, the French attacked Minorca with an army of 15,000 men. The small British force under Lt-Gen William Blakeney held out for seventy days. There was an attempt to relieve the garrison under the incompetent direction of Admiral Byng who, as is well known, was court-martialled, condemned and shot, *pour encourager les autres*. Blakeney on the other hand was given a peerage as Baron Blakeney in the peerage of Ireland, a colonelcy in the 27th Foot, the Red Ribbon (K.B.) and eventually a burial in Westminster Abbey. He was eighty-four at the time of the siege, lived to eighty-nine and 'must dispute with Marshal Radetsky and the Eunuch Narses the reputation of being the most extraordinary old man known to history' (Lord, *op cit*, p 119). At the Peace of Paris in 1763 Minorca was restored to Britain, though in return Britain restored to Spain both Cuba and the Philippines, which curiously enough were the last Spanish colonies remaining at the time of the Spanish-American War of 1898. During the later tenure of the island in 1770, it is interesting to note that a Russian fleet put into Port Mahon, a remote foreshadowing of the presence of the Russian navy in the Mediterranean today.

Again, in 1782, the French succeeded in recapturing Minorca. The British government would never agree to garrison the island with sufficient troops, and in this second siege the British were outnumbered ten to one. Moreover, this capitulation took place in the closing stages of the war with the American colonies. France and Spain had declared war against Britain, which had temporarily lost command of the sea. At the Peace of Paris in 1784, Minorca remained Spanish. Apart from its value as a base, it was an important place for harrying French commerce, so that when Britain was again at war with France in 1798, the recapture of Minorca was a very popular move. Gen Sir Charles Stuart captured it easily but it was finally ceded to Spain by the Treaty of Amiens in 1802. Its importance as a base controlling British passage of the Mediterranean was lessened by the capture of Malta in 1800.

The shifting nature of the British presence in the Mediterranean can be gauged from the following table which shows the places garrisoned from England from the reign of Charles II to that of Victoria.

1661-1684	Tangier
1684-1704	No base
1704-1713	Gibraltar
1713-1756	Minorca and Gibraltar
1756-1763	Gibraltar
1763-1782	Minorca and Gibraltar
1782-1794	Gibraltar
1794-1797	Corsica and Gibraltar
1798-1800	Minorca and Gibraltar
1800-1802	Malta, Minorca and Gibraltar
1802-1811	Malta and Gibraltar
1811-1814	Sicily, Malta and Gibraltar
1815-1863	The Ionian Islands, Malta and Gibraltar
1863-1879	Malta and Gibraltar
1878-1882	Cyprus, Malta and Gibraltar
1882-1945	Alexandria, Cyprus, Malta and Gibraltar

In the eighteenth century, war with France was so frequent that she began to assume the appearance of an hereditary enemy of England. Canada became British in 1763, and Britain was paramount in India. In a war of revenge the French were instrumental in causing Britain to lose the American colonies, but the great financial drain occasioned by this war on France's already strained resources brought on the bankruptcy which accelerated the French Revolution. The internal weakness of the republic which followed the old French monarchy exposed it to the ambitions of its First Consul, Napoleon. He, like later dictators, could not maintain his position at home save by launching schemes of conquest abroad, and thus France embarked on her final struggle with England which was terminated after more than twenty years of warfare (broken only by the 'Munich' peace of Amiens in 1802) by the decisive battle of Waterloo in 1815.

From this struggle there resulted important consequences. At its conclusion France was no longer a rival of Britain, which had by then achieved absolute supremacy at sea. From 1815-1914 Britain, by virtue of her sea-power, industrial wealth and huge empire, was the world's chief power. It is probably true that even without the growth of the USA, Germany, Japan and Russia, this position would have been undermined by the inventions of weapons of war—the submarine and the aeroplane—which militated against the omnipotence of a surface fleet. Another consequence for Britain of Napoleon's career was her realisation of the importance of the Mediterranean as a highway of empire. After the loss of the American colonies, fresh dominions were being created in India, Canada and Australia, and though the Indian Empire was only in its beginnings, Britain had become the dominant European power in India. In those days, possessions in India meant a flow of treasure and goods to the ruling power, unlike the present time when Britain is debtor to India. Napoleon conceived the plan of establishing French influence in Asia and at the same time breaking the back of the British Empire. Like Hitler and Mussolini in 1940-42, he struck at Egypt. His expedition in 1798 was well planned, and only British sea power prevented it from being a success. On his way to Egypt, Napoleon captured Malta, which was still ruled by the Knights of St John, but Nelson was hot on his heels and Malta was soon cleared of its French garrison. Nelson perceived the value of Malta. 'I consider it,' he said, 'as a most important outwork to India. I hope we shall never give it up.'

At the conclusion of the war with France, Malta remained in the British Empire, mainly, it is true, owing to the Maltese themselves, who did not wish to return to the rule of the Knights of St John, rather than to any far-sighted policy of imperial expansion.

The fleet which had escorted Napoleon's army to Egypt had been wiped out by Nelson at the battle of the Nile, thus stranding the French forces in Egypt. But there was no British army ready to deal with them and Napoleon decided to try to carry out his plans without possessing command of the sea. He defeated the rulers of Egypt at the battle of the Pyramids, and having left a force to occupy Egypt as his base, marched boldly into Palestine. His plan was to reduce the important seaport of Acre and then, by enlisting Mohammedan support, to carry out his original scheme of striking at India, perhaps by proceeding overland to the Persian Gulf and thence by sea. Though his plans bear a striking resemblance to those of Hitler, this is no mere matter of historical coincidence but the natural strategy imposed upon a great continental land power trying to overcome the sea power of Britain. Napoleon, in 1798, had found invasion of Britain impracticable, as Hitler was to discover in 1940-41. They both, therefore, struck with all their might at Egypt, the neck of land connecting the land masses of the Old World. Once in possession of Egypt they would bestride the communications of the British Empire. Even before the cutting of a canal through the isthmus, possession of Egypt by a European power hostile to Britain was a menace to her empire, since means could then be found to transport troops against India by a much shorter route than the British could use to send reinforcements round the Cape of Good Hope. Napoleon was foiled at Acre by a resistance inspired by Capt Sir Sidney Smith, the man he considered to have caused him to miss his destiny,* and realising the futility of his schemes in the east he abandoned his army in Egypt and returned to France.

Napoleon's forces in Egypt were subsequently overcome by the British, but the tradition of French interest in the Levant persisted and it was through French initiative and by French engineers that the Suez Canal was cut in 1869. The story of the canal is far older than that of the modern waterway which was the creation of Ferdinand de Lesseps. Whereas the present Suez Canal reached its centenary in 1969, canals across the Isthmus of Suez had lasted for several centuries, and many attempts were made to link the Mediterranean with the Red Sea. The natural meeting-place of three continents and the gateway between east and west, Egypt was the key to empire and after a period of 2,500 to 3,000 years in which the country of the Pharaohs was a great and splendid power, one empire after another has controlled Egypt—Persia, Greece, Rome, the Arabs, the Turks, the French for a few years, and then the British for over seventy years.

---

* A captain in the Royal Navy in 1782, William Sidney Smith was knighted for his services in 1790-92 in advising the king of Sweden in the war with Russia. His life was colourful and adventurous. Captured by the French in 1796, he escaped in 1798. He was sent on a diplomatic mission to Turkey, whence he went to Acre and to what was his most important assignment. Smith served in the Napoleonic wars in several spheres of operations and was later made an admiral and a KCB. Brave and energetic, he was yet a sore trial to several of his superior officers. He died in 1840 in Paris and was buried there in the Père Lachaise cemetery.

Q

The Isthmus of Suez is a narrow neck of land joining Egypt to Asia, and in olden times the waters of the Red Sea came even nearer to the Mediterranean than they do now. The Nile reaches the open sea through several mouths in the delta and the Pelusiac branch entered the Mediterranean near the isthmus. As far back as the reign of Sesostris, a Pharaoh of the 20th Dynasty about 2000 BC, Egyptian engineers constructed a canal which linked the Pelusiac branch of the Nile eastward through the Wadi Tumilat and then turned south into the Bitter Lakes to reach the Red Sea. This canal, despite its somewhat devious and twisting course, none the less served its purpose of allowing shipping to cross the isthmus. It had a long life for it did not apparently fall into disuse until the seventh century BC. Then the Pharaoh Necho, of 612 BC, began the recutting of the canal but is reputed to have desisted because of a warning that invaders could use it to penetrate his country. It was under the rule of the Persian conquerors of Egypt that the canal was restored to use. When the Greek dynasty of the Ptolemies took over the country, the idea of cutting straight through the isthmus was rejected on the ground that the level of the Red Sea was higher than that of the Mediterranean and that the cutting of the canal would mean the flooding of the country. This misconception as to the different levels of the two seas persisted into modern times. The Ptolemies therefore contented themselves with reconditioning the old canal, and under Roman rule the canal was again repaired and given a new direction over part of its course. It was united with the main stream of the Nile at Babylon, the modern Cairo. The reconstruction was named from the Emperor Trajan who reigned AD 98-117, and it remained navigable until the third or fourth century. After some centuries of neglect it was reopened by Amru, the Arab governor of Egypt in 641-42 and not disused until 776, when it was closed by orders of the then Caliph. Thus the isthmus remained closed to shipping for 1,100 years. Other ways of reaching the riches of the east had been found, as described in previous chapters, by the voyages of the Europeans in the fifteenth to the eighteenth centuries, voyages which opened up the world as we know it now.

The project of the Suez Canal was not, however, forgotten and it was due to the French that it ultimately became a reality. Both commercial and military reasons combined to make the idea attractive. The decline of the Mediterranean ports when the Cape route became known and usable had not left Marseilles and the south of France unaffected. France would stand greatly to gain if she could deal directly with the eastern world by sea through the Mediterranean instead of by the tedious and costly transportation of goods at Suez by camel until they were placed on ship again at the north of the isthmus. During the whole of the eighteenth century Britain and France were rivals for empire, and the possession of Egypt, or at least of the isthmus, would strike a blow against Britain's possessions in the east. Hence the importance of Napoleon's invasion of Egypt.

A French engineer on Napoleon's staff, J. M. Lepère, reported against the direct route for the canal because of the persistent belief in the differing levels of the seas, north and south. Lepère wanted to reopen the ancient canal of the Pharaohs. At last, in 1855, a concession was granted by the Viceroy of Egypt, the Khedive Mohammed Pasha Al-Said, to Ferdinand de Lesseps giving him permission to establish a company to finance the scheme, and to cut a canal through the Isthmus of Suez. It was after the Khedive Mohammed Said that Port Said, at the northern end of the canal, was named. In 1858 the shares of the Suez Canal Company were put on the market; 80,000 were allotted to Great Britain and 20,000 to the USA. Neither of the allocations was taken up, though there were many small applications from other countries, giving the venture a truly international flavour. The French took 207,160 shares and the Egyptian government (ie the Khedive) 177,642. The Americans were apparently not interested and, as for the British, they did everything in their power to prevent the canal being made, a curious attitude in view of the canal's subsequent importance in Britain's foreign policies. The all-powerful legendary Lord Stratford de Redcliffe, the British Ambassador to Turkey, produced delay after delay in the granting of the concession, and as an alternative, the British proposed a scheme for linking Alexandria with Suez by rail. But at last the hour came and on 25 April 1859 de Lesseps started work on the Pelusiac shore of the Mediterranean. The canal was completed in the summer of 1869. It was then 100 miles in length with a width varying at the surface from 150 to 300ft. The depth was 26ft and the width at bottom 72ft. The course was very direct, having only fourteen curves over its whole length.

The ocean power which possessed a huge empire in India, Africa and the Pacific was now confronted with a serious problem. A voyage to India through the new canal saved 4,000 miles, or a fortnight's steaming by the standards of 1869, thus presenting unmistakable strategic and commercial advantages to Britain. The canal was open to vessels of all nations, but the empire could not well be dependent upon the goodwill of a trading company or on the uncertain favour of the Turkish nominal viceroy, the Khedive or ruler of Egypt. So, in 1875, Disraeli bought for Britain from the luxury-loving and wasteful Khedive a major interest in the shares of the Suez Canal Company for £4 million.

Egypt has always possessed a nationalist party ready to use violence against Europeans who seek to exploit the country. In 1882, the Gladstone government was compelled to intervene in Egypt with the practical result that it became a British protectorate although still nominally part of the now decadent Turkish Empire. Egypt depends on the Nile, and the upper reaches of the river were controlled by the Mahdi and his Dervishes who had destroyed General Gordon at Khartoum in 1885. Public opinion in England, combined with the need to control the headwaters of the Nile, resulted in the despatch of a British force against the Sudan, which was conquered at the battle of Omdurman in 1898 when the forces of the Mahdi were destroyed. Another part of the crumbling Turkish realm—Cyprus—had been leased from Turkey in 1878, thus adding yet another to Britain's line of potential bases in the Mediterranean. In 1839 Aden had been taken over as a coaling station on the route to India, and in 1886 Socotra also was annexed.

The position in the Near East during the nineteenth century was complicated by the decline of the Turkish Empire, a decline which as already noted in Chapter 14, had begun with their repulse from Vienna in 1683. The second siege of Vienna marked the furthest advance into Europe of the Turkish armies. Some forty years before that the Turkish Empire had reached its greatest extent—the whole of the Balkans, Greece and the islands of the Aegean, the full length of the North African seaboard, Egypt, Palestine, Syria, Asia Minor and the Arabian peninsula. In the first half of the sixteenth century Turkish naval power was supreme in the western Mediterranean as well as the eastern portion of the sea. In 1538 Khair-ed-Din, Barbarossa, the Sultan's admiral, defeated Andrea Doria, admiral of the fleets of Spain, the Empire and Venice. This Barbarossa and his brother Aruj and their successors rendered the North African coastline hostile to all European shipping until the French captured Algiers in 1831. It was not until the successful defence of Malta (1565) and the Christian victory of Lepanto (1571) that Turkish naval power was forced to a stalemate in the Mediterranean.

The Turkish Empire had expanded for nearly 300 years, but after 1683 its fortunes ebbed. There were several wars with the Christian states—Austria and Russia—and though the fortunes of war varied, the Turks made no more advances and in some territories were compelled to retire. The growing Russian power was the greatest threat to the Turks during the eighteenth century, and by 1781 Catharine the Great had made an arrangement with Austria, the first of many such plans, to divide the dominions of the 'Sick Man of Europe', as the Sultan came to be called. In 1783 Catharine annexed the Crimea, and by 1792 the Russian frontier had reached the Dniester. But while Russian pressure steadily ate into the Turkish Empire, it was a threat from another direction which proved most dangerous in the nineteenth century. For 300 years the Balkan peoples had endured Turkish rule. After the French Revolution, no European country was unaffected. All wanted their independence. Greece was the first in the fight for freedom, and from 1821 to 1829 the Greeks strove for their liberty. More than once the strong and well-disciplined forces of the Sultan nearly succeeded in overcoming the Greek patriots, and but for the inter-vention of the European powers, and particularly of England, the Greek revolt would most likely have been suppressed. The official attitude of the governments of Britain, France and Russia was often ambivalent, but not the sentiment of their peoples and of other Christian nations. Greece will never forget the sacrifices made by Lord Byron, who fought in the war on the side of the Greeks and gave his life, worn out by sickness and hardship, at Missolonghi. He was by no means the only distinguished Briton to serve Hellas. The famous British seaman, Thomas Cochrane, and General Sir Richard Church were elected by the Greek National Assembly to be their commanders-in-chief on sea and land respectively. (Byron had even been offered the Crown of Greece!)

At length, however, the three powers, Britain, France and Russia, issued terms to the Sultan. His troops occupied the Peloponnese under the command of Ibrahim, the son of that Mehemet Ali (an Albanian) who ruled Egypt in the Sultan's name. Many horrible atrocities were committed by the Turks, including an especially dreadful massacre on the island of Chios. The British government appointed Vice-Admiral Sir Edward Codrington, KCB, to carry out its very imprecise orders. He was to get Ibrahim to stop atrocities, slavery and transportation of Greeks to other lands. His instrument to effect this was the British fleet in the Mediterranean, supplemented by a French and a Russian squadron, both under his command. The Turkish and Egyptian fleets under Ibrahim were in the Bay of Navarino on the western coast of the Peloponnese, and on 20 October 1827, Codrington led his British, French and Russian warships into the Bay of Navarino, took up position opposite the Turkish and Egyptian fleets, gave them a last ultimatum and then opened fire. No allied ship was lost, and at least sixty enemy vessels were destroyed with great loss of life. An Egyptian squadron was later allowed to proceed to Alexandria. The victory was decisive, and as a result the Turks had to evacuate the Peloponnese and Greece became an independent country, Turkey having no other course but to recognise its freedom.

In Britain there was great popular rejoicing, but the government was not so sure. In a speech from the Throne on 22 January 1828 at the opening of Parliament, it was stated that 'a collision wholly unexpected by His Majesty took place in the port of Navarino, between the fleets of the Contracting Powers and that of the Ottoman Porte'. In the same speech the battle was referred to as 'this untoward event'. Untoward or not, the battle of Navarino not only saved Greek independence but started the liberation movement in the rest of the Balkan peninsula. Incidentally, it was the only major sea battle of the Royal Navy between 1815 and 1914. In 1829 Serbia became an autonomous state under Turkish suzerainty. In 1856 Rumania became independent, and Bulgaria in 1878. All three states, Serbia, Greece and Bulgaria, were enlarged at Turkish expense, and by 1914 Albania was independent. After the Treaty of Lausanne in 1923 Turkey in Europe was reduced to Constantinople and a strip of eastern Thrace.

In 1914, when Turkey joined Germany against Britain, Cyprus was formally annexed by Britain, and Egypt declared a British protectorate. The Turkish army attacked the Suez Canal but was beaten back, and in their turn the British crossed the Desert of Sinai and conquered Palestine. Egypt became an independent kingdom under the rule of King Fuad in 1922, but important reservations were made by the British with regard to the Suez Canal and the right to keep British troops in the Canal Zone. With possession of Gibraltar, Malta and Cyprus, a mandate from the new League of Nations over Palestine, a treaty with Egypt, and the major share in controlling the Suez Canal Company, Britain's route through the Mediterranean might seem to have been assured.

One of the great Mediterranean peoples had, however, achieved political unity only as late as 1870. Italy was thus, of necessity, excluded from participation in the European scramble for Africa and Asia. The most that newly united Italy could obtain was Tripoli, which she seized from Turkey in 1911, and two barren strips of territory in East Africa, Eritrea and Italian Somaliland, which no other European power had seen fit to annex. The Italians also attempted to invade Abyssinia, but were repulsed in the battle of Adowa in 1896. With a population that was increasing rapidly, and natural resources which did not promise a wealthy future, Italy was eager for a share in what appeared to be the assured European supremacy over the coloured races. The scraps which she had obtained did not, and could not, satisfy her, and many of her people emigrated to the United States and to Australia. Italy suffered from the curse of many other nations whose present condition does not correspond to their past greatness—an historical memory. The modern Italians can claim only a limited blood relationship with the ancient Romans for, like other European nations, Italy was formed from the mixing of many peoples in the early Middle Ages. Nevertheless, the Italian language is directly descended from Latin; under the Roman Empire, Italy had been the centre of the classical world; the Mediterranean had been *mare nostrum*, an Italian lake, and with the passage of the centuries the city of Rome, thanks to the Papacy, had acquired greater fame. Not all Italians, or even perhaps a majority of them, held these views, but living in a country which had had such immense influence on the world, it was almost impossible for Italians to avoid thinking of the past greatness of their country and evolving schemes for extending her boundaries.

In the war of 1914-18 Italy, as again in 1939-45, hesitated, waiting to see which side should prove the stronger. In 1915 she chose the western allies and was thus enabled to sit at the peace conference as one of the victors. Materially she gained little from the war. The fighting quality of her troops bore no resemblance to the bravery and endurance of the Roman legions, and after Caporetto in 1917 Italy had had to be succoured by troops from hard-pressed France and Britain. Her navy had played a negligible part in the war, and in Tripoli the Senussi had cleared Italian influence from all but the coastal strip. The territories on the Adriatic which Italy had been promised by the other allies were not granted to her and all that she could point to as a result of her war was the possession, after much murky intrigue, of the Dodecanese Islands off the coast of Asia Minor. In addition Italy, like all other belligerents, was distracted by post-war social and economic problems. She had not the necessary experience of democracy to pass, as Britain has so frequently done, through revolutionary periods without revolution. Whether she would have broken down in anarchy the world will never know, for the possibilities of anarchy and democracy alike for over twenty years were brought to an end on the seizure of power in 1922 by Benito Mussolini at the head of his blackshirted gangsters, the fascists.

Owing to the weakness of the Italian monarchy, the army was not used against the fascists, who gained control of Rome. The king invited Mussolini to become premier, but he was in reality a dictator and democracy in Italy became a thing of the past. Some of Mussolini's democratic opponents were murdered, some imprisoned, others driven into exile, and the new Italian state was organised in corporations and controlled guilds on fascist lines. Fascism might perhaps be described as the dictatorship of a few gangsters allied with the wealthy classes who were in fear of socialist or communist revolution. Whatever the definitions of the system, its results were clear in the control of the life of the nation by the state and the denial of liberty to the individual. At the apex of the new state stood the great dictator whose mind was filled with aspirations to be another Julius Caesar or Augustus. It is the fashion to speak now of the sawdust Caesar, but in the days before he embarked on his adventure of foreign conquest Mussolini was regarded as one of the greatest statesmen in Europe. He certainly gripped Italy and with decisive energy forced through schemes of improvement which a weak democratic government would have taken treble the time to accomplish. The works of *Il Duce* stand in the midst of the ruins which his own suicidal foreign policy brought upon the Italians, but there is no gainsaying that Mussolini did many things which were much needed in Italy. Everyone has heard of the draining of the Pontine marshes, but very few know that this famous piece of land reclamation was only one of many. Large associations of sheep farmers were formed in the plains of Italy and in Cyrenaica, and one can travel for miles along the roads between these farms, and every few miles come across a small civic centre neatly and cleanly organised around a church. This latter feature is always present in any Mussolinian settlement, which may go far to explain the Papal silence over his misdemeanours.

Nor did *Il Duce's* restless energy concern itself only with agricultural improvements. Everywhere he made changes, all designed to make Italy foremost among the nations. At Naples and Rome, for instance, there were plenty of fine buildings built in the year V or X of the fascist era. They usually had a map of the Italian Empire in the entrance halls—sometimes with territory marked on them which never did belong to Italy or even to ancient Rome.

The brittle quality of the fascist achievement is well brought out in another of Mussolini's triumphs, the sea front at Bari. To anyone approaching from the sea in those days, Bari had a splendid appearance, with fine buildings, including some civic ones such as the magnificent police headquarters. But anyone driving in from the interior of Italy comes first upon the older Bari, where there are plenty of slums and the usual dirt of an Italian town. In the midst of this squalor is the ancient cathedral with its Byzantine paintings and elaborate waxworks of the saints. Perhaps Mussolini would have prevented the citizens of Bari from spoiling their ancient cathedral's appearance if he had had more time, just as he cleaned up the main streets of Rome. Possibly his most enduring memorial will be the fine thoroughfares he built in Rome, the Via del Impero running through the Forum, and the street leading up to St Peter's church.

Mussolini was successful in the internal affairs of Italy for some ten or twelve years, from about 1922 to 1934, mainly because of the inability of the Italians to respond to democratic government. His form of rule was in the tradition of the Italian governments for many ages, beginning with that of the Roman emperors. There were episodes like that of the Florentine republic, or Rienzi's government in Rome, which were more nearly akin to democracy, but despotism found a fair field on the whole. Unfortunately for Italy, the world from 1930 onwards was involved in a series of economic disasters. This applied to all countries, democracies and dictatorships alike, but whereas a democratic government can admit that it is wrong a dictator cannot, and the temptation inevitably presents itself to escape from awkward positions at home by embarking on foreign adventures.

Mussolini with his theatrical outlook and his mind filled with ideas about ancient Rome did not need much temptation to set out on foreign conquests. Already, at the beginning of his career, he had used violence against the Greeks at Corfu, but in 1923 there was still a conscience among the nations and Mussolini did not proceed with further schemes. He did, it is true, recover for Italy the territory in North Africa which had lapsed to the Senussi, and in the campaigns by which they subdued the natives of Tripoli, the Italians showed signs of the particular brand of atrocity they were to use later against the Abyssinians. Indicative of Mussolini's determination to stir up racial memories was his alteration of the name of Tripoli to Libya, which had been the old Roman name of the country. He also strengthened Italy's armaments in every department, and in 1935, after looking around the Mediterranean world for an antagonist sufficiently profitable and at the same time sufficiently weak, he decided to attack Abyssinia. In one respect it was a bold decision, for although Italy could probably overwhelm Abyssinia without much difficulty, to attack her at all meant a direct threat to Britain's position in the Mediterranean. Britain had fought wars in Egypt and the Sudan with the purpose of preventing a hostile power from dominating the Nile valley and the Suez Canal. Mussolini's control of Abyssinia would mean the creation of a huge Italian sphere of influence in the region of the Sudan and the Red Sea. Joined with the presence of a powerful Italian garrison in Libya, facing the Egyptian frontier, and the existence of a strong Italy possessed of numerous bases, it was clear that for the first time in more than a century a Mediterranean power could attempt to close the Mediterranean to Britain.

Opposition from Britain to Italy's move against Abyssinia was therefore to be expected, but Mussolini had chosen his time well. The armed forces of Britain had been drastically reduced after the war of 1914-18 and were now scarcely more than a police force barely sufficient to keep order in the vast empire. The temper of the British people had never been militaristic and there was a strong reaction in the period after 1918 from patriotism, or anything resembling aggressive imperialism. The great economic difficulties of the country, the sudden development of democratic government by the grant of male and later female suffrage, the growth of socialism, and the mood of weariness which comes inevitably upon a people which has had great power for a long time, all combined to prevent any proper provision of the military force essential to carry out the worldwide responsibilities of Britain. It is probable that a government in Britain which, previous to 1938, had embarked on a programme of rearmament would have been driven from office by its opposition, yet paradoxically enough, at the same time that Britain's military power was reduced, many leading Britons were advocating support of the League of Nations, which inevitably led to interference with powers such as Italy. The result was that, under public pressure, the government of the day challenged Italy's advances against Abyssinia, well knowing that it could not interfere effectively. Not only were economic sanctions invoked against Italy by the League of Nations, the chief members of which were France and Britain but, more dangerous still, the bulk of the British fleet was ordered into the Mediterranean. This was presumably intended as a threat to Mussolini that his communications with Italy from Abyssinia would be cut. If so, he disregarded the threat and, relying on the power of his air force to wreck the British fleet in the narrow Mediterranean, calmly went on with his conquest of Abyssinia.

Here was the test case for the dictators of Europe and from 1935, when Abyssinia was invaded, the whole European situation progressively deteriorated. Civil war broke out in Spain and both Mussolini and Hitler interfered to support the rebels against the legitimate republican government. Mussolini thought that he was on the threshold of realising his ambitions. With the victory of the Spanish rebels he had secured a footing in Spain; his incessant agitations for French territory in Nice, Corsica and Tunisia must, he felt, produce concessions; on Good Friday in 1938 he attacked and occupied Albania. Posing as the champion of Islam, he fomented difficulties for Britain in the Arab world. After his victory over Abyssinia he felt that Egypt, Malta and Palestine were nearly his, and that he would be able to assist in carving up the British Empire. Thus, within the space of a few years, a species of bogus Roman Empire began to appear, although the bulk of it consisted of claims to portions of territory belonging to other powers such as Britain, France, Greece, Egypt and Turkey, which were unwilling or too weak to go to war with fascist Italy, and which might therefore be blackmailed into giving up part of their possessions.

The true measure of Mussolini's power was seen in the short space of four years from 1934 to 1938 in his handling of the problem of Austria. Hitler had come to power in 1933, but in the following year was too weak to intervene against the marshalled forces of Mussolini in Austria upon the death of Dollfuss. Four years later Hitler took over Austria without any opposition from Mussolini, who was compelled to accept the position of underling.

When, in September 1939, Britain was forced to declare war on Germany, the menace of Mussolini's Italy to British communications in the Mediterranean was at once apparent. The British Admiralty forbade British merchant shipping to use the routes through the Mediterranean, and some French and British forces were necessarily detained in the Mediterranean area to deal with possible Italian advances. Fortunately for the freedom of the world, Germany and Italy, as later they and Japan, had no concerted strategy and Mussolini was able to sit on the fence until the fall of France was in sight, when, fearful of losing his share of the French and British empires, he hurriedly declared war. On the face of things he seemed to have chosen wisely. France collapsed in June 1940, a few days after Italy had declared war. Britain had thus to contend against Germany and Italy, both of which had been building up their armaments for several years, whereas Britain had hardly begun to rearm. The battle for the Mediterranean was renewed and the struggle which followed was greater than anything which had occurred there in the past.

That struggle was to prove yet again, however, that the power which held the entrance and exit from the Mediterranean had a better chance of winning control of its waters than had any other country. Gibraltar was one key to the Mediterranean, the other was the control of the Suez Canal. The two keys were quite unlike. The one a grim rock rising as a landmark to seamen ever since man first navigated the waters and, at the other end of the Mediterranean, an Egyptian ditch cut through the sand, a delicate piece of work which could probably be wrecked by bombing (but little sense in this if the enemy hopes one day to use it himself) and without natural defences unless one includes the deserts stretching on either side of it. Yet this second key was no less potent than the other because the power which could use it had freedom of communication throughout half the world and could save thousands of miles in sea journeys, in addition to preventing the union of its enemies.

Great as the influence of the Suez Canal must have been in peace, its influence on the course of human history through its use in war must be even greater. Ferdinand de Lesseps, with all his giant genius, could not have foreseen the full consequences of his work. His statue at the Mediterranean end of the canal at Port Said once beckoned genially to the mariners and passengers as their vessels entered the ditch but is now no more, having been dynamited on 24 December 1956 by the Egyptians in celebration of the departure of the British and French troops two days earlier. It was a particularly futile gesture, because Egypt has derived great wealth from the canal which transformed a barren area of desert and swamp into one of flourishing towns and industry.

NOTE : Under the Convention dated 29 October 1888 and agreed between Great Britain, Germany, Austria, Hungary, Spain, France, Italy, the Netherlands, Russia and Turkey, the Suez Canal was always to remain free and open, in time of war as in time of peace, to every vessel of commerce or of war, without distinction of flag. The canal was never to be subjected to the exercise of the right of blockade.. This is the gist of Article 1 of the Convention and, if anything, the tenour of Article 4 is even stronger. In time of war Britain has certainly not allowed free passage of belligerents' vessels through the canal and has been in a position through her control of the sea to prevent even the approach of enemy vessels. British troops held the canal against Turkish attacks in 1914-15, and in the Second World War, during which the Germans bombed the canal, the British had plans to destroy it if they were forced to leave Egypt. When Nasser controlled the canal, he refused to allow Israeli shipping to pass through it, one of the causes of war between Egypt and Israel.

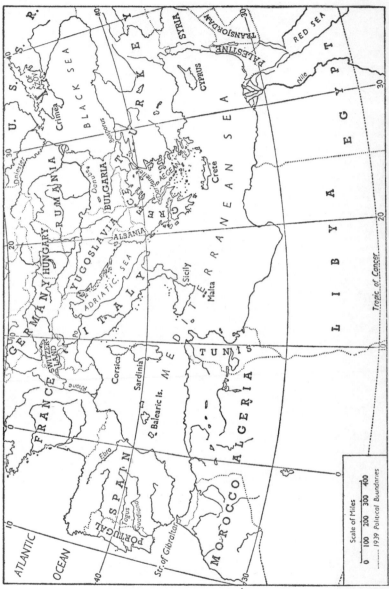

Map 9: The Mediterranean World showing Political Divisions in 1939

CHAPTER SEVENTEEN

THE BATTLE FOR
THE MEDITERRANEAN 1939-1945

WITH THE declaration of war by Italy, the Mediterranean was closed to British merchant shipping until such time as British sea and air power could control its waters, and the chance of doing that seemed very remote in the first years of the war.

In the quarter of a century since the Second World War much serious thought has been given to its problems and one feature of the Axis war effort which emerges is that the Axis nations did not fight with a properly co-ordinated strategy. We cannot tell whether Hitler was pleased with Italy's entry into the war in 1940, or whether he would have preferred her to stay in the vague and ambiguous state of 'non-belligerency', which would have necessitated the British maintaining in idleness in the Mediterranean, forces which would have been very useful against Germany. As it was, Mussolini decided for war and this being so, it would have been well for him, and ultimately for Hitler, had Germans and Italians struck jointly against Britain in the Mediterranean. Instead, in the second half of 1940 the Italians were allowed to conduct a half-hearted campaign on the borders of Egypt, which, indeed, they invaded; but at the end of that year they were driven from Egypt by Wavell's vastly inferior forces, their Libyan army destroyed, large numbers being captured and the whole of Cyrenaica was occupied early in 1941. In addition, they began to suffer severe losses at the hands of the British navy and air force. It is possible that the rest of Italian North Africa might have been conquered by Wavell's army had he not been forced to divert many of his troops to the support of the Greeks who had been attacked,

R

first by Italy, and then by Germany. For Mussolini, not content with the proposed liquidation of the British Empire, had also decided to push on from his base in Albania to conquer Greece. His troops had been beaten again and again by the much less well-equipped Greeks despite the preponderance of the Italian air force.

British assistance by air and sea was at once forthcoming for the Greeks, but the British army was not launched in Greece until Germany had threatened to attack her. Away to the south, in Abyssinia and Somaliland, the Italian armies after a brilliant victory over the police force of British Somaliland were driven on to the defensive and finally wiped out by British and Dominion troops. The Italian navy received a very severe mauling from Admiral Cunningham's squadrons in the battle of Cape Matapan, and again Germans had to come to Italy's assistance by putting some of their own seamen on board her ships to act as a stiffening to the Italian naval personnel. Individual Italian seamen showed great daring and skill, as with their frogmen's attacks on British warships, but as a fleet the Italian navy failed badly. These efforts of the Germans should have been made contemporary with Italy's entry into war; in the meantime, whilst the Germans were learning the true value of their southern ally, the Italians had sustained heavy losses and a most valuable fillip to the morale of the British people had been given in some of the darkest hours they had ever experienced.

Still, Germany's participation in the war in Libya was serious enough. The appearance of German troops in considerable numbers on the borders of Cyrenaica caused the retreat of Wavell's weakened army and within a short time the territorial gains of his brilliant 1940-41 campaign were lost, while the forces despatched to Greece were, after severe fighting, likewise forced to retreat. The evacuation of Greece by the British forces was followed by a brilliant German air invasion of Crete, in which German air supremacy was pitted against the British navy and army. The Royal Navy suffered severely as the Germans were in possession of nearby land bases for their bombing aircraft, while British fighters in Egypt were out of range and no carrier-borne aircraft were available. By June 1941, the British position in the Mediterranean was very grim. Between Gibraltar and Malta, Britain possessed no bases, and Malta could not be used by shipping for any length of time owing to the strict siege maintained by the Axis forces, and the very heavy air bombardment. In the eastern Mediterranean, German forces had overrun Greece, captured Crete and invaded Egypt. Turkey was neutral, but French-mandated Syria was full of Axis agents, and its invasion seemed the next step for the Germans to take, unless they preferred to drive towards Cairo or to assail Cyprus as they had Crete.

In the meantime British reinforcements and supplies had come up, but those from the United Kingdom or North America had been compelled to make a very long sea voyage around the Cape of Good Hope, whereas the Axis troops had merely to cross the narrow channel between Sicily and Africa. Vichy France was in the grip of Germany, and French North Africa was not neutral in the struggle.

The British, however, after recovering from their several defeats, struck the first blow in the new battle. They invaded and took over Syria. A rebellion in Iraq, fomented by Axis agents, had already been suppressed by them, and, later in 1941 in a joint operation with the Russians, they invaded Persia, where dangerous Axis sympathies were being manifested by the governing class. The world's attention was in the meantime diverted from events in the Mediterranean by the stupendous news that Hitler had invaded Russia. From the Axis point of view victory in the Mediterranean might seem postponed by this step, and just when German and Italian strategy had been co-ordinated the necessary supplies of men and material would be diverted to Russia. Nevertheless, the position continued to be serious for the British. They launched an offensive in November 1941 to regain Libya. At first, after grim fighting, they drove back the Germans, who were led by the much publicised Rommel, and they succeeded in reaching the limits of Cyrenaica, as had Wavell before them. Rommel's armoured divisions were not broken, though, and after a hard-fought battle, in which the troops of both sides were exhausted, Rommel managed to bring his army into play again before the British. The territorial gains of the campaign were lost once more, together with much equipment and many prisoners. The Germans advanced deeper into Egypt than ever before until they were at last halted a mere seventy miles from Alexandria, on the edge of the Quattara depression where the western desert comes very close to the sea. Here was a 'backs to the wall' position, and the British army responded as nobly as ever in its history. The enemy was held at El Alamein.

On the wider stage of the world, the end of 1941 witnessed the entry into the war of the last of the great powers. Japan struck, and the full force of the United States, mostly potential as yet, was irrevocably committed to the side of the United Nations*. For several months the news was melancholy for the Allies—a succession of Axis victories—until in 1942 the armies of Germany and Japan were halted on their various battle fronts. A mere halt could not secure victory to the Allies, but it gave them a breathing space with which to prepare for the final struggle. The year 1942 was the year of decision. In that year the Axis advance in Russia, in the Pacific, on the borders of India and at El Alamein was stopped, and from then on the Allied task was to recover lost ground.

In October, 1942 the Allied offensive was opened at El Alamein, and the advance was begun which was to clear the Germans from Africa. Soon afterwards, in November, a great Anglo-American armada bore down on North Africa and within a short time the main ports from Casablanca to Algiers were secured. During the winter of 1942-3 the Allies struggled with the Axis for the possession of Tunisia, while Montgomery's army advanced nearer and nearer from the east. At last, a juncture of the two Allied forces was effected and the Axis troops surrendered at Cape Bon in May 1943. The Italian fleet surrendered to Admiral Cunningham, after being bombed by its former German allies on its way to Africa.

The consequences were immediately felt. Africa was cleared of Axis armies, the southern coastline of the Mediterranean was in Allied hands, and, most important of all, the long voyage round the Cape of Good Hope could be saved. Large convoys began to pass through the Mediterranean, heavily escorted at first and subjected to fierce attacks, but in no great time the attacks lessened, and after the conquest of Sicily, the invasion of Italy, and the expulsion of the Axis from Sardinia and Corsica, control of the Mediterranean could be said to be in Allied hands. It was to become more complete with the passing of each month, until at length the first surrender of a German command in Europe was made in the Italian theatre of operations.

Had the Allies failed at El Alamein, what would have been the results? Very probably the loss of the war for the United Nations. If Rommel had bridged the gap of seventy miles which separated him from Alexandria, he would not only have deprived the British fleet of its great Egyptian base, not only destroyed the British armies in Egypt, but would also have sat astride the Suez Canal and the land area which is the key to Europe, Asia and Africa. The communications of the British Empire would have been hopelessly disrupted and the Axis forces in possession of Egypt could have radiated east and south to break up the British armies in the Middle East. Reinforcements for Rommel would have come across the narrow Mediterranean, subject to less or no menace from British submarines which would have had no bases save Gibraltar, for Malta would no doubt have succumbed to encirclement. The invasion of French North Africa could hardly have taken place, or at the best have been a forlorn hope.

Furthermore, had the Japanese been spurred to even greater efforts by the victory of their friends in Egypt they might have forced their way into and across India to join up with the German and Italian forces advancing across the Middle East. The Allies had fortunately learned to co-ordinate their strategy, but the furthest that the Axis had gone in this direction had been the subordination of Italy to Germany. As between Germany and Japan there was no unified plan. The mutual jealousies of these would-be world rulers, which revealed themselves behind official politeness and friendship, perhaps prevented any concerted action by the general staffs of Germany and Japan. Nevertheless, had Rommel secured Egypt and continued to advance, and had the Japanese gained a firm footing in India, an Axis link-up on the Persian Gulf might well have resulted, that is, on the ruins of the British Empire.

Not since the time of Napoleon has a more strenuous effort to overthrow a sea power been made by land powers than in the Second World War. Germany, except for her U-boat fleet, had never been in the list of great sea powers, and the Italian navy, although fairly large and composed of swift ships, could not, as events proved, compete with a really first-class fleet. Primarily, the war in the Mediterranean was a struggle by the air forces and armies of Germany and Italy against the British sea and air hold on the route to India. Victory for the Axis there would have meant permanent disruption of the communications of the empire (and therefore, its destruction), the breaking of the British blockade of Europe, the final sundering of the great Allies, and so on to the end of the war on Axis terms. Conversely, the Allied victory in North Africa and Libya freed the Mediterranean from Axis control and was the beginning of final victory.

NOTE : *The term 'United Nations' was frequently used in the years 1941-45 to denote Britain, the United States, Russia, etc, though it was not until hostilities had ceased that the United Nations Organisation was set up, deriving its title from the earlier period.

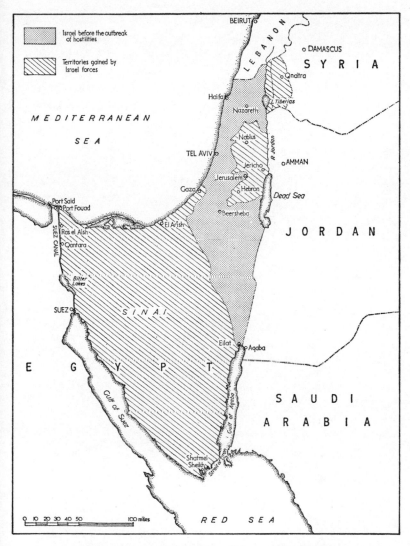

CHAPTER EIGHTEEN

HISTORY SINCE 1945

AT THE END of World War II, the Mediterranean had become once more the focal point of concern in a titanic struggle, instead of being merely an historic sea around whose shores lay the ruins of past empires. Many British people had read in newspapers and books that the British route to India lay through the Mediterranean, and took the statement for granted, forgetting that an aggressive Italy might well threaten the lifeline of imperial communications. British possession of Gibraltar, Malta, Suez, Aden, Ceylon, Singapore etc was accepted as a matter of course, or, at most, regarded as a well-earned legacy from the days of empire-building. It required the Axis threat to Alexandria and even more serious disaster in the fall of Singapore for British folk to realise that the hitherto neglected chain of bases was a vital link in the exchange of supplies and men between the leading members of the United Nations; and that the collapse of British imperialism would herald an Axis victory and the domination of the civilisation which is derived from the shores of the Mediterranean by a ruthless totalitarianism.

It was not only with the Second World War that the Inland Sea came once more to be a danger spot, and an area of supreme importance in the world's affairs. The end of that war brought no lessening in its importance, and today the eastern end of the Mediterranean is one of the most dangerous areas in the world, a place where great powers can very easily be involved almost without being aware of approaching catastrophe. This very serious state of affairs is largely bound up with the astonishing emergence of the state of Israel, and also with the control of the Suez Canal.

The British position in the Mediterranean, which had been maintained in the area for 300 years, has now been completely eliminated, or at least eliminated as far as any intervention in power politics is concerned. Gibraltar is still under the British flag, but Malta is independent and is no longer of importance as a naval base. There are no other British possessions in the Mediterranean lands. The former Mediterranean Fleet has ceased to exist. While the two super-powers, the USA and the USSR, maintain large naval forces in the sea, Britain is sometimes represented by two ships, which may on occasion be augmented to six. The details of this removal of British influence are important as showing the many changes which have occurred in this part of the world.

Leaving for the moment the establishment of Israel as an independent state, which is a special case requiring explanation, the departure of the British really followed the renunciation of British sovereignty over India in 1947. The chain of bases through the Mediterranean and right over to the Indian Ocean was required in order to maintain passage to India. With India gone, there could be little point in hanging on to outlying possessions, but the process of disentanglement from the imperial past was unfortunately accompanied by much loss of life. The British presence in Egypt was ended following the withdrawal of British troops from the Canal Zone on 13 June 1956. Egypt's constitution had been changed in the preceding four years. King Farouk abdicated in 1952 and for a year Egypt continued as a monarchy under his infant son, proclaimed as King Ahmed Fuad II. The monarchy was, however, abolished in 1953, and the prime minister, Neguib, proclaimed Egypt a republic with himself as president. In 1954 he was replaced by President Nasser, who held his position until his death in 1970. During these changes Egyptian hostility to the British presence continued, and led to constant terrorist attacks on the British garrison in the Canal Zone.

Less than five weeks after the British withdrawal, Britain and the USA refused to finance Nasser's project of building a new high dam at Aswan, which they had previously more or less agreed to support. Nasser was thrown back on the only other source of finance,

Soviet Russia, which in the event had to pay for the entire project. The American and British refusal was made on 19 July 1956 and a week later, on 26 July, Nasser nationalised the Suez Canal. The news was brought to the British premier, Sir Anthony Eden (now Earl of Avon), while he was entertaining an old friend, King Feisal of Iraq (who was murdered not long after, on 14 July 1958, with his premier, Nuri-es-Said), to dinner at 10 Downing Street. Efforts were made to substitute an international board for the operation of the canal. This was the proposal of a twenty-two nations conference held in London (16-23 August 1956) and the American politician Foster Dulles had the idea of a Suez Canal Users' Association. The Suez Canal Company withdrew its (foreign) pilots by 15 September, but the Egyptians succeeded in working the canal with the aid of volunteer pilots from all over the world.

The British and French governments were those most concerned with use of the canal, especially as they feared that its nationalisation might endanger the supplies of oil which they drew from the Persian Gulf and other sources. The two governments began to concert plans for military action in order to 'bring Nasser to his senses' as Eden stated in a wire to President Eisenhower (27 July 1956). There was talk of the danger in failing to resist aggression, as had been the case in 1938, but the American government refused to sanction the use of force in any form.

The upshot of the matter was that Britain and France made an abortive invasion of the Canal Zone, as a result of which both countries lost all stake or influence in Egypt. The details will come more appropriately below in the account of the second Israeli-Egyptian war.

Loss of Egypt was followed, in 1960, by renunciation of British rule over Cyprus, which became an independent state and a republican member of the Commonwealth. Arrangements were made for bases in Cyprus, but this, of course, depends on the goodwill of the Cypriot government. Provision for bases in Libya was ended by the government of that country. On a larger field, British armed presence east of Suez had ceased by the end of 1972.

The story of the British involvement in the affairs which led to the establishment of the present state of Israel goes back to 1917,

when British troops conquered Palestine from the Turks. The
Turkish Empire had been in a shaky condition for some time and,
owing to Turkish participation on the German side in the 1914-18
war, their outlying provinces had been taken from them. On
2 November 1917, Arthur Balfour (later Lord Balfour), then Foreign
Secretary, made a declaration, which bears his name, to the effect
that the British government favoured the setting-up of a national
home for the Jews in Palestine. This was endorsed by the chief
Allied powers and it was laid down by the Treaty of Sèvres★ that
the government of Palestine should be conducted by mandate
(granted to Britain) under the League of Nations. On 1 July 1920,
a civil administration was established in Palestine with Sir Herbert
Samuel as first High Commissioner. The British mandate lasted until
1948, and involved immense trouble for the administering power.
To some extent the British authorities had themselves to blame,
for in the Balfour Declaration itself they had stated that nothing
was to be done to prejudice the rights of existing non-Jewish
communities in the country. The Arabs of Palestine, who had after
all been there for over a thousand years, were not to lose their
lands, yet space was to be found in Palestine for large numbers of
immigrant Jews. Someone would have to give place and it was
fairly obvious that the mandatory power would incur the hatred
of both Jew and Arab.

Apart from any question of natural justice, the British attitude
towards the Arabs was necessary in view of the part taken by the
latter in the campaigns which had brought down the Turkish
Empire. There are about a dozen Arab states around the Mediterranean, the Red Sea and the Persian Gulf, but only two or three of
these can really be classed as Arab in a racial sense. They owe their
existence, as mentioned in Chapter 12, to the emergence of the
Islamic religion 1,300 years ago. They are Islamic in faith and
Arabic-speaking. In the 1914 war the exploits of the almost legend-

---

★ This treaty proved abortive in many respects and the relations between
the Allied powers of World War I and Turkey were regulated by the
Treaty of Lausanne, signed in July 1923. By this latter treaty the Turks
obtained better terms as regards their European territory, but the treaty did
not affect the Allied dispositions concerning Palestine.

ary Col Lawrence of Arabia brought some of the desert tribes into the war on the Allied side, and greatly assisted the campaigns of Allenby in Palestine. Promises had been made to the Arab leaders which were only partially fulfilled when some of them became heads of such independent states as Iraq, Transjordania or Jordan, and Saudi Arabia. Incidentally, there has been for over 100 years a curious strain of romanticism among a few persons in Britain as to the character of the Arabs. Travellers like the famous Doughty, the equally famous Burton, one of the Wavell family, and Lawrence himself all tended to romanticise the wild Bedouin of the desert, a tendency which was caricatured in the 1920s in England with novels and the Hollywood films of the Rudolph Valentino type, in which the 'sheikh' is a figure of sexual gallantry and manly bravery.

Later writers of greater knowledge and experience, eg Sir John Glubb, have proved this conception to be fictitious, and the correctness of their views was demonstrated (see below) in the poor showing of Arabs against Israelis in the three wars.

The double promises made to Arabs and Jews first caused trouble with the former. In 1936 there was much fighting in Palestine with the Arabs, and British forces had to be strengthened. Lord Peel headed a royal commission of inquiry in the autumn of 1936, and among its recommendations were that the mandate should be terminated, that Palestine should be divided between Jews and Arabs, and that the Holy Places—dear to the adherents of the three religions, Jews, Christians and Moslems—should be reserved as a mandatory territory. It was not until 1948 that the mandate was ended and Palestine partitioned, but not by peaceful means.

On the outbreak of war in 1939 the Palestine troubles were submerged beneath the much greater wave of disasters let loose in Europe. As a result of Hitler's persecution of the Jews, many of them fled to other lands. The survivors were often men and women of superior intelligence, hardihood or courage—they could not have survived unless they had been such. Many of them tried to get into Palestine, and were aided financially by British Jewry and even more by the large Jewish community in the United States.

It has been estimated that 6,000,000 Jews perished in the Hitlerite persecutions and certainly the Jewish population of Europe was very much decreased; those that remained usually came into the category of displaced persons, having lost everything, including their nationality. Rehabilitation in European lands was usually impossible, and the thoughts of the displaced turned towards Britain, the USA, or the revival of their ancient home in Palestine.

From the beginning of the British administration one of the most vexed questions had been that of how many Jewish immigrants were to be permitted to enter Palestine. The estimate was that in 1914 only 60,000 Jews lived in Palestine. By 1931, after some fourteen years of effective British rule (the mandate dated officially from 1923), the number of Jews had risen to 175,000. In 1946 the population of Palestine was estimated at 1,500,000, of whom 500,000 were Jews; today there are said to be 2,773,000 Jews in the Holy Land. These large increases in numbers were not due only to illegal immigrant ships crossing the Mediterranean from Italian or French ports after 1945. The British government had permitted the entry of more and more Jews before 1939; this being in fact the cause very largely of the British-Arab clash in 1936. The newcomers bought land from the Arabs and developed it with financial shrewdness. All the world knows of the Jaffa orange; many are aware of the potash deposits near the Dead Sea (a beautiful sight are the works: they look like a vast magnification of a child's paint box, with the squares containing a range of colours from a lovely eau-de-nil to a glorious deep turquoise), but not all are aware that Tel-Aviv is a modern city built up by Jewish ingenuity and labour from what, in 1923, was a collection of mudhuts.

The 1939 war did lead, despite terrible Jewish suffering in Europe, to the growth of the Jewish state. The British government had not accepted the recommendations of the Peel Commission, but in May 1939 had outlined a plan of a compromise nature whereby the Arabs and Jews were to become partners in an independent Palestinian democratic state. As the British could please neither side in the Palestine problem, they stood to be shot at or bombed by both. Gradually the open hostility to the British expressed in violent deeds shifted to the Jews rather than to the Arabs. Palestine is a land made for ambuscades and innumerable opportunities arose for attacks on British troops. The outbreak of war in 1939 did suspend the struggle, as clearly the Jews were on the same side as the British in opposition to Hitler. Soon the Palestinian Jews were organised on military lines and obtained weapons. As in so many countries where resistance groups were organised to combat Hitler's men, the organisations developed ulterior motives and gained control of much-needed arms. The Jews of Palestine could now look forward to the successful defence of their settlements in the country, and even to the re-establishment of Israel in its ancient boundaries.

When peace came in 1945, Britain had a peculiarly hard problem in Palestine. Despite all the efforts of the Palestine administration and of the Royal Navy, illegal immigrants continued to be landed. The murders of British troops, police and officials continued. A particularly horrible incident occurred in 1946 when two British sergeants were found hanged in a eucalyptus grove at Nathanya. This murder was carried out by Jewish terrorists as a reprisal for the legal trial and execution of other Jewish terrorists, and it became clear that the mandate must be given up. It ended on 14 May 1948, when the last British governor left the country on a British cruiser, but British departure did not mean peace. On the afternoon of the 14th, while General Cunningham (the governor) was on board the ship, the Jews proclaimed 'the establishment of the Jewish state in Palestine to be called Israel'. To many Jews, and to many non-Jews, there must have come a reminiscence of Hosea's words. 'The children of Israel shall abide many days without a king, and without a prince, and without a sacrifice, and without an image, and without an ephod and without teraphim. Afterwards shall the children of Israel return and seek the Lord their God and David their king; and shall fear the Lord and His goodness in the latter days.'

For the moment the Jews had their state of Israel, after 2,000 years of subjection to the Gentiles, but it was immediately menaced by the Arabs. On the day following the proclamations of the new Israel, the armies of Syria, Iraq, Transjordan and Egypt invaded Palestine. Then it was that the prophets were loud and exact in their forecasts. The Arabs would sweep the Jews into the sea; how could men drawn mostly from the ghettoes of eastern Europe stand against the fierce sons of the desert? The exploits of the Stern gang and other Jewish societies had been performed against isolated British soldiers in ambushes and street incidents. Gangsters were not soldiers. Those who knew the Near East were not so assured. They knew that the sons of the desert are a minority among modern Arabs; that the Jews had carefully trained and disciplined themselves for future war while serving with the British in the Second World War; and above all that the superiority of weapons would probably lie with the Jews.

In the result, this reasoning was proved right. The only force which won any success of real value against the Jews was the British-trained and led Arab Legion of Transjordan. The performance of the Egyptian, Syrian and Iraqi armies was feeble. Not only did the Arabs lose this, the first of the three modern wars with Israel, but large numbers of the Palestinian Arabs fled from their homes or were expelled, and became inhabitants of the refugee camps which still exist.

After a few months of warfare the state of Israel had been not only proclaimed but firmly established. The recognition of the world followed and President Truman of the USA led the way. Flushed with victory, Israeli forces even pressed on to the Gulf of Akaba and entrenched themselves opposite a British force. A Jewish air force had secretly been formed and scored many successes against its Arab enemies, while its reconnaissance extended far and wide. In these early days of independence, the Israelis made out a claim for the whole of the Negev, the apparently barren portion of southern Palestine on the borders of Egypt.

The war of 1948 had been won by Israel, but no one supposed that it could be final. The victory guaranteed the existence of the new state, but it did nothing more. Israel was ringed round by hostile states, except on her western side. She had no proper boundaries, save the Mediterranean. Her territory was pinched in by Jordan which, holding part of the west bank of the river Jordan, rendered Israel little more than ten miles wide near Tel-Aviv. There was a strip round Gaza in Egyptian occupation. Nor was peace complete after the end of open warfare in November 1948. Guerilla activities harassed the Israelis from the frontiers of Egypt and Jordan, and perhaps worst of all, as years passed, from Syria.

The second war between Israel and the Arabs was closely connected with the British and French absorption with the nationalisation of the Suez Canal. While the two governments were making military preparations for an expedition against Egypt, and while the American attitude continued to be, to say the least, discouraging to Franco-British military effort, the Israelis resolved the dilemma of fighting or not fighting. On 28 October 1956, Israel announced her mobilisation. This was in answer to the preparations for an offensive which were being made by the Arab states, and was also motivated by Israeli determination to stop the raids and other guerilla activities of the Arabs. In the 1956 operations the Israelis achieved the most important objective in war—surprise. It was generally thought that Israel would strike against Jordan, but on 29 October the Israeli forces attacked across the Sinai desert against Ismailia and Suez. Upon this the British and French governments issued an ultimatum requiring a ceasefire and the withdrawal of both Egyptian and Israeli forces to ten miles on either side of the canal. Failing the acceptance of the ultimatum, the Allied troops would occupy the Canal Zone from Port Said to Suez. On 31 October Allied planes bombed the Egyptian airfields. By 2 November the Israelis had achieved their aims, sealing off the Gaza strip and destroying the Egyptian forces in Sinai. They had wiped out the Egyptian air force and went on to bomb military installations in the Canal Zone. They had also seized Sharm-el-Sheikh at the tip of the Sinai peninsula, which enabled them to reopen the Gulf of Akaba. This allowed shipping access to the Israeli port of Eilat, whereas Nasser had previously blockaded the straits of Tirana which lead to the Gulf.

The exemplary swiftness of the Israeli military operations was in marked contrast to the tardiness of the Allied proceedings. The bombing of the Egyptian airfields began on 2 November; on 4 and 5 November Allied paratroopers landed at Port Fuad, which was quickly captured, and at Port Said where resistance was prolonged. On 6 November the Allied forces landed in the Port Said area, overcoming bitter Egyptian resistance, and the invaders were able

s

to advance along the canal to El Cap, twenty-three miles south of Port Said.

Meanwhile a storm of criticism against Britain and France had arisen at the United Nations, in the United States, in Canada, among the Afro-Asian nations, and internally in Britain. The upshot was that the Security Council of the United Nations ordered a ceasefire, as did the General Assembly of the same body, in a vote of 64 to 5 with 6 abstentions. The Allied troops were well on their way to the southern end of the canal when they were halted by their governments' acceptance of the UN ceasefire order. The Russians had talked of sending volunteers to aid the Egyptians and even of using atomic weapons against London and Paris, but the main reason for failure to go on with the campaign was the opposition of the United States. The extreme slowness of Allied operations contributed to the failure of the whole project, for had the Allies acted with the same speed as was shown by the Israelis the world would probably have accepted the *fait accompli* of an Allied occupation of the Canal Zone.

The consequences of the fiasco were numerous and far-reaching. The Allied forces withdrew from Egypt on 22 December 1956, being replaced by a multi-racial United Nations security force. During the seven weeks' occupation there were terrorist attacks on British troops, and a notable incident was the murder of Lt Moorhouse. On 24 December the Egyptians blew up De Lesseps statue and the debris was sunk in the harbour at Port Said. The canal was now well and truly blocked by about fifty sunken ships and other obstacles. Fourteen foreign vessels were caught in the canal and its installations had suffered immense damage. Salvage work was begun by British and French teams, but was completed by the United Nations clearance bodies. Nasser refused the latter permission to begin salvage operations until the Allied troops were withdrawn, and he also refused any Egyptian assistance until the Israelis gave up the Gaza Strip and Sharm-el-Sheikh. At the latter place they were replaced by the UN force.

By 8 April 1957 the canal was reopened for normal traffic. Oil supplies were held up for Britain and France; in Britain petrol rationing was imposed. Nasser's position as Egyptian leader was confirmed. Instead of his departure from politics, it was Sir Anthony Eden who had to resign from his position as Britain's premier.

France's Mediterranean empire in North Africa has gone as well as that of Britain, despite keen opposition from French governments before the advent of Gen De Gaulle to power in Paris. The weight of world power formerly borne by Britain and France passed, as far as the democratic nations were concerned, to the United States. That great champion of democracy has, however, found, like Hercules when he changed places with Atlas, that responsibility for world policing is a very heavy and undesirable burden. The participation by the United States in the wars in Korea, and above all in Vietnam, has brought the Americans to detest the position of a world power, entailing as it does the necessity for costly warfare in distant parts of the world.

The second Israeli-Arab war had given the Arab states a very sharp lesson in military tactics, but either this schooling was lost upon them, or else they had not the ability to profit from it. Nasser set about the task of empire-building, as well as reconstructing his forces. On 1 February 1958 he made a treaty with Syria under which the two countries were linked as the United Arab Republic. A few months later there followed a revolution in Iraq, but the new regime was not friendly to Nasser. Ironically, in view of American opposition to Suez, the USA had to send marines into the Lebanon in July 1958 to prevent subversion, and to allow British paratroopers to be air-lifted to Jordan in the same month and for the same purpose.

The United Arab Republic collapsed in the autumn of 1961 when Syria seceded. Next year Nasser involved Egypt in the affairs of the Yemen. The Imam of the Yemen, the hereditary priest king, was overthrown but the Yemenites refused to accept Egyptian rule. In spite of the use of poison gas and of modern bombing techniques, the Egyptians could not subdue the Yemen, and Nasser's financial difficulties were increased. In the sphere of the Suez Canal he could, however, claim a justified success. 'In 1955 the last full year of operation by the Suez Canal Company, 14,666 ships used the canal, totalling 115¾m net tons and yielding a revenue of £E32m. In 1966, the number of vessels at 21,250 showed a 50 per cent in-

s*

crease, tonnage was more than doubled at 274⅓m and—most important from Egypt's point of view—receipts were trebled at £E95m.' (*The Suez Canal*, by H. J. Schonfield, 1969, p 164.)

Then, in July 1966, it was announced that there was to be a new six-year programme of development which would allow navigation of the canal by vessels as large as 110,000 tons loaded tankers. It seemed very likely that by 1980 the canal would even permit the passage of ships of 200,000 tons, a development of great importance considering the launching of the giant Japanese tanker, the *Idemitsu Maru* (209,000 tons), forerunner of even larger vessels. Work began on the six-year programme in February 1967, but less than five months later the canal was blocked as it had been in 1956. Blocked it remains, with Egypt losing the £E100m revenues her careful canal management had built up. Nor is this all. The Suez oil refineries have been drastically reduced in output, and the towns along the canal are now battered by shells and bombs. As for the western European nations, their oil supplies now come from other sources in countries like Libya and Algeria, and by voyage round the Cape in tankers far too large for the canal passage.

What is the reason for this state of affairs? The third Israeli-Arab war, and the Arabs' refusal to accept the Israeli state as a permanent neighbour. From 1957 onwards there were continual raids into Israel by Arab guerillas, especially the Syrians. Israel put complaints before the United Nations of 422 such raids between 1957 and 1962. Batteries on the Syrian heights were also constantly shelling the Israeli farmlands in the plains below. Nasser rebuilt his forces with Russian money and equipment, part of the growth of Russian influence in the area (see below) and Russian experts and volunteers were sent over to Egypt in large numbers. Nasser never ceased to proclaim hostility towards Israel and encouraged the preaching of the Islamic concept of the jihad or holy war. 'Even Pope Kyrillos VI, head of the Coptic Orthodox Church in Egypt, joined in it. He supported all steps taken by Egypt to "regain Palestine from those who crucified Christ".' (*The Six Day War*, by R. S. and W. S. Churchill, 1967, p 47.) All this agitation, accompanied by active military movements by the Egyptians, and the withdrawal of the UN security force at Nasser's request in May 1967, did not fail to have its effect upon the Israeli government. Moyshe Dayan was chief of staff in the Sinai operation of 1956 and had become in Jewish eyes the symbol of patriotism and victory. Late on 1 June 1967 he had been appointed Minister of Defence, and on 5 June at 0745 hours began the Israeli air strikes which, in a matter of a few hours, eliminated the Egyptian air force and made victory over the Egyptian army certain.

Comparison of the armed strengths of Israel and the Arab nations is instructive. Egypt had 240,000 soldiers, 1,200 tanks, and 450 combat planes. Jordan had 50,000 soldiers, 200 tanks, and 40 planes; Syria had 50,000 soldiers, 400 tanks, and 120 planes. The only other Arab state which need be mentioned is Iraq with 70,000 troops, 400 tanks, and 200 planes. The Iraqis did move troops into Jordan, but the other Arab powers, like Algeria, Lebanon or Saudi Arabia, did not render military aid. The population of Israel had risen from the half-million of 1946 to two and a half million by 1967. Against this, the population of the Arab states was forty millions. In the spring of 1967 the Israeli army numbered 50,-60,000, of whom 10,-20,000 were regulars, the rest national servicemen. With complete mobilisation, the total force was 264,000, one-tenth of the population. In addition men over forty-five, who were out of the armed forces, served in civil defence. Women also served, sometimes as combatants. National servicemen served for thirty months and then went on the reserve. Mobilisation was efficiently and quickly effected, like all Israeli military operations. Israel had 800 tanks and 300 combat aircraft, and all infantry was motorised. The aircraft were fighter-bombers, mostly French. Their rate of turn round was fantastically high—a squadron would be refuelled and their cannon reloaded in $7\frac{1}{2}$ minutes from landing. There was also a small Israeli navy, consisting in 1961 of three destroyers, three submarines, one anti-submarine craft and eight motor torpedo boats. It succeeded in protecting the coast of Israel from attack.

Nasser was ostentatiously preparing his forces for war but did not expect the Israeli onslaught. Perhaps he thought that the Israelis would attack the Syrian heights, whereas it was against the Egyptian forces that Israel struck. Within a few hours the Egyptian air force was eliminated, and thereafter the Egyptian army in Sinai had to fight without air assistance. Under the strafing of the Israeli planes, guns and tanks, the Egyptian army broke, the officers being often the first to run. At the Mitla Pass the Egyptian army was massacred. Its remnants made their painful way to the canal, the length of which was held by the Israelis. Meanwhile their forces had stood firm in Jerusalem and on the west bank of the Jordan against Jordanian and Iraqi troops. Only here did Arab forces fight well, but without success. The Old City of Jerusalem passed to the Israelis, as did the west bank of the Jordan. The Gaza Strip and the whole of the Sinai peninsula were clear of living Egyptians; of the many who fell there, probably as many died from thirst as from bombs or bullets. The UN Security Council ordered a ceasefire which was accepted by the Israelis and Syrians on Saturday, 10 June, at 1930 hours, but before this some of the Israeli forces had been switched to the northern front. There the Syrian heights were captured and the nineteen-year-old menace to the Jewish settlements was removed.

As a result of this third war Israel held the whole area from the banks of the Suez Canal right up to the borders of Lebanon, part of western Syria, all the west bank of the Jordan, the Gaza Strip, and the Sinai peninsula down to the strait of Tirana. Israel emerged from the struggle as the strongest power in the Near East. Jerusalem, old and new, is now in Israeli hands. Jerusalem has indeed been trodden down of the nations, but after nineteen centuries—from 70 to 1967—Jerusalem is again in Jewish hands.

It should be made clear that the modern people of Israel in Palestine do not represent in any entirety the whole of the ancient people of the same name. In 786 BC, as mentioned in Chapter 10, the larger part of the population of Palestine, then included in the northern kingdom of Israel, was carried away captive after defeat by the Assyrians. Among them were all the leaders or potential leaders. Consequently these ten lost tribes, as they have come to be known, were indeed lost in the nations of the world. Modern Jewry acknowledges this and recognises that present-day Jews are derived from the tribes of Judah, Benjamin and Levi, plus a large intermixture of Gentile folk who, over the ages, have become Jews. As far back as the last century BC, the Edomites, or Idumeans, were forcibly converted to Judaism—hence the claim of Herod the Great, an Idumean by birth, to be King of the Jews, as being a Jew himself. In addition, during later centuries a number of Caucasian tribes became Jews by voluntary association. The existence of many different types of physical appearance, and even of colour, among modern Jews proves that the Jewish community of our time is far from being of one race. The modern Jewish belief is that the lost tribes are hidden among the nations, to be revealed at a later day. Their last mention in the Scriptures is in 2 Esdras, chapter XIII, verses 40-42, where they are reported as migrating to a distant territory. Conjectures as to the identity of these lost tribes today divide between the possibility of the Afghans and/or the British being their lineal representatives.

Allowing, however, that the modern Israeli does not represent more than a fraction of the original twelve tribes of Israel, the reoccupation of the Holy Land by the Jews and the establishment of a modern state is almost a miracle. A people excluded from their homeland for 1,900 years have regained it. Even the most determined sceptic must feel that Old Testament and New Testament prophecies find here their fulfilment.

The wars between Israel and the Arabs are the more important because they have drawn in the great powers. The removal of British influence from the Mediterranean has not left a power vacuum. The gap has been filled by the two super states, the United States of America and Soviet Russia. From almost the close of World War II the USA has maintained a large naval force in the Mediterranean, the famous Sixth Fleet. This is now confronted by a large Russian fleet which is permanently at cruise in the sea. The USSR's great assistance to Egypt, financially, technically, and militarily in the shape of volunteers, has already been mentioned and stems from a desire to counter American aid to smaller countries.

From the first rise of Russian power under the autocratic Tzars, the aim of Russian policy has been to secure a warm-water port and to gain worldwide influence. In this as in most other matters of foreign policy, Soviet Russia has continued the policy of the Tzars, but with much more efficiency and success. The Soviet

Russian Empire extends even further now than under the imperial rule, and its control of its subject peoples is far more secure, as witness the vain attempts of Hungary, Czecho-Slovakia and Poland, to say nothing of East Germany, to break away from the Soviet circle. Only Yugo-Slavia has got free of Moscow's control.

Now Soviet Russian naval policy has secured a freedom of action on the high seas which Imperial Russia never approached. Russian war vessels sail in every major sea, and over all the oceans, and since 1949 the USSR has had atomic bombs, with all their fearful possibilities. Since 1961 she has been able to demonstrate a great technological advance in space flight; on 4 October 1957 Sputnik I was sent into orbit, and in 1961 Yuri Gagarin, in spacecraft Vostok I, was the first man in space. So spectacular were the Russian achievements that it seemed as if the United States would be completely surpassed, but the vast efforts made under the late President Kennedy's directives resulted in America being the first to get men to the moon and back.

When, therefore, consideration is given to the possibility of great power strife in the Near East, with the USSR espousing the Arab cause and the USA aiding that of the Israelis, it has to be remembered that any potential conflict would have almost cosmic consequences. Man has succeeded in passing out of what appeared for so long to be his only element and is invading the cosmos; it is quite likely, given the rivalry in the space race of Soviet Russia and America, and resulting stimulation, that the greater part of the solar system will have received at least unmanned probes before the end of the century.

Yet all these advances, which would have appeared miraculous to our forefathers not so many generations ago, have been achieved in an atmosphere, not of international amity but of continual bitterness, hostility and suspicion. What is to be the end of the matter?

Prophecy is usually a vain exercise, though it holds a deep attraction for the human soul. There are strangely converging lines of prophecy which point to the Near East and to Palestine in 'an end of the age' as the year 2000 draws near. One writer whose work was published in 1936 had this to say :

'The Pyramid dating does not run beyond the year 2001. Nostradamus fixes the year 1999 as the time for an attack and one of the terrible destructions of the city of Paris, by a strange people coming from the north, perhaps from Asia. St Malachi and the Monk of Padua predict the burning of Rome, at the end of the Papacy, which seems to fall at about the same period. Many other prophecies point to the "End of the Age" as falling within the present century. One cannot but recall the words of the Gospel according to St Mark, "Verily I say unto you that this generation shall not pass, till all these things be done".' (*The Story of Prophecy*, by H. J. Forman, 1936, p 155.)

To which may be added this excerpt from *The Times* (1 July 1966, fourth centenary of the death of Nostradamus), by James Laver:

'Even allowing for the libraries of nonsense which have been written about Nostradamus, there is a residue which those of us who believe in human free will cannot help finding a little disturbing. In the words of Napoleon III, who was well acquainted with the writings of Nostradamus, "Ça épouvante et énerve l'imagination".'

The reference above to St Malachi is to the prophecy of that name which gives a motto for each Pope, certainly from the sixteenth century and which leaves only four more on the list to come after the present pontiff. This is sometimes curiously interpreted as denoting the destruction of the Papacy, but the author of the prophecy meant only that the Papacy, like all other institutions, could not survive the end of the world.

The strangest feature of the present age is that modern thought is frequently quite apocalyptic in its outlook. Forty years ago a person who made reference to such a topic as the end of the world would have been regarded as beyond the intellectual pale. Today a very different attitude prevails. Not only has the century been marked by two most terrible wars, but there has been the discovery of the atomic bomb and its later refinements which have given to human beings the power of unparalleled destruction. Not only that but the problems of pollution of the environment are beginning to be grasped. To quote one example only: the widely-publicised book by Gordon Rattray Taylor—*The Doomsday Book*—is explicitly limited in its purview to the next thirty years. After discussing the population explosion, which, says the author, could come to fifteen billion people in the lifetime of those now living, he writes: 'It is my belief that the collapse will come considerably before this level is reached, perhaps quite soon' (p 23). Again (p 249) Taylor, in referring to the expectation of demographers that the world's population will reach twenty-five billion by 2070, says cheerfully: 'Personally I doubt if we shall make it to 2070.' This same author prefaces his book with a long quotation from the *Revelation of St John*.

Science and religion have often been described as at war, but here in prophecies of trouble looming up into a storm due to break towards the end of the century, science and religion have combined with the spirit of prophecy to present mankind with a terrifying picture.

Whatever the ultimate fate of humanity in its perilous but at the same time thrilling course, it can be taken as certain that the Mediterranean is likely to remain at the centre of our destiny. It is an astonishing reflection that, after so many ages, a tiny land to the east of the Inland Sea is the focus of attention of the two most powerful states on our planet. After many hundreds of years during which Palestine was of little consequence in the battles of the nations, events taking place within its narrow boundaries again draw upon it the attention of mankind and make it the focus of human interest.

SOURCES

Only the main sources and outstanding reference works can be named here, but these will serve those who want to read further as each contains numerous references to other authorities. Many works are mentioned in the text and others in the notes, to which reference should be made.

CHAPTERS 1 & 2
Articles in the *Encyclopedia Britannica* and *Chambers's Encyclopedia*, on the Mediterranean.

CHAPTER 3
For the early relations between Persians and Greeks, the prime authority is the *History of Herodotus*. Literal translations are available, perhaps that of Bohn is as good as any. One of the classic editings of Herodotus is that of George Rawlinson. As to the ancient civilisations, some useful and entertaining books are: *Gods, Graves and Scholars, the Story of Archaeology*, C. W. Ceram (1952), the author has also produced a picture history of archaeology, *The Living Past*, by Ivar Lissner (1957); and *The Bible as History*, by Werner Keller (1956).

CHAPTER 4
Prof J. B. Bury, *The History of Greece* (1922), gives perhaps the best summary from the earliest times to the death of Alexander. It is well illustrated. For the Platonic Dialogues there is the fine translation by the great Victorian scholar, Dr Benjamin Jowett. *The Legacy of Greece* (1922) is admirable in assessments by Greek scholars. For a particular study which sheds light on the life of Athens and of Sparta, the fascinating biography of *Alcibiades* by E. F. Benson is well worth reading.

CHAPTER 5

Xenophon's *Anabasis or the Going Up of the Ten Thousand* gives a good account of what campaigning against the Persians was like. Numerous versions exist in English. For Alexander's warfare in India, in addition to Bury, see, from the Indian point of view, E. B. Havell's *History of Aryan Rule in India*.

CHAPTER 6

J. Wells's *A Short History of Rome* gives the story from the earliest times to the end of the republic and the establishment of the empire; also H. L. Havell, *Republican Rome*; Prof Bury's *Roman Empire* is very useful. For an interesting and popular study of the conspiracy of Cataline, see the chapter on this in Hector Bolitho's *Twelve Against the Gods. The Legacy of Rome* (1923-57) is valuable for all details.

CHAPTERS 6-9

Needless to remark, a vast literature exists on the rise and development of the Roman republic and empire, and its relations with Carthage. The career of Hannibal is treated in many works. A good guide to the historians of both Greece and Rome, with evaluations of each of them, is in *The Historians of Greece and Rome*, by Stephen Usher (1969). The Loeb Classical Library contains most of the works referred to in this last book. In this library the original text is given with an English translation opposite. Other very useful translations are to be found in the Penguin Classical Library. One of the best studies of Roman affairs under the early empire is in Robert Graves's novel, *I Claudius* and its sequel *Claudius the God*. Should any of the statements in these works of fiction be thought far-fetched, the reader can easily check them, eg in Tacitus, the greatest Roman historian, as far as style is concerned. The *Annals* and the *Histories* of Tacitus give a fine picture of the early emperors, though possibly biassed from an aristocratic standpoint. Baring Gould's *House of the Caesars* is not only good reading but gives considerable detail. No one should fail to read Gibbon's *Decline and Fall of the Roman Empire*. It does not deal in detail, however, with the period before the death of Marcus Aurelius, for which see Prof Bury's *Roman Empire*. A matchless study of the period of Marcus Aurelius is *Marius the Epicurean*, by Walter Pater. A recent work of great interest, dealing with the establishment of the Augustan regime, is *Cleopatra* by Jack Lindsay, 1971. Major Gen J. C. Fuller's *Julius Caesar* is most stimulating.

CHAPTER 10

The literature on the rise and progress of Christianity is so great that it is difficult to single out suitable works for general reading. For a brief history of the Church, C. P. S. Clarke's *History of the Christian Church* can be recommended. For the early centuries, see B. J. Kidd, *History of the Church* to 461, also Mgr L. Duchesne, *Histoire Ancienne de l'Eglise*. Another Roman Catholic history is by Canon Philip Hughes, *A History of the Church* (1948) and on Broad Church lines, *An Outline of Christianity*, 5 vols circa 1925. For the life of Christ, the only recommendation is that the reader should study the Gospels for himself, read representative works on Christ's life and times and then return to the Gospels. It is possible that the sanity of the little Gospel of Mark (considered to be the earliest of the four) may assert itself over the fancies of the critics. Farrar's *Life of Christ*, which has been recently reprinted, is a painstaking composition. Renan's *Life of Jesus* is a romance, and Papini's *Story* is another but written from very different premises. Westcott and Hort supplied a much-used Greek text of the New Testament, and there is now the text by R. V. G. Tasker, issued by Oxford and Cambridge University Presses, 1964. Canon Streeter in his study, *The Four Gospels*, went at length into the problem of their origins. *The New Commentary on Holy Scripture* is worthy of close study.

The change-over mentioned in the chapter from the Jewish Dispensation to that of Christianity is perhaps best summed up under the term Parousia, by which the coming of Christ is referred to in the New Testament. There are some good works dealing with this momentous matter. They are: T. H. Passmore's *St Peter's Charter as Peter read it* (1925), and also the same author's *The New and Living Way* (1929). This author died in 1941; why his works have been so consistently ignored is hard to understand, as he was a man of scholarship and literary power, being poet, novelist, translator, and humorist, as well as theologian and philosopher. On the subject of the interpretation of the New Testament on the lines indicated in the text, Passmore is lucidity itself. To supplement his work, attention should be given to: *The Parousia, A Critical Inquiry into the New Testament Doctrine of Our Lord's Second Coming*, by J. Stuart Russell (1887); also *The Christ Has Come*, by E. Hampden Cooke (1894). A writer who is diametrically opposed in his religious beliefs to those cited, Ernest Renan, in his *Histoire des Origines du Christianisme, Livre Quatrième, L'Antechrist* (1876) reaches substantial agreement with them, however, as to the interpretation of facts in the early history of the Church.

On the history of the Jews there are both learned and popular works. W. O. E. Osterley, *A History of Israel* (2 vols) is most instructive, and Dean Milman's *History of the Jews* is still worth reading. *A Short History of Israel from Abraham to Bar Cochba*, by M. A.

Beek (1957) and *The Legacy of Israel* (1928) are very useful.

On the Papacy there are many small works and some voluminous ones. John Farrow's *Pageant of the Popes* is a very useful one-volume survey. Leopold Ranke, *History of the Popes*, gives the story in the sixteenth and seventeenth centuries, after a brief resumé of earlier times. Bishop Mandel Creighton wrote five volumes on *The Papacy from 1378 to the Reformation*.

CHAPTER 11

On Mithraism, see Franz Cumont, *The Mysteries of Mithra*. Cumont was a professor in the University of Ghent. The work is translated by T. J. McCormack (1903). On China, two good books are: *The Legacy of China* edited by Raymond Dawson, and *The Birth of Communist China* by C. P. Fitzgerald (1964).

CHAPTER 12

Good books on Mohammed and the religion which he founded are as numerous as those on any other great subject. Out of the mass can be selected some which have proved helpful to the writer. *The Life of Mohammed* by Sir William Muir is a monument of industry (1858-61) which contains much that is useful even now. *The Life and Times of Muhammad* by Sir John Glubb (Glubb Pasha), published in 1970, is right up-to-date and written from an appreciative standpoint as Muir's was not. Thomas Carlyle wrote of Mohammed in his *Heroes and Hero Worship* (1841) with The Hero as Prophet. In 1896, a Moslem, Syed Ameer Ali, gave a modern view of the Prophet's life and teaching in *The Spirit of Islam*.

For the Koran, the best known version is that of George Sale, which first appeared in 1734 but of which a modern printing, with an introduction by Sir Edward Dennison Ross, was published by Frederick Warne and Co without a date. There is also the translation made by the Rev J. M. Rodwell, which is published in Everyman's Library. On the Caliphate there are: Sir William Muir's study, that by T. W. Arnold (1924) and *The Course of Empire*, by Sir John Glubb (1965).

Also on Chapters 5 to 11, may be added Prof Bury's *History of the Later Roman Empire 395 to 565*, and from the death of Theodosius I to the death of Justinian (2 vols, 1923); and his *History of the Eastern Roman Empire* (1912). A very fine work on the Eastern Empire is *The Byzantine Achievement*. Useful is N. H. Baines's *The Byzantine Empire*.

NOTES

CHAPTER 2

Page 34: One of the Minor Prophets. Amos I, v. 1; 'The words of Amos . . . which he saw . . . in the days of Jeroboam, king of Israel, two years before the earthquake'.

Page 36: A Mediterranean race. Almost any popular modern work on the subject of the races of man will contain references to the Mediterranean race, eg in his essay in the *Outline of Modern Knowledge* (1932), Prof C. G. Seligman writes of the Nordic, Alpine and Mediterranean races comprising the White, or 'to use a conventional but extremely convenient term, Caucasian Man'. He adds: 'The Mediterranean race includes not only such obviously related strains as the Hamite and the Arab, but is enlarged by some authorities to embrace the Dravidians of Southern India and Ceylon, with aberrant types of their own as extreme as the Todas, distribution going far beyond that admitted by Sergi, whose work, *The Mediterranean Race* (1901), is the *locus classicus* for the use of the term'.

CHAPTER 4

Page 57: A word which the Romans erroneously bestowed. See Goodwin's *Greek Grammar* (1924), Introduction: 'In the historic period, the people of this race (ie the Greeks), called themselves by the name Hellenes, and their language Hellenic. We call them Greeks, from the Roman name, Graeci'. Compare this with the following passage from Helmholt's *The World's History* (1902), vol 4, p270: 'The word Hellenes was taken from the small tribe that Achilles had governed in Thessalia . . . In the fifth century BC this term was applied to the entire Greek people. The name Greek, on the other hand, derived from Graecoi (a Latinisation of the tribal name of the Graeci who dwelt on the Euripus, and who once lived in the North-West), was first introduced into Greece from Italy during the days of Aristotle, as shown by the Latin termination. (Grai-icoi as Op-icoi), and its spread marks the triumph of a tribal name'.

Page 64: Their economic position was based on a slave population . . . Half of the population were slaves. See J. B. Bury's *History of Greece* (Macmillan, 1922), p378: 'About this time (ie, 450 BC) the whole number of the inhabitants of Attica seems to have been about 250,000. But nearly half of these inhabitants were slaves'.

Page 64: The founder of European thought was Thales of Miletus. See any history of philosophy, eg, that by Clement C. J. Webb in the Home University Library.

Page 68: Socrates is still calmly drinking and continuing a philosophical discussion with two other survivors. See the dialogue of Plato—the *Symposium*—in which Alcibades is featured.

Page 68: 'Offer a cock to Aesculapius'. The exact words were: 'Crito, I owe a cock to Aesculapius, do not forget to pay it'. See the dialogue of Plato, called the *Phaedo*.

Page 69: He also advanced the progress of the sciences by the necessary task of sub-division. See the *7th Book of the Republic* (Davies's and Vaughan's translation). I do not mean that Plato invented the various sciences, but that he made the first clear division between them.

Page 69: Supreme Lords of the Human Mind. I am guilty here of bestowing a phrase upon Coleridge, and can only plead that I have a recollection of the use of such a phrase by the poet. Here is the actual passage in the *Table Talk* (Bohn's Standard Library, 1896), under 2 July 1830: 'Every man is born an Aristotelian or a Platonist. I do not think it possible that anyone born an Aristotelian can become a Platonist; and I am sure that no born Platonist can ever change into an Aristotelian. They are the two classes of men, beside which it is next to impossible to conceive a third . . . Aristotle was, and still is, the sovereign lord of the understanding: the faculty, judging by the senses. He was a conceptualist, and never could raise himself into that higher state which was natural to Plato, and has been so to others, in which the understanding is distinctly contemplated, and as it were, looked down upon from the throne of actual ideas, or living, inborn, essential truths. Yet what a mind was Aristotle's—only not the greatest that ever animated the human form—the parent of science, properly so called, the master of criticism, and the founder or editor of logic'.

Page 69: In Dante's Poem. See Cary's *Translation of Dante, the Inferno*. Canto IV, lines 127-141.

CHAPTER 5

Page 79: Philip, the heir to the throne, should come as a hostage to Thebes. See Bury's *History of Greece*, p614: 'Among the young

Macedonian nobles who were sent as pledges to Thebes was the boy Philip, who was now to be trained in the military school of Boeotia, under the eye of Epaminondas himself'.

Page 81 : The word 'myriads'. But we have extended the meaning of the original Greek *murias* which meant 10,000 until in our usage it equals an indefinitely great number. The Greeks usually used the word, however, only in connection with the hosts of Persia as their own armies were not often of a size sufficient to require it.

Page 83 : In the words of Esther. See the Book of Esther, ch 1, verse i.

Page 83 : Alexander's passage with his army into the Punjab. See Bury's *History of Greece*, ch 18, and E. B. Havell's *History of Aryan Rule in India*, chs 4 & 5.

CHAPTER 6

Page 96 : The story of Regulus : see Horace *Carmna* III, 5. For a modern criticism see *The Dawn of Empire : Rome's Rise to World Power*, by R. M. Errington.

CHAPTER 8

Page 126 : On the career of Julius Caesar, see two very different works : *The House of the Caesars*, by Rev S. Baring-Gould, a piece of unadulterated hero-worship of Caesar, and Major-Gen J. F. C. Fuller's study of Julius. (See Sources.)

CHAPTER 9

Page III : Tacitus's phrase. See the *History of Cornelius Tacitus* —*Historarium Liber Primus*, cap. 1, '*postquam bellatum apud Actium atque omnem potentiam ad unum conferri pacis interfuit*'. Rendered thus by Church and Brodribb: 'After the conflict at Actium, when it became essential to peace that all power should be centred in one man'.

Page 130 : Troops ceased to be responsible Romans. Gibbon, *Decline and Fall*, ch 1. 'The legions themselves, even at the time when they were recruited in the most distant provinces were supposed to consist of Roman citizens ... but a more serious regard was paid to essential merit of age, strength and military stature.'

Page 139 : On the Jewish avoidance of the Arch of Titus the following is of interest. It comes from *Black Sabbath* by Robert Katz (1969). No Jew would ever go through the Arch, but after the establishment of the state of Israel, they did so. On p313 the author writes: 'For nineteen centuries Jews had refused to pass through the Arch, which commemorated the conquest of Judea by the Roman Empire. Now, however, wrote the Italian Jewish historian

Attilio Milano, "history had made a complete cycle and the humiliation could be considered cancelled" '. This was three days after the United Nations voted for the establishment of Israel in Palestine.

Page 139: On the emperor Severus there is an elaborate study: *Septimius Severus, The African Emperor*, by Anthony Burley.

CHAPTER 10

Page 142: Tacitus's account of the Jews. 'Even a brilliant historian such as Tacitus makes astounding mis-statements about the Jews, their origin, history and religion.' See the *Histories of Tacitus*, Book 5, where a garbled version of Jewish history can be read, including the origin of the Jews from Crete, their advance under their leaders, Jerusalem and Judah, and their worship of an ass.

Page 143: 'Romans, such as Pompey the Great, who forced their way into the Holy of Holies'. Again Tacitus, *Histories*, Book 5, ch 9, '*Romanorum primus Gn. Pompeius Judaeos domuit, templumque jure victoriae ingressus est. Inde volgatum nulla intus deum effigie vacuam sedem et inania arcana*'.

Page 145: The Queen of Sheba. The legend of the Queen of Sheba, the Queen of the South, is given by Sir E. A. Wallis Budge (though he does not, of course, vouch for its accuracy) in his monumental *History of Ethiopia, Nubia and Abyssinia*, two volumes (1928) p194: 'The Visit of the Queen of Sheba to Solomon'.

Page 148: 'From the time of the return from captivity the Jews possessed no prophetic voices'. This was the period between the Old and New Testaments, that of Apocrypha, the collection of books (including Maccabees), which in the English Bible comes between the two Testaments. They cannot be better described than in the words of the sixth of the thirty-nine Articles of the Church of England: 'The other books the Church doth read for example of life and instruction of manners; but yet doth it not apply them to establish any doctrine'. To this day no Bible may be used on a lectern in a Church of England place of worship unless it contains the Apocrypha. James Bridie's play *Tobias and the Angel* has popularised one of the books of the Apocrypha.

Page 152: 'He could even quote Greek poets'. Cf. The Acts of the Apostles, ch 17, verse 28. 'As certain also of your own poets have said, For we are also his offspring' and Epistle to Titus, ch 1, verse 12, 'One of themselves even a prophet of their own, said, The Cretans are always liars, evil beasts, slow bellies'. The first quotation is from a Cicilian poet, Aratus; the second from the Cretan poet, Epimenides.

Page 157: The rock of Masada. So deeply is the memory of Masada engraved on modern Israel that recruits to the Israeli Army take their oath of allegiance on the summit of the rock.

CHAPTER 11

Page 164: 'The worship of Mithras the soldiers' god from the East'. It is very interesting in this connection to note that the Church of St Clement at Rome is not only built on the site of the house of St Clement (who was once Bishop of Rome, was mentioned in St Paul's Epistle to the Philippians, ch 4, verse 3, and wrote the Letter to the Corinthians, which is the first Christian writing outside the New Testament) but also covers a Mithraic cave or temple where the statue of Mithras can be seen in good preservation. How far the Mithraic worship extended may be gauged by its existence in Roman London, ie, the temple discovered in the city.

Page 170: St Augustine. A good translation of the *City of God* is in Everyman, 2 vols. For those wishing to study his life but not his theology, there is Peter Brown's *Augustine of Hippo* (1967).

CHAPTER 12

Page 175: As Sir Edward Creasy called them. Actually, the words are a quotation from Michelet's *Histoire Romaine* which occur in Sir Edward Creasy's *Fifteen Decisive Battles of the World*, ch 4. Battle of the Metaurus: 'The Arabs, that formidable rearguard of the Semitic world, dashed forth from their deserts'.

Page 176: Readers of Horace will remember. See the Odes, Book 1, ch 29, *beatis Arabum gazis* and Book 2, ch 12, 24, *plenas Arabum domos*, and Book 3, 24, 1, *intactis opulentior thesauris Arabum*.

Page 176: The Jewish king and the *jus primae noctis*. See the volume in the 'Heroes of the Nations' series: *Mohammed*, by D. S. Margoliouth (1905), p187: 'There was a Jewish kingdom at Yathrib in Western Arabia, where one Jewish chieftain (with the curious name of Bedchamber) even exacted the *jus primae noctis*. By an expedient which rarely failed in anecdotes of this style, the brother of one of the brides, disguised in bridal attire, assassinated the tyrant'. On p26 of the same work, Margoliouth says of Southern Arabia: 'In South Arabia ... some Sabaen king having been won over by the Jews of Yathrib, and for once men of the Jewish persuasion had possessed the courage to fight and even to die. A conquering state, governed by the laws of Moses. That Jewish state was, indeed, of short duration. Like other religious communities which preach toleration when oppressed, they became persecutors when they had acquired sovereignty'. A force was sent from Christian Abyssinia against those who burned Christians 'defeated by some accident the Jewish king died a hero's death'. Among the stories of scattered Jewish communities, which may be found in various parts of the world, this must surely be one of the most peculiar, if only for the likeness between the habits of the Jewish king and the old French seigneurs with their rights over their vassals' womenfolk.

Page 178: As Gibbon says, the Creed of Mohammed contains an eternal truth and a necessary fiction. See *Decline and Fall of the Roman Empire*, ch 50.

Page 184: The distinction between Sunnites and Shi'ites is very clearly defined in the article on Islam in the *Encyclopedia Britannica*, where the numbers of the Sunnites are given as approximately 150 millions, whereas the Shi'ites are said to be no more than 12 millions. An alternative spelling of Ommiyade is Umayyad.

Page 185: Trade in the Mediterranean after the rise of Islam. On this subject there is an article in *Speculum: A Journal of Medieval Studies*. (The Medieval Academy of America, Massachusetts, April 1948). This discusses one of Henri Pirenne's works, *Mohammed and Charlemagne*, and he considered that the expansion of the Islamic Arab Empire meant the disruption of Mediterranean trade, so that few, if any goods from eastern countries, or the south of the Mediterranean, reached western Europe. This thesis is strongly contested in the article mentioned. In connection with the history of Islam, the works of Sir John Glubb should be consulted.

CHAPTER 13

Page 189: The strong central monarchy established by William the Conqueror. Compare Trevelyan's *History of England*, p123. 'The Conqueror ... successfully prevented England from falling into the anarchy of political feudalism prevalent on the Continent. And he had cleared the ground for the gradual development of a great monarchical bureaucracy'. Trevelyan adds, however, 'He did not enjoy unlimited despotic power, nor by right did anyone who ever succeeded him on the throne of England'.

Page 190: By the hand of the only Englishman who was ever Pope, the land of Ireland was bestowed upon Henry II. Compare again, Trevelyan's *History of England*, p202, 'Adrian IV, the only English Pope in history, had commissioned Henry II to conquer the island if he liked, as the best means of bringing it into the Roman fold'.

Page 190: Donation of Ireland to the English king. The text in English of the Bull *Laudabiliter* by which the pope, Adrian IV, gave Ireland to the English king, Henry II, is printed in *Irish Historical Documents* 1172-1922, edited by Edmund Curtis and R. B. McDowell (1968). So also are the Constitution of the Synod of Cashel, 1172, and the three letters of Pope Alexander III, 1172. The last-mentioned confirms the validity of Henry II's conquest of

Ireland. On the work of Scotus Eringera and other medieval philosophers see the excellent *Cambridge History of Late Greek and
Early Medieval Philosophy.*
Page 191 : The Holy Roman Empire. The masterpiece on this
subject is, of course, *The Holy Roman Empire* by James, Viscount
Bryce (Macmillan, 1922). Although this admirable work is concerned with the development of the Holy Roman Empire in the
first instance, other matters are inevitably introduced, and the
whole history of Europe could be brought in. Bryce gives references
to several monumental works which have already been mentioned, such as Gibbon's *Decline and Fall* and Milman's *Latin
Christianity*; others are Hodgkin, *Italy and Her Invaders*, Bury's
History of the Later Roman Empire, Ranke's *History of the World*,
and Gregorovius's work on the *City of Rome in the Middle Ages.*
    The latest work on the subject of the Holy Roman Empire is by
a German scholar, Heer, *Holy Roman Empire* (1969), but owing to
difficulties in the English translation is not available in England.
Page 193 : Urban, the successor of Gregory VII. See Milman,
History of Latin Christianity, vol 4, book 7, chs 4 & 5. Gregory was
succeeded by Victor III, but the latter held the Pontificate only
some six months before the election of Urban II.
Page 198 : All the crusades failures. The success of the enterprise
of Frederick II can hardly be reckoned as fulfilling the crusading
ideal or aims, since the Holy City remained in non-Christian hands.
Page 203 : An excellent short account of the crusades is by Sir
Ernest Barker. The full length treatment of the subject is in Sir
Steven Runciman's work in three volumes.

CHAPTER 15
Page 217 : The great Portuguese national epic, the *Lusiad*, written
by Camoens in ten books (1572). Described by Dr Brewer in the
Reader's Handbook as 'this really classic epic in ten books, worthy
to be ranked with *Virgil's Aeneid*, has been translated into English
verse by Auberton in 1878 : Fanshawe in 1655 : by Mickle in 1775
and Sir Richard Burton in 1880.'
Page 217 : The latest translation of Camoens is in the Penguin
Classics.
Page 218 : 'For some 150 years Portugal was thus the world's
leading power, and her remaining colonies in Africa and Asia show
the former extent of her empire'. After the consolidation of the
Portuguese monarchy in the first years of the fifteenth century,
there began a period of expansion overseas with the capture of
Ceuta in Morocco. During the period 1415-99, Portugal led the way
in the discoveries which opened up the African continent and the
sea way to India. In 1500, King Emanuel assumed the title 'Lord of

the Conquest, Navigation and Commerce of India, Ethiopia, Arabia and Persia' and this was confirmed by Pope Alexander VI in 1502. All the way along the coast of Africa to India and beyond, the outposts of the Portuguese Empire stretched, and this empire remained independent of foreign conquest until 1580 when Portugal was conquered by Spain. For the modern extent of the Portuguese colonies at the beginning of the twentieth century, Portugal was the fourth on the list of colonial powers, Britain, France and Germany being the first, second and third respectively. The total area of Portugal overseas was 812,606 square miles.

Page 219: 'For 60 years was herself actually annexed to the Spanish crown'. From 1580 to 1640 Portugal was under the rule of Spain, and this period is known as the Sixty Years' Captivity. It was not until 1668 that Spain recognised the independence of Portugal, when the House of Braganza into which the English Charles II married had obtained the throne.

CHAPTER 18

Page 260: In the history of the Zionist Movement in the early years of this century. Palestine was not the only goal of the Jews. The British government in 1903 offered a Jewish Home in Uganda (British East Africa) to the Jews of Eastern Europe who were suffering from Russian persecution. This offer was considered at the Sixth Zionist Congress at Kattowitz, but did not commend itself to the majority of the Jews there represented. English Jewry tended toward acceptance of such an offer (there was another British offer of territory on the borders of Egypt) but, as we all know, nothing came of this. For full details of this matter the reader is referred to *Trial and Error* by Chaim Weizmann, First President of Israel (1949). Other works which may be consulted are *A History of Palestine from A.D. 135 to Modern Times* by James Parkes (1949), and Arthur Koestler's *Promise and Fulfilment*. All these works are marked by anti-British feeling; the offers and efforts of the British government have produced a most ungrateful reaction.

CHRONOLOGICAL TABLE

VARIOUS ATTEMPTS have been made to mark the passage of time, and one of the great difficulties of historians is to reconcile the different systems of chronology which have prevailed among the nations. At the present time the numbering of the year is usually based on the system for so long in use among the nations of Western Europe, and 1973 would be used as the date of the present year among most educated men and women throughout the world. This does not prevent certain bodies from maintaining their own system of chronology, eg the Jews date the year from what they consider to have been the date of the creation of the world, their year 5733/4 corresponding roughly to 1973-74. The Moslems reckon time from the Hegira, the date of the flight of Mohammed from Mecca. The Christian system is based, of course, on a division of time before and after the date of the cardinal event in the Christian religion, the birth of Christ, hence our BC and AD. The date which still appears in the margin of most copies of the Authorised version of the Bible, namely, 4004 BC, was the result of a great effort by Archbishop Ussher in the seventeenth century to reconcile the existing systems of chronology and to reach a reasonable system for dating the events of Biblical history. This date and systems have been subjected to much stupid ridicule, but it is not easy to understand how Ussher, in the absence of the knowledge about the past of man and the antiquity of the world which has been acquired since his time, could have worked out any other system.

The table set out below does not enable the reader to follow the growth of intellectual movements, such as Scholasticism or Protestantism, because such movements are difficult to pin-point with particular dates, nor is it possible to give precise dates for the growth of the vast Mongol power in the thirteenth century, or again, to show the gradual decline of Venice or Genoa.

The table is given principally to aid the reader and to assist him in bearing in mind the lapse of time between events narrated in various chapters, but it ought to be stated that some of the dates given, eg the date of the founding of Carthage or of Rome, are only approximations at best.

BC 1000. Era of David and Solomon.
    800. Founding of Carthage.
    753. Founding of Rome.
    722. Fall of Samaria, and end of the ancient Kingdom of Israel. Israel carried captive by the Assyrians.
588-586. Fall of Jerusalem, and captivity of Kingdom of Judah by King of Babylon.
    550. Cyrus the Persian begins his career.
    536. Cyrus permits the Jews to return to Palestine.
    521. Darius, King of Persia, rules Persian Empire.
    508. Treaty between Rome and Carthage.
    490. Battle of Marathon.
    480. Battles of Thermopylae and Salamis.
    479. Battles of Platea and Mycale.
431-404. Peloponnesian War.
    401. Retreat of 10,000 under Xenophon from Persia.
    399. Death of Socrates.
    371. Battle of Leuctra.
    359. Philip became King of Macedonia.
    336. Death of Philip: Succession of Alexander.
    334. Battle of the Granicus.
    333. Battle of Issus.
    331. Battle of Arbela.
    323. Death of Alexander the Great.
    281. Pyrrhus, King of Epirus, declares war on Rome.
    275. Battle of Beneventum.
    265. First Punic War begins.
    241. End of First Punic War.
    219. Second Punic War begins. Siege and capture of Saguntum.
    216. Battle of Cannae.
    202. Battle of Zama.
    198. Antiochus Epiphanes becomes ruler of Palestine.
168-7. Revolt of the Maccabees.
    149. Third Punic War begins.
    146. Carthage destroyed. Corinth destroyed.
    133. Attalus, King of Pergamum, bequeathed his kingdom to Rome. Tiberius Gracchus and his legislation; his assassination.
    102. Marius destroys the Teutones.
    101. Marius destroys the Cimbri.
    82. Sulla, dictator of Rome.
73-71. Revolt of Spartacus, finally defeated by Crassus.

63. Pompey conquers Syria and captures Jerusalem.
48. Julius Caesar defeated Pompey at Pharsalos.
44. Julius Caesar murdered.
4. Birth of Jesus Christ. (The computation on which the chronology of the Christian Era is founded was made by Dionysus Exiguus in the sixth century AD and, owing to certain miscalculations, the date of the Christian Era was set four years later than in reality.)

AD
9. Defeat of Varus and his legions by the Germans.
14. Death of Augustus.
29. Crucifixion of Christ. (Dates given vary from AD 29-33.)
68. Year of Four Emperors at Rome.
70. Destruction of Jerusalem by Titus.
117. Roman Empire reached greatest extent under Trajan.
180. Death of Marcus Aurelius.
220. In China period of disorder begins at end of Han Dynasty.
284. Diocletian became Emperor.
323. Constantine the Great became sole Emperor of Rome.
325. Council of Nicaea. Nicene Creed drawn up.
410. Rome captured and sacked by Alaric.
452. Foundation of Venice.
453. Death of Attila.
476. Fall of the Western Roman Empire.
527. Justinian became Emperor.
528-534. Revision of Roman Law by Justinian.
569-570. Birth of Mohammed.
622. Beginning of the Hegira or Mohammedan Era.
632. Death of Mohammed. Abu Bekr Caliph.
637. Battle of Kadessia.
661. Death of Ali (Fourth Caliph) and beginning of Uwayyad Caliphate.
711. Invasion of Spain by the Moslems.
717. Defeat of Moslems at Constantinople.
732. Battle of Tours.
749. Abbasid Caliphate begins.
800. Charlemagne crowned Emperor by the Pope.
814. Death of Charlemagne.
1095. Urban II preached the First Crusade.
1099. Jerusalem captured by the Crusaders.
1147. Second Crusade.
1189. Third Crusade.
1202. Fourth Crusade.
1204. Constantinople captured by the Crusaders.

1217.	Fifth Crusade.
1228.	Sixth Crusade.
1248.	Seventh Crusade.
1378.	The Great Schism in the Western Church.
1453.	Capture of Constantinople by the Turks.
1486.	Bartholomew Diaz rounded the Cape of Good Hope.
1492.	Columbus discovered America.
1497.	Cabot sailed from Bristol to discover Newfoundland.
1498.	Vasco Da Gama sailed to India round the Cape of Good Hope.
1521.	Luther began independent teaching. Magellan discovered the Philippines.
1577.	Drake sailed round the world.
1588.	Defeat of the Armada.
1656.	Blake in the Mediterranean.
1658.	Death of Cromwell.
1704.	British capture Gibraltar.
1775-83.	American War of Independence.
1789.	French Revolution began.
1798.	Napoleon Bonaparte's expedition to Egypt. Battle of the Nile.
1799.	Napoleon besieged Acre, but was repulsed.
1801.	Battle of Alexandria won by British. French leave Egypt.
1814.	Malta joins British Empire.
1839.	Aden becomes British coaling station.
1869.	Suez Canal opened to commercial traffic.
1869-70.	First Vatican Council.
1870.	Victor Emmanuel became King of all Italy.
1875.	Disraeli acquired for Britain controlling interest in Suez Canal shares.
1878.	Cyprus leased to Britain by Turkey.
1882.	England intervened in Egypt.
1914.	Outbreak of World War I.
1918.	End of World War I.
1922.	Mussolini became Dictator of Italy.
1933.	Hitler became Dictator of Germany.
1939.	Beginning of World War II.
1945.	End of World War II.
1948.	Establishment of State of Israel. First Arab-Israeli War.
1949.	Announcement by Britain and USA that Russia has atomic bomb.
1952.	Abdication of King Farouk of Egypt.
1953.	Abolition of Egyptian Monarchy.
1954.	Nasser became President of Egypt.

1956. Withdrawal of British forces from Canal Zone (13 June).
Nasser nationalised Canal (26 July).
Israeli forces struck against Egypt (29 October).
Anglo-French operations to seize Canal Zone
(31 October-6 November)
Allied Forces withdrew from Egypt (22 December).
Canal blocked and closed until
1957. 8 April.
Russia sent up Sputnik I (4 October).
1958. Nasser made treaty with Syria by which United Arab
Republic was set up.
USA sent marines into Lebannon. British paratroopers
air-lifted into Jordan (July).
1960. British renounced sovereignty over Cyprus.
1961. Russian Yuri Gagarin first man in space.
Syria seceded from UAR.
1962. Nasser intervened in the affairs of the Yemen.
1962. Second Vatican Council.
1966. Announcement of Egyptian Six Year Programme for
Suez Canal (July).
1967. Work began on Six Year Programme (February).
Israeli air strike against Egyptian Air Force (5 June).
1969. Neil Armstrong, Michael Collins and Edwin Aldrin, of
the USA, first men on the Moon (20 July).
1970. Guerilla hostilities continued between Israelis and Arab
states. Israelis in occupation of Syrian heights. Gaza
Strip, Jordan west bank, and Old City of Jerusalem.
Death of President Nasser (28 September).
1972. Murder of Israeli athletes at Olympic Games in Munich
by Arab terrorists, followed by Israeli reprisals against
Lebanon.

INDEX